Mastering Python for Data Science

Explore the world of data science through Python and learn how to make sense of data

Samir Madhavan

[PACKT] open source
community experience distilled
PUBLISHING

BIRMINGHAM - MUMBAI

Mastering Python for Data Science

First published: August 2015

Production reference: 1260815

Published by Packt Publishing Ltd.
Livery Place
35 Livery Street
Birmingham B3 2PB, UK.

ISBN 978-1-78439-015-0

www.packtpub.com

Credits

Author
Samir Madhavan

Reviewers
Sébastien Celles
Robert Dempsey
Maurice HT Ling
Ratanlal Mahanta
Yingssu Tsai

Commissioning Editor
Pramila Balan

Acquisition Editor
Sonali Vernekar

Content Development Editor
Arun Nadar

Technical Editor
Chinmay S. Puranik

Copy Editor
Sonia Michelle Cheema

Project Coordinator
Neha Bhatnagar

Proofreader
Safis Editing

Indexer
Monica Ajmera Mehta

Graphics
Disha Haria
Jason Monteiro

Production Coordinator
Arvindkumar Gupta

Cover Work
Arvindkumar Gupta

About the Author

Samir Madhavan has been working in the field of data science since 2010. He is an industry expert on machine learning and big data. He has also reviewed *R Machine Learning Essentials* by Packt Publishing. He was part of the ubiquitous Aadhar project of the Unique Identification Authority of India, which is in the process of helping every Indian get a unique number that is similar to a social security number in the United States. He was also the first employee of Flutura Decision Sciences and Analytics and is a part of the core team that has helped scale the number of employees in the company to 50. His company is now recognized as one of the most promising Internet of Things—Decision Sciences companies in the world.

I would like to thank my mom, Rajasree Madhavan, and dad, P Madhavan, for all their support. I would also like to thank Srikanth Muralidhara, Krishnan Raman, and Derick Jose, who gave me the opportunity to start my career in the world of data science.

About the Reviewers

Sébastien Celles is a professor of applied physics at Universite de Poitiers (working in the thermal science department). He has used Python for numerical simulations, data plotting, data predictions, and various other tasks since the early 2000s. He is a member of PyData and was granted commit rights to the pandas DataReader project. He is also involved in several open source projects in the scientific Python ecosystem.

Sebastien is also the author of some Python packages available on PyPi, which are as follows:

- openweathermap_requests: This is a package used to fetch data from OpenWeatherMap.org using Requests and Requests-cache and to get pandas DataFrame with weather history
- pandas_degreedays: This is a package used to calculate degree days (a measure of heating or cooling) from the pandas time series of temperature
- pandas_confusion: This is a package used to manage confusion matrices, plot and binarize them, and calculate overall and class statistics
- There are some other packages authored by him, such as pyade, pandas_datareaders_unofficial, and more

He also has a personal interest in data mining, machine learning techniques, forecasting, and so on. You can find more information about him at `http://www.celles.net/wiki/Contact` or `https://www.linkedin.com/in/sebastiencelles`.

Robert Dempsey is a leader and technology professional, specializing in delivering solutions and products to solve tough business challenges. His experience of forming and leading agile teams combined with more than 15 years of technology experience enables him to solve complex problems while always keeping the bottom line in mind.

Robert founded and built three start-ups in the tech and marketing fields, developed and sold two online applications, consulted for Fortune 500 and Inc. 500 companies, and has spoken nationally and internationally on software development and agile project management.

He's the founder of Data Wranglers DC, a group dedicated to improving the craft of data wrangling, as well as a board member of Data Community DC. He is currently the team leader of data operations at ARPC, an econometrics firm based in Washington, DC.

In addition to spending time with his growing family, Robert geeks out on Raspberry Pi's, Arduinos, and automating more of his life through hardware and software.

Maurice HT Ling has been programming in Python since 2003. Having completed his PhD in bioinformatics and BSc (Hons) in molecular and cell biology from The University of Melbourne, he is currently a research fellow at Nanyang Technological University, Singapore. He is also an honorary fellow of The University of Melbourne, Australia. Maurice is the chief editor of Computational and Mathematical Biology and coeditor of The Python Papers. Recently, he cofounded the first synthetic biology start-up in Singapore, called AdvanceSyn Pte. Ltd., as the director and chief technology officer. His research interests lie in life itself, such as biological life and artificial life, and artificial intelligence, which use computer science and statistics as tools to understand life and its numerous aspects. In his free time, Maurice likes to read, enjoy a cup of coffee, write his personal journal, or philosophize on various aspects of life. His website and LinkedIn profile are `http://maurice.vodien.com` and `http://www.linkedin.com/in/mauriceling`, respectively.

Ratanlal Mahanta is a senior quantitative analyst. He holds an MSc degree in computational finance and is currently working at GPSK Investment Group as a senior quantitative analyst. He has 4 years of experience in quantitative trading and strategy development for sell-side and risk consultation firms. He is an expert in high frequency and algorithmic trading.

He has expertise in the following areas:

- Quantitative trading: This includes FX, equities, futures, options, and engineering on derivatives
- Algorithms: This includes Partial Differential Equations, Stochastic Differential Equations, Finite Difference Method, Monte-Carlo, and Machine Learning
- Code: This includes R Programming, C++, Python, MATLAB, HPC, and scientific computing
- Data analysis: This includes big data analytics (EOD to TBT), Bloomberg, Quandl, and Quantopian
- Strategies: This includes Vol Arbitrage, Vanilla and Exotic Options Modeling, trend following, Mean reversion, Co-integration, Monte-Carlo Simulations, ValueatRisk, Stress Testing, Buy side trading strategies with high Sharpe ratio, Credit Risk Modeling, and Credit Rating

He has already reviewed *Mastering Scientific Computing with R*, *Mastering R for Quantitative Finance*, and *Machine Learning with R Cookbook*, all by Packt Publishing.

You can find out more about him at `https://twitter.com/mahantaratan`.

Yingssu Tsai is a data scientist. She holds degrees from the University of California, Berkeley, and the University of California, Los Angeles.

www.PacktPub.com

Support files, eBooks, discount offers, and more

For support files and downloads related to your book, please visit www.PacktPub.com.

Did you know that Packt offers eBook versions of every book published, with PDF and ePub files available? You can upgrade to the eBook version at www.PacktPub.com and as a print book customer, you are entitled to a discount on the eBook copy. Get in touch with us at service@packtpub.com for more details.

At www.PacktPub.com, you can also read a collection of free technical articles, sign up for a range of free newsletters and receive exclusive discounts and offers on Packt books and eBooks.

PACKTLIB™

https://www2.packtpub.com/books/subscription/packtlib

Do you need instant solutions to your IT questions? PacktLib is Packt's online digital book library. Here, you can search, access, and read Packt's entire library of books.

Why subscribe?

- Fully searchable across every book published by Packt
- Copy and paste, print, and bookmark content
- On demand and accessible via a web browser

Free access for Packt account holders

If you have an account with Packt at www.PacktPub.com, you can use this to access PacktLib today and view 9 entirely free books. Simply use your login credentials for immediate access.

Table of Contents

Preface

Data science is an exciting new field that is used by various organizations to perform data-driven decisions. It is a combination of technical knowledge, mathematics, and business. Data scientists have to wear various hats to work with data and derive some value out of it. Python is one of the most popular languages among all the languages used by data scientists. It is a simple language to learn and is used for purposes, such as web development, scripting, and application development to name a few.

The ability to perform data science using Python is very powerful as it helps clean data at a raw level to create advanced machine learning algorithms that predict customer churns for a retail company. This book explains various concepts of data science in a structured manner with the application of these concepts on data to see how to interpret results. The book provides a good base for understanding the advanced topics of data science and how to apply them in a real-world scenario.

What this book covers

Chapter 1, Getting Started with Raw Data, teaches you the techniques of handling unorganized data. You'll also learn how to extract data from different sources, as well as how to clean and manipulate it.

Chapter 2, Inferential Statistics, goes beyond descriptive statistics, where you'll learn about inferential statistics concepts, such as distributions, different statistical tests, the errors in statistical tests, and confidence intervals.

Chapter 3, Finding a Needle in a Haystack, explains what data mining is and how it can be utilized. There is a lot of information in data but finding meaningful information is an art.

Chapter 4, Making Sense of Data through Advanced Visualization, teaches you how to create different visualizations of data. Visualization is an integral part of data science; it helps communicate a pattern or relationship that cannot be seen by looking at raw data.

Chapter 5, Uncovering Machine Learning, introduces you to the different techniques of machine learning and how to apply them. Machine learning is the new buzzword in the industry. It's used in activities, such as Google's driverless cars and predicting the effectiveness of marketing campaigns.

Chapter 6, Performing Predictions with a Linear Regression, helps you build a simple regression model followed by multiple regression models along with methods to test the effectiveness of the models. Linear regression is one of the most popular techniques used in model building in the industry today.

Chapter 7, Estimating the Likelihood of Events, teaches you how to build a logistic regression model and the different techniques of evaluating it. With logistic regression, you'll be able learn how to estimate the likelihood of an event taking place.

Chapter 8, Generating Recommendations with Collaborative Filtering, teaches you to create a recommendation model and apply it. It is similar to websites, such as Amazon, which are able to suggest items that you would probably buy on their page.

Chapter 9, Pushing Boundaries with Ensemble Models, familiarizes you with ensemble techniques, which are used to combine the power of multiple models to enhance the accuracy of predictions. This is done because sometimes a single model is not enough to estimate the outcome.

Chapter 10, Applying Segmentation with k-means Clustering, teaches you about k-means clustering and how to use it. Segmentation is widely used in the industry to group similar customers together.

Chapter 11, Analyzing Unstructured Data with Text Mining, teaches you to process unstructured data and make sense of it. There is more unstructured data in the world than structured data.

Chapter 12, Leveraging Python in the World of Big Data, teaches you to use Hadoop and Spark with Python to handle data in this chapter. With the ever increasing size of data, big data technologies have been brought into existence to handle such data.

What you need for this book

The following softwares are required for this book:

- Ubuntu OS, preferably 14.04
- Python 2.7
- The pandas 0.16.2 library
- The NumPy 1.9.2 library
- The SciPy 0.16 library
- IPython 4.0
- The SciKit 0.16.1 module
- The statsmodels 0.6.1 module
- The matplotlib 1.4.3 library
- Apache Hadoop CDH4 (Cloudera Hadoop 4) with MRv1 (MapReduce version 1)
- Apache Spark 1.4.0

Who this book is for

If you are a Python developer who wants to master the world of data science, then this book is for you. It is assumed that you already have some knowledge of data science.

Conventions

In this book, you will find a number of styles of text that distinguish between different kinds of information. Here are some examples of these styles, and an explanation of their meaning.

Code words in text, database table names, folder names, filenames, file extensions, pathnames, dummy URLs, user input, and Twitter handles are shown as follows: "The `json.load()` function loads the data into Python."

Any command-line input or output is written as follows:

```
$ pig ./BigData/pig_sentiment.pig
```

New terms and **important words** are shown in bold.

[Warnings or important notes appear in a box like this.]

[Tips and tricks appear like this.]

Reader feedback

Feedback from our readers is always welcome. Let us know what you think about this book—what you liked or may have disliked. Reader feedback is important for us to develop titles that you really get the most out of.

To send us general feedback, simply send an e-mail to `feedback@packtpub.com`, and mention the book title via the subject of your message.

If there is a topic that you have expertise in and you are interested in either writing or contributing to a book, see our author guide on `www.packtpub.com/authors`.

Customer support

Now that you are the proud owner of a Packt book, we have a number of things to help you to get the most from your purchase.

Downloading the example code

You can download the example code files for all Packt books you have purchased from your account at `http://www.packtpub.com`. If you purchased this book elsewhere, you can visit `http://www.packtpub.com/support` and register to have the files e-mailed directly to you.

The codes provided in the code bundle are for both IPython notebook and Python 2.7. In the chapters, Python conventions have been followed.

Downloading the color images of this book

We also provide you a PDF file that has color images of the screenshots/diagrams used in this book. The color images will help you better understand the changes in the output. You can download this file from: `http://www.packtpub.com/sites/default/files/downloads/01500S_ColorImage.pdf`.

Errata

Although we have taken every care to ensure the accuracy of our content, mistakes do happen. If you find a mistake in one of our books—maybe a mistake in the text or the code—we would be grateful if you would report this to us. By doing so, you can save other readers from frustration and help us improve subsequent versions of this book. If you find any errata, please report them by visiting `http://www.packtpub.com/submit-errata`, selecting your book, clicking on the **errata submission form** link, and entering the details of your errata. Once your errata are verified, your submission will be accepted and the errata will be uploaded on our website, or added to any list of existing errata, under the Errata section of that title. Any existing errata can be viewed by selecting your title from `http://www.packtpub.com/support`.

Piracy

Piracy of copyright material on the Internet is an ongoing problem across all media. At Packt, we take the protection of our copyright and licenses very seriously. If you come across any illegal copies of our works, in any form, on the Internet, please provide us with the location address or website name immediately so that we can pursue a remedy.

Please contact us at `copyright@packtpub.com` with a link to the suspected pirated material.

We appreciate your help in protecting our authors, and our ability to bring you valuable content.

Questions

You can contact us at `questions@packtpub.com` if you are having a problem with any aspect of the book, and we will do our best to address it.

1
Getting Started with Raw Data

In the world of data science, raw data comes in many forms and sizes. There is a lot of information that can be extracted from this raw data. To give an example, Amazon collects click stream data that records each and every click of the user on the website. This data can be utilized to understand if a user is a price-sensitive customer or prefer more popularly rated products. You must have noticed recommended products in Amazon; they are derived using such data.

The first step towards such an analysis would be to parse raw data. The parsing of the data involves the following steps:

- **Extracting data from the source**: Data can come in many forms, such as Excel, CSV, JSON, databases, and so on. Python makes it very easy to read data from these sources with the help of some useful packages, which will be covered in this chapter.
- **Cleaning the data**: Once a sanity check has been done, one needs to clean the data appropriately so that it can be utilized for analysis. You may have a dataset about students of a class and details about their height, weight, and marks. There may also be certain rows with the height or weight missing. Depending on the analysis being performed, these rows with missing values can either be ignored or replaced with the average height or weight.

In this chapter we will cover the following topics:

- Exploring arrays with NumPy
- Handling data with pandas
- Reading and writing data from various formats
- Handling missing data
- Manipulating data

The world of arrays with NumPy

Python, by default, comes with a data structure, such as List, which can be utilized for array operations, but a Python list on its own is not suitable to perform heavy mathematical operations, as it is not optimized for it.

NumPy is a wonderful Python package produced by Travis Oliphant, which has been created fundamentally for scientific computing. It helps handle large multidimensional arrays and matrices, along with a large library of high-level mathematical functions to operate on these arrays.

A NumPy array would require much less memory to store the same amount of data compared to a Python list, which helps in reading and writing from the array in a faster manner.

Creating an array

A list of numbers can be passed to the following array function to create a NumPy array object:

```
>>> import numpy as np


>>> n_array = np.array([[0, 1, 2, 3],
                 [4, 5, 6, 7],
                 [8, 9, 10, 11]])
```

A NumPy array object has a number of attributes, which help in giving information about the array. Here are its important attributes:

- `ndim`: This gives the number of dimensions of the array. The following shows that the array that we defined had two dimensions:

  ```
  >>> n_array.ndim
  2
  ```

  `n_array` has a rank of `2`, which is a 2D array.

- `shape`: This gives the size of each dimension of the array:

  ```
  >>> n_array.shape
  (3, 4)
  ```

  The first dimension of `n_array` has a size of `3` and the second dimension has a size of `4`. This can be also visualized as three rows and four columns.

- `size`: This gives the number of elements:

  ```
  >>> n_array.size
  12
  ```

  The total number of elements in `n_array` is 12.

- `dtype`: This gives the datatype of the elements in the array:

  ```
  >>> n_array.dtype.name
  int64
  ```

  The number is stored as `int64` in `n_array`.

Mathematical operations

When you have an array of data, you would like to perform certain mathematical operations on it. We will now discuss a few of the important ones in the following sections.

Array subtraction

The following commands subtract the `a` array from the `b` array to get the resultant `c` array. The subtraction happens element by element:

```
>>> a = np.array( [11, 12, 13, 14])
>>> b = np.array( [ 1, 2, 3, 4])
>>> c = a - b
>>> c
Array[10 10 10 10]
```

Do note that when you subtract two arrays, they should be of equal dimensions.

Squaring an array

The following command raises each element to the power of `2` to obtain this result:

```
>>> b**2
[1  4  9 16]
```

A trigonometric function performed on the array

The following command applies cosine to each of the values in the `b` array to obtain the following result:

```
>>> np.cos(b)
[ 0.54030231 -0.41614684 -0.9899925  -0.65364362]
```

Conditional operations

The following command will apply a conditional operation to each of the elements of the `b` array, in order to generate the respective Boolean values:

```
>>> b<2
[ True False False False]
```

Matrix multiplication

Two matrices can be multiplied element by element or in a dot product. The following commands will perform the element-by-element multiplication:

```
>>> A1 = np.array([[1, 1],
                   [0, 1]])


>>> A2 = np.array([[2, 0],
                   [3, 4]])


>>> A1 * A2
[[2 0]
[0 4]]
```

The `dot` product can be performed with the following command:

```
>>> np.dot(A1, A2)
[[5 4]
[3 4]]
```

Indexing and slicing

If you want to select a particular element of an array, it can be achieved using indexes:

```
>>> n_array[0,1]
1
```

The preceding command will select the first array and then select the second value in the array. It can also be seen as an intersection of the first row and the second column of the matrix.

If a range of values has to be selected on a row, then we can use the following command:

```
>>> n_array[ 0 , 0:3 ]
[0 1 2]
```

The `0:3` value selects the first three values of the first row.

The whole row of values can be selected with the following command:

```
>>> n_array[ 0 , : ]
[0 1 2 3]
```

Using the following command, an entire column of values need to be selected:

```
>>> n_array[ : , 1 ]
[1 5 9]
```

Shape manipulation

Once the array has been created, we can change the shape of it too. The following command flattens the array:

```
>>> n_array.ravel()
[ 0  1  2  3  4  5  6  7  8  9 10 11]
```

The following command reshapes the array in to a six rows and two columns format. Also, note that when reshaping, the new shape should have the same number of elements as the previous one:

```
>>> n_array.shape = (6,2)
>>> n_array
[[ 0  1]
[ 2  3]
[ 4  5]
[ 6  7]
[ 8  9]
[10 11]]
```

The array can be transposed too:

```
>>> n_array.transpose()
[[ 0  2  4  6  8 10]
[ 1  3  5  7  9 11]]
```

Empowering data analysis with pandas

The pandas library was developed by Wes McKinny when he was working at AQR Capital Management. He wanted a tool that was flexible enough to perform quantitative analysis on financial data. Later, Chang She joined him and helped develop the package further.

The pandas library is an open source Python library, specially designed for data analysis. It has been built on NumPy and makes it easy to handle data. NumPy is a fairly low-level tool that handles matrices really well.

The pandas library brings the richness of R in the world of Python to handle data. It's has efficient data structures to process data, perform fast joins, and read data from various sources, to name a few.

The data structure of pandas

The pandas library essentially has three data structures:

1. Series
2. DataFrame
3. Panel

Series

Series is a one-dimensional array, which can hold any type of data, such as integers, floats, strings, and Python objects too. A series can be created by calling the following:

```
>>> import pandas as pd
>>> pd.Series(np.random.randn(5))

0    0.733810
1   -1.274658
2   -1.602298
3    0.460944
4   -0.632756
dtype: float64
```

The `random.randn` parameter is part of the NumPy package and it generates random numbers. The series function creates a pandas series that consists of an index, which is the first column, and the second column consists of random values. At the bottom of the output is the datatype of the series.

The index of the series can be customized by calling the following:

```
>>> pd.Series(np.random.randn(5), index=['a', 'b', 'c', 'd', 'e'])


a    -0.929494
b    -0.571423
c    -1.197866
d     0.081107
e    -0.035091
dtype: float64
```

A series can be derived from a Python dict too:

```
>>> d = {'A': 10, 'B': 20, 'C': 30}
>>> pd.Series(d)


A     10
B     20
C     30
dtype: int64
```

DataFrame

DataFrame is a 2D data structure with columns that can be of different datatypes. It can be seen as a table. A DataFrame can be formed from the following data structures:

- A NumPy array
- Lists
- Dicts
- Series
- A 2D NumPy array

A `DataFrame` can be created from a dict of series by calling the following commands:

```
>>> d = {'c1': pd.Series(['A', 'B', 'C']),
         'c2': pd.Series([1, 2., 3., 4.])}
>>> df = pd.DataFrame(d)
>>> df

   c1  c2
0    A   1
1    B   2
2    C   3
3  NaN   4
```

The DataFrame can be created using a dict of lists too:

```
>>> d = {'c1': ['A', 'B', 'C', 'D'],
     'c2': [1, 2.0, 3.0, 4.0]}
>>> df = pd.DataFrame(d)
>>> print df
 c1  c2
0 A   1
1 B   2
2 C   3
3 D   4
```

Panel

A `Panel` is a data structure that handles 3D data. The following command is an example of panel data:

```
>>> d = {'Item1': pd.DataFrame(np.random.randn(4, 3)),
     'Item2': pd.DataFrame(np.random.randn(4, 2))}
>>> pd.Panel(d)

<class 'pandas.core.panel.Panel'>
Dimensions: 2 (items) x 4 (major_axis) x 3 (minor_axis)
Items axis: Item1 to Item2
Major_axis axis: 0 to 3
Minor_axis axis: 0 to 2
```

The preceding command shows that there are 2 DataFrames represented by two items. There are four rows represented by four major axes and three columns represented by three minor axes.

Inserting and exporting data

The data is stored in various forms, such as CSV, TSV, databases, and so on. The pandas library makes it convenient to read data from these formats or to export to these formats. We'll use a dataset that contains the weight statistics of the school students from the U.S..

We'll be using a file with the following structure:

Column	**Description**
`LOCATION CODE`	Unique location code
`COUNTY`	The county the school belongs to
`AREA NAME`	The district the school belongs to
`REGION`	The region the school belongs to
`SCHOOL YEARS`	The school year the data is addressing
`NO. OVERWEIGHT`	The number of overweight students
`PCT OVERWEIGHT`	The percentage of overweight students
`NO. OBESE`	The number of obese students
`PCT OBESE`	The percentage of obese students
`NO. OVERWEIGHT OR OBESE`	The number of students who are overweight or obese
`PCT OVERWEIGHT OR OBESE`	The percentage of students who are overweight or obese
`GRADE LEVEL`	Whether they belong to elementary or high school
`AREA TYPE`	The type of area
`STREET ADDRESS`	The address of the school
`CITY`	The city the school belongs to
`STATE`	The state the school belongs to
`ZIP CODE`	The zip code of the school
`Location 1`	The address with longitude and latitude

CSV

To read data from a `.csv` file, the following `read_csv` function can be used:

```
>>> d = pd.read_csv('Data/Student_Weight_Status_Category_
        Reporting_Results__Beginning_2010.csv')
>>> d[0:5]['AREA NAME']

0    RAVENA COEYMANS SELKIRK CENTRAL SCHOOL DISTRICT
1    RAVENA COEYMANS SELKIRK CENTRAL SCHOOL DISTRICT
2    RAVENA COEYMANS SELKIRK CENTRAL SCHOOL DISTRICT
3                         COHOES CITY SCHOOL DISTRICT
4                         COHOES CITY SCHOOL DISTRICT
```

The `read_csv` function takes the path of the `.csv` file to input the data. The command after this prints the first five rows of the `Location` column in the data.

To write a data to the `.csv` file, the following `to_csv` function can be used:

```
>>> d = {'c1': pd.Series(['A', 'B', 'C']),
    'c2': pd.Series([1, 2., 3., 4.])}
>>> df = pd.DataFrame(d)
>>> df.to_csv('sample_data.csv')
```

The DataFrame is written to a `.csv` file by using the `to_csv` method. The path and the filename where the file needs to be created should be mentioned.

XLS

In addition to the pandas package, the `xlrd` package needs to be installed for pandas to read the data from an Excel file:

```
>>> d=pd.read_excel('Data/Student_Weight_Status_Category
        _Reporting_Results__Beginning_2010.xls')
```

The preceding function is similar to the CSV reading command. To write to an Excel file, the `xlwt` package needs to be installed:

```
>>> df.to_excel('sample_data.xls')
```

JSON

To read the data from a JSON file, Python's standard `json` package can be used. The following commands help in reading the file:

```
>>> import json
>>> json_data = open('Data/Student_Weight_Status_Category
        _Reporting_Results__Beginning_2010.json')
>>> data = json.load(json_data)
>>> json_data.close()
```

In the preceding command, the `open()` function opens a connection to the file. The `json.load()` function loads the data into Python. The `json_data.close()` function closes the connection to the file.

The pandas library also provides a function to read the JSON file, which can be accessed using `pd.read_json()`.

Database

To read data from a database, the following function can be used:

```
>>> pd.read_sql_table(table_name, con)
```

The preceding command generates a DataFrame. If a table name and an SQLAlchemy engine are given, they return a DataFrame. This function does not support the DBAPI connection. The following are the description of the parameters used:

- `table_name`: This refers to the name of the SQL table in a database
- `con`: This refers to the SQLAlchemy engine

The following command reads SQL query into a DataFrame:

```
>>> pd.read_sql_query(sql, con)
```

The following are the description of the parameters used:

- `sql`: This refers to the SQL query that is to be executed
- `con`: This refers to the SQLAlchemy engine

Data cleansing

The data in its raw form generally requires some cleaning so that it can be analyzed or a dashboard can be created on it. There are many reasons that data might have issues. For example, the Point of Sale system at a retail shop might have malfunctioned and inputted some data with missing values. We'll be learning how to handle such data in the following section.

Checking the missing data

Generally, most data will have some missing values. There could be various reasons for this: the source system which collects the data might not have collected the values or the values may never have existed. Once you have the data loaded, it is essential to check the missing elements in the data. Depending on the requirements, the missing data needs to be handled. It can be handled by removing a row or replacing a missing value with an alternative value.

In the `Student Weight` data, to check if the location column has missing value, the following command can be utilized:

```
>>> d['Location 1'].isnull()
0        False
1        False
2        False
3        False
4        False
5        False
6        False
```

The `notnull()` method will output each row of the value as `TRUE` or `FALSE`. If it's `False`, then there is a missing value. This data can be aggregated to find the number of instances of the missing value:

```
>>> d['Location 1'].isnull().value_counts()
False    3246
True       24
dtype: int64
```

The preceding command shows that the `Location 1` column has `24` instances of missing values. These missing values can be handled by either removing the rows with the missing values or replacing it with some values. To remove the rows, execute the following command:

```
>>> d = d['Location 1'].dropna()
```

To remove all the rows with an instance of missing values, use the following command:

```
>>> d = d.dropna(how='any')
```

Filling the missing data

Let's define some DataFrames to work with:

```
>>> df = pd.DataFrame(np.random.randn(5, 3), index=['a0', 'a10',
                      'a20', 'a30', 'a40'],
                      columns=['X', 'Y', 'Z'])
>>> df
            X         Y         Z
a0  -0.854269  0.117540  1.515373
a10 -0.483923 -0.379934  0.484155
a20 -0.038317  0.196770 -0.564176
a30  0.752686  1.329661 -0.056649
a40 -1.383379  0.632615  1.274481
```

We'll now add some extra row indexes, which will create null values in our DataFrame:

```
>>> df2 = df2.reindex(['a0', 'a1', 'a10', 'a11', 'a20', 'a21',
                  'a30', 'a31', 'a40', 'a41'])
>>> df2

            X         Y         Z
a0  -1.193371  0.912654 -0.780461
a1        NaN       NaN       NaN
a10  1.413044  0.615997  0.947334
a11       NaN       NaN       NaN
a20  1.583516  1.388921  0.458771
a21       NaN       NaN       NaN
a30  0.479579  1.427625  1.407924
a31       NaN       NaN       NaN
a40  0.455510 -0.880937  1.375555
a41       NaN       NaN       NaN
```

If you want to replace the null values in the `df2` DataFrame with a value of zero in the following case, execute the following command:

```
>>> df2.fillna(0)

            X         Y         Z
a0  -1.193371  0.912654 -0.780461
```

```
a1    0.000000  0.000000  0.000000
a10   1.413044  0.615997  0.947334
a11   0.000000  0.000000  0.000000
a20   1.583516  1.388921  0.458771
a21   0.000000  0.000000  0.000000
a30   0.479579  1.427625  1.407924
a31   0.000000  0.000000  0.000000
a40   0.455510 -0.880937  1.375555
a41   0.000000  0.000000  0.000000
```

If you want to fill the value with forward propagation, which means that the value previous to the null value in the column will be used to fill the null value, the following command can be used:

```
>>> df2.fillna(method='pad') #filling with forward propagation

            X         Y         Z
a0  -1.193371  0.912654 -0.780461
a1  -1.193371  0.912654 -0.780461
a10  1.413044  0.615997  0.947334
a11  1.413044  0.615997  0.947334
a20  1.583516  1.388921  0.458771
a21  1.583516  1.388921  0.458771
a30  0.479579  1.427625  1.407924
a31  0.479579  1.427625  1.407924
a40  0.455510 -0.880937  1.375555
a41  0.455510 -0.880937  1.375555
```

If you want to fill the null values of the column with the column mean, then the following command can be utilized:

```
>>> df2.fillna(df2.mean())

            X         Y         Z
a0  -1.193371  0.912654 -0.780461
a1   0.547655  0.692852  0.681825
a10  1.413044  0.615997  0.947334
a11  0.547655  0.692852  0.681825
a20  1.583516  1.388921  0.458771
```

```
a21   0.547655   0.692852   0.681825
a30   0.479579   1.427625   1.407924
a31   0.547655   0.692852   0.681825
a40   0.455510  -0.880937   1.375555
a41   0.547655   0.692852   0.681825
```

String operations

Sometimes, you would want to modify the string field column in your data. The following technique explains some of the string operations:

- **Substring**: Let's start by choosing the first five rows of the `AREA NAME` column in the data as our sample data to modify:

  ```
  >>> df = pd.read_csv('Data/Student_Weight_Status_Category_
          Reporting_Results__Beginning_2010.csv')
  >>> df['AREA NAME'][0:5]

  0     RAVENA COEYMANS SELKIRK CENTRAL SCHOOL DISTRICT
  1     RAVENA COEYMANS SELKIRK CENTRAL SCHOOL DISTRICT
  2     RAVENA COEYMANS SELKIRK CENTRAL SCHOOL DISTRICT
  3                         COHOES CITY SCHOOL DISTRICT
  4                         COHOES CITY SCHOOL DISTRICT
  Name: AREA NAME, dtype: object
  ```

  In order to extract the first word from the `Area Name` column, we'll use the `extract` function as shown in the following command:

  ```
  >>> df['AREA NAME'][0:5].str.extract('(\w+)')

  0     RAVENA
  1     RAVENA
  2     RAVENA
  3     COHOES
  4     COHOES
  Name: AREA NAME, dtype: object
  ```

In the preceding command, the `str` attribute of the series is utilized. The `str` class contains an `extract` method, where a regular expression could be fed to extract data, which is very powerful. It is also possible to extract a second word in `AREA NAME` as a separate column:

```
>>> df['AREA NAME'][0:5].str.extract('(\w+)\s(\w+)')
        0         1
0  RAVENA  COEYMANS
1  RAVENA  COEYMANS
2  RAVENA  COEYMANS
3  COHOES      CITY
4  COHOES      CITY
```

To extract data in different columns, the respective regular expression needs to be enclosed in separate parentheses.

- **Filtering**: If we want to filter rows with data on `ELEMENTARY` school, then the following command can be used:

```
>>> df[df['GRADE LEVEL'] == 'ELEMENTARY']
```

- **Uppercase**: To convert the area name to uppercase, we'll use the following command:

```
>>> df['AREA NAME'][0:5].str.upper()
0    RAVENA COEYMANS SELKIRK CENTRAL SCHOOL DISTRICT
1    RAVENA COEYMANS SELKIRK CENTRAL SCHOOL DISTRICT
2    RAVENA COEYMANS SELKIRK CENTRAL SCHOOL DISTRICT
3                        COHOES CITY SCHOOL DISTRICT
4                        COHOES CITY SCHOOL DISTRICT
Name: AREA NAME, dtype: object
```

Since the data strings are in uppercase already, there won't be any difference seen.

- **Lowercase**: To convert `Area Name` to lowercase, we'll use the following command:

```
>>> df['AREA NAME'][0:5].str.lower()
0    ravena coeymans selkirk central school district
1    ravena coeymans selkirk central school district
2    ravena coeymans selkirk central school district
3                        cohoes city school district
4                        cohoes city school district
Name: AREA NAME, dtype: object
```

- **Length**: To find the length of each element of the `Area Name` column, we'll use the following command:

```
>>> df['AREA NAME'][0:5].str.len()
0    47
1    47
2    47
3    27
4    27
Name: AREA NAME, dtype: int64
```

- **Split**: To split `Area Name` based on a whitespace, we'll use the following command:

```
>>> df['AREA NAME'][0:5].str.split(' ')

0    [RAVENA, COEYMANS, SELKIRK, CENTRAL, SCHOOL, D...
1    [RAVENA, COEYMANS, SELKIRK, CENTRAL, SCHOOL, D...
2    [RAVENA, COEYMANS, SELKIRK, CENTRAL, SCHOOL, D...
3                     [COHOES, CITY, SCHOOL, DISTRICT]
4                     [COHOES, CITY, SCHOOL, DISTRICT]
Name: AREA NAME, dtype: object
```

- **Replace**: If we want to replace all the area names ending with `DISTRICT` to `DIST`, then the following command can be used:

```
>>> df['AREA NAME'][0:5].str.replace('DISTRICT$', 'DIST')

0    RAVENA COEYMANS SELKIRK CENTRAL SCHOOL DIST
1    RAVENA COEYMANS SELKIRK CENTRAL SCHOOL DIST
2    RAVENA COEYMANS SELKIRK CENTRAL SCHOOL DIST
3                      COHOES CITY SCHOOL DIST
4                      COHOES CITY SCHOOL DIST
Name: AREA NAME, dtype: object
```

The first argument in the replace method is the regular expression used to identify the portion of the string to replace. The second argument is the value for it to be replaced with.

Merging data

To combine datasets together, the `concat` function of pandas can be utilized. Let's take the `Area Name` and the `County` columns with its first five rows:

```
>>> d[['AREA NAME', 'COUNTY']][0:5]

                                  AREA NAME     COUNTY
0  RAVENA COEYMANS SELKIRK CENTRAL SCHOOL DISTRICT   ALBANY
1  RAVENA COEYMANS SELKIRK CENTRAL SCHOOL DISTRICT   ALBANY
2  RAVENA COEYMANS SELKIRK CENTRAL SCHOOL DISTRICT   ALBANY
3                     COHOES CITY SCHOOL DISTRICT   ALBANY
4                     COHOES CITY SCHOOL DISTRICT   ALBANY
```

We can divide the data as follows:

```
>>> p1 = d[['AREA NAME', 'COUNTY']][0:2]
>>> p2 = d[['AREA NAME', 'COUNTY']][2:5]
```

The first two rows of the data are in `p1` and the last three rows are in `p2`. These pieces can be combined using the `concat()` function:

```
>>> pd.concat([p1,p2])

                                  AREA NAME     COUNTY
0  RAVENA COEYMANS SELKIRK CENTRAL SCHOOL DISTRICT   ALBANY
1  RAVENA COEYMANS SELKIRK CENTRAL SCHOOL DISTRICT   ALBANY
2  RAVENA COEYMANS SELKIRK CENTRAL SCHOOL DISTRICT   ALBANY
3                     COHOES CITY SCHOOL DISTRICT   ALBANY
4                     COHOES CITY SCHOOL DISTRICT   ALBANY
```

The combined pieces can be identified by assigning a key:

```
>>> concatenated = pd.concat([p1,p2], keys = ['p1','p2'])
>>> concatenated
                       AREA NAME           COUNTY
p1 0  RAVENA COEYMANS SELKIRK CENTRAL SCHOOL DISTRICT     ALBANY
   1  RAVENA COEYMANS SELKIRK CENTRAL SCHOOL DISTRICT     ALBANY
p2 2  RAVENA COEYMANS SELKIRK CENTRAL SCHOOL DISTRICT     ALBANY
   3                     COHOES CITY SCHOOL DISTRICT    ALBANY
   4                     COHOES CITY SCHOOL DISTRICT    ALBANY
```

Using the keys, the pieces can be extracted back from the concatenated data:

```
>>> concatenated.ix['p1']

                                         AREA NAME     COUNTY
0  RAVENA COEYMANS SELKIRK CENTRAL SCHOOL DISTRICT    ALBANY
1  RAVENA COEYMANS SELKIRK CENTRAL SCHOOL DISTRICT    ALBANY
```

Data operations

Once the missing data is handled, various operations can be performed on the data.

Aggregation operations

There are a number of aggregation operations, such as average, sum, and so on, which you would like to perform on a numerical field. These are the methods used to perform it:

- **Average**: To find out the average number of students in the `ELEMENTARY` school who are obese, we'll first filter the `ELEMENTARY` data with the following command:

  ```
  >>> data = d[d['GRADE LEVEL'] == 'ELEMENTARY']
  213.41593780369291
  ```

  Now, we'll find the mean using the following command:

  ```
  >>> data['NO. OBESE'].mean()
  ```

  The elementary grade level data is filtered and stored in the data object. The `NO. OBESE` column is selected, which contains the number of obese students and using the `mean()` method, the average is taken out.

- **SUM**: To find out the total number of elementary students who are obese across all the school, use the following command:

  ```
  >>> data['NO. OBESE'].sum()
  219605.0
  ```

- **MAX**: To get the maximum number of students that are obese in an elementary school, use the following command:

  ```
  >>> data['NO. OBESE'].max()
  48843.0
  ```

- **MIN**: To get the minimum number of students that are obese in an elementary school, use the following command:

```
>>> data['NO. OBESE'].min()
5.0
```

- **STD**: To get the standard deviation of the number of obese students, use the following command:

```
>>> data['NO. OBESE'].std()
1690.3831128098113
```

- **COUNT**: To count the total number of schools with the `ELEMENTARY` grade in the `DELAWARE` county, use the following command:

```
>>> data = df[(d['GRADE LEVEL'] == 'ELEMENTARY') &
          (d['COUNTY'] == 'DELAWARE')]
>>> data['COUNTY'].count()
19
```

  The table is filtered for the `ELEMENTARY` grade and the `DELAWARE` county. Notice that the conditions are enclosed in parentheses. This is to ensure that individual conditions are evaluated and if the parentheses are not provided, then Python will throw an error.

Joins

SQL-like joins can be performed on the DataFrame using pandas. Let's define a lookup DataFrame, which assigns levels to each of the grades using the following command:

```
>>> grade_lookup = {'GRADE LEVEL': pd.Series(['ELEMENTARY',
               'MIDDLE/HIGH', 'MISC']),
               'LEVEL': pd.Series([1, 2, 3])}


>>> grade_lookup = DataFrame(grade_lookup)
```

Let's take the first five rows of the GRADE data column as an example for performing the joins:

```
>>> df[['GRADE LEVEL']][0:5]
      GRADE LEVEL
0  DISTRICT TOTAL
1      ELEMENTARY
2     MIDDLE/HIGH
3  DISTRICT TOTAL
4      ELEMENTARY
```

The inner join

The following image is a sample of an inner join:

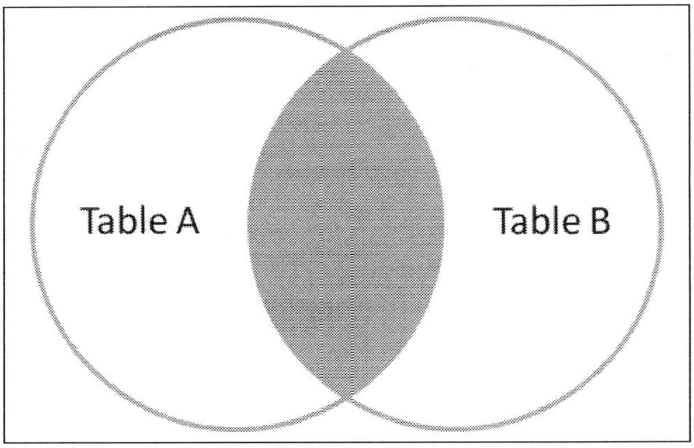

An inner join can be performed with the following command:

```
>>> d_sub = df[0:5].join(grade_lookup.set_index(['GRADE LEVEL']),
          on=['GRADE LEVEL'], how='inner')
>>> d_sub[['GRADE LEVEL', 'LEVEL']]

  GRADE LEVEL  LEVEL
1   ELEMENTARY      1
4   ELEMENTARY      1
2  MIDDLE/HIGH      2
```

The join takes place with the `join()` method. The first argument takes the DataFrame on which the lookup takes place. Note that the `grade_lookup` DataFrame's index is being set by the `set_index()` method. This is essential for a join, as without it, the join method won't know on which column to join the DataFrame to.

The second argument takes a column of the `d` DataFrame to join the data. The third argument defines the join as an inner join.

The left outer join

The following image is a sample of a left outer join:

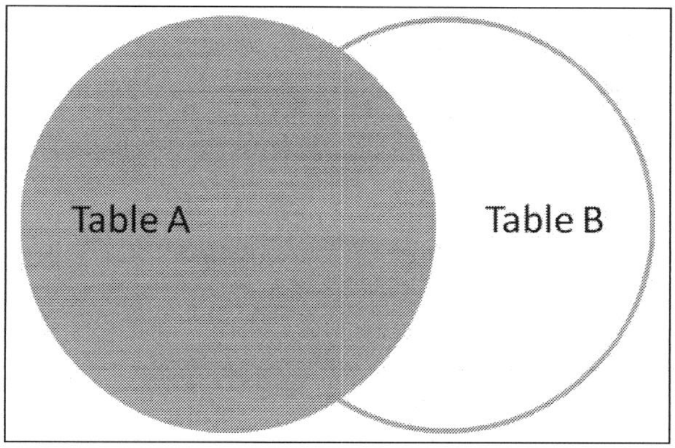

A left outer join can be performed with the following commands:

```
>>> d_sub = df[0:5].join(grade_lookup.set_index(['GRADE LEVEL']),
on=['GRADE LEVEL'], how='left')
>>> d_sub[['GRADE LEVEL', 'LEVEL']]

      GRADE LEVEL  LEVEL
0  DISTRICT TOTAL    NaN
1      ELEMENTARY      1
2     MIDDLE/HIGH      2
3  DISTRICT TOTAL    NaN
4      ELEMENTARY      1
```

You can notice that `DISTRICT TOTAL` has missing values for a level column, as the `grade_lookup` DataFrame does not have an instance for `DISTRICT TOTAL`.

The full outer join

The following image is a sample of a full outer join:

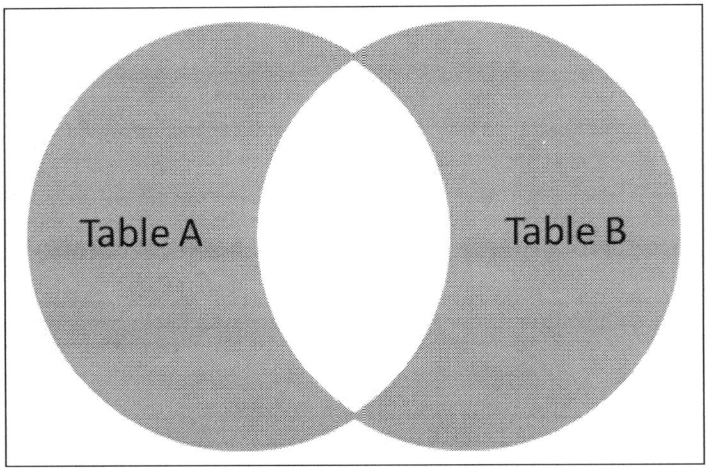

The full outer join can be performed with the following commands:

```
>>> d_sub = df[0:5].join(grade_lookup.set_index(['GRADE LEVEL']),
            on=['GRADE LEVEL'], how='outer')
>>> d_sub[['GRADE LEVEL', 'LEVEL']]
```

```
     GRADE LEVEL  LEVEL
0  DISTRICT TOTAL    NaN
3  DISTRICT TOTAL    NaN
1      ELEMENTARY      1
4      ELEMENTARY      1
2     MIDDLE/HIGH      2
4            MISC      3
```

The groupby function

It's easy to do an SQL-like group by operation with pandas. Let's say, if you want to find the sum of the number of obese students in each of the grades, then you can use the following command:

```
>>> df['NO. OBESE'].groupby(d['GRADE LEVEL']).sum()
GRADE LEVEL
```

```
DISTRICT TOTAL     127101
ELEMENTARY          72880
MIDDLE/HIGH         53089
```

This command chooses the number of obese students column, then uses the group by method to group the data-based group level, and finally, the sum method sums up the number. The same can be achieved by the following function too:

```
>>> d['NO. OBESE'].groupby(d['GRADE LEVEL']).aggregate(sum)
```

Here, the aggregate method is utilized. The sum function is passed to obtain the required results.

It's also possible to obtain multiple kinds of aggregations on the same metric. This can be achieved by the following command:

```
>>> df['NO. OBESE'].groupby(d['GRADE LEVEL']).aggregate([sum, mean,
        std])
                   sum         mean          std
GRADE LEVEL
DISTRICT TOTAL  127101   128.384848   158.933263
ELEMENTARY       72880    76.958817   100.289578
MIDDLE/HIGH      53089    59.251116    65.905591
```

Summary

In this chapter, we got familiarized with the NumPy and pandas packages. We understood the different datatypes in pandas and how to utilize them. We learned how to perform data cleansing and manipulation, in which we handled missing values and performed string operations. This chapter gives us a foundation for data science and you can dive deeper into NumPy and pandas by clicking on the following links:

- **NumPy documentation**: `http://docs.scipy.org/doc/`
- **pandas documentation**: `http://pandas.pydata.org/`

In the next chapter, we'll learn about the meaning of inferential statistics and what they do, and also how to make sense of the different concepts in inferential statistics.

2
Inferential Statistics

Before getting understanding the inferential statistics, let's look at what descriptive statistics is about.

Descriptive statistics is a term given to data analysis that summarizes data in a meaningful way such that patterns emerge from it. It is a simple way to describe data, but it does not help us to reach a conclusion on the hypothesis that we have made. Let's say you have collected the height of 1,000 people living in Hong Kong. The mean of their height would be descriptive statistics, but their mean height does not indicate that it's the average height of whole of Hong Kong. Here, inferential statistics will help us in determining what the average height of whole of Hong Kong would be, which is described in depth in this chapter.

Inferential statistics is all about describing the larger picture of the analysis with a limited set of data and deriving conclusions from it.

In this chapter, we will cover the following topics:

- The different kinds of distributions
- Different statistical tests that can be utilized to test a hypothesis
- How to make inferences about the population of a sample from the data given
- Different kinds of errors that can occur during hypothesis testing
- Defining the confidence interval at which the population mean lies
- The significance of p-value and how it can be utilized to interpret results

Various forms of distribution

There are various kinds of probability distributions, and each distribution shows the probability of different outcomes for a random experiment. In this section, we'll explore the various kinds of probability distributions.

A normal distribution

A normal distribution is the most common and widely used distribution in statistics. It is also called a "bell curve" and "Gaussian curve" after the mathematician Karl Friedrich Gauss. A normal distribution occurs commonly in nature. Let's take the height example we saw previously. If you have data for the height of all the people of a particular gender in Hong Kong city, and you plot a bar chart where each bar represents the number of people at this particular height, then the curve that is obtained will look very similar to the following graph. The numbers in the plot are the standard deviation numbers from the mean, which is zero. The concept will become clearer as we proceed through the chapter.

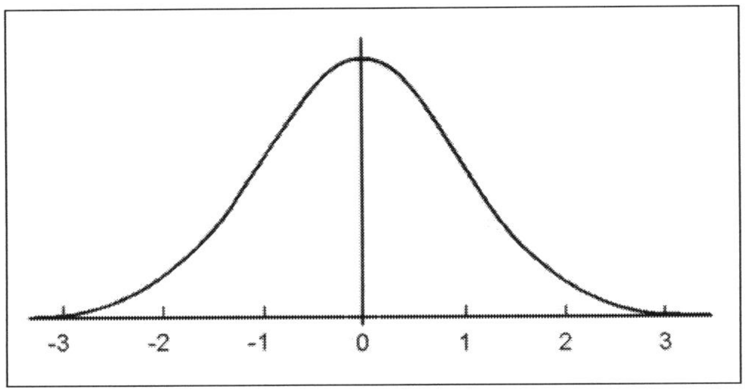

Also, if you take an hourglass and observe the way sand stacks up when the hour glass is inverted, it forms a normal distribution. This is a good example that shows how normal distribution exists in nature.

Take the following figure: it shows three curves with normal distribution. The curve **A** has a standard deviation of 1, curve **C** has a standard deviation of 2, and curve **B** has a standard deviation of 3, which means that the curve **B** has the maximum spread of values, whereas curve **A** has the least spread of values. One more way of looking at it is if curve **B** represented the height of people of a country, then this country has a lot of people with diverse heights, whereas the country with the curve **A** distribution will have people whose heights are similar to each other.

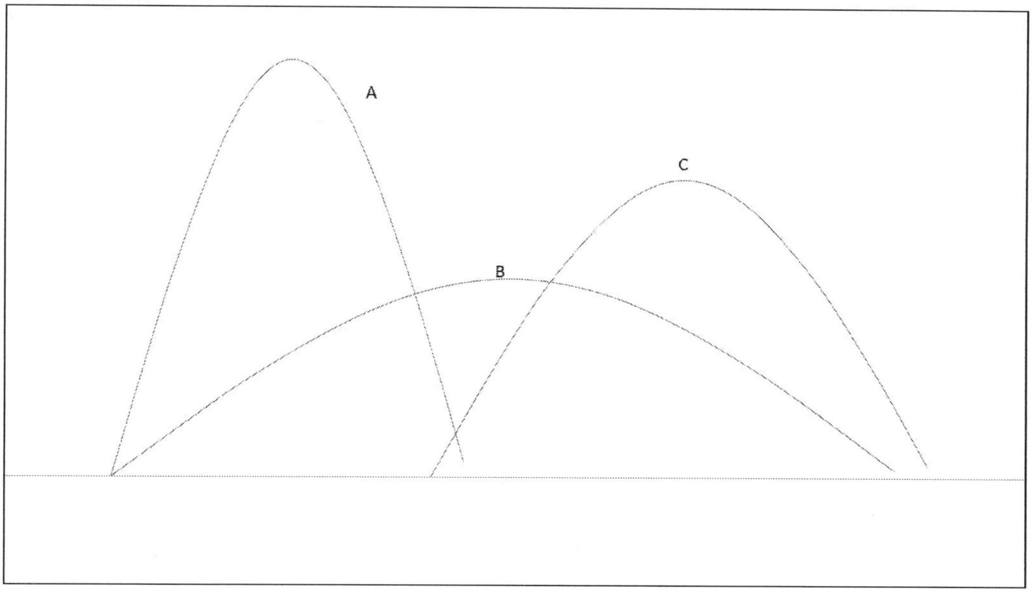

A normal distribution from a binomial distribution

Let's take a coin and flip it. The probability of getting a head or a tail is 50%. If you take the same coin and flip it six times, the probability of getting a head three times can be computed using the following formula:

$$P(x) = \frac{n!}{x!(n-x)!} p^x q^{n-x}$$

$$\textit{and } x \text{ is the number of successes desired}$$

In the preceding formula, n is the number of times the coin is flipped, p is the probability of success, and q is $(1-p)$, which is the probability of failure.

The SciPy package of Python provides useful functions to perform statistical computations. You can install it from `http://www.scipy.org/`. The following commands helps in plotting the binomial distribution:

```
>>> from scipy.stats import binom
>>> import matplotlib.pyplot as plt


>>> fig, ax = plt.subplots(1, 1)
>>> x = [0, 1, 2, 3, 4, 5, 6]
>>> n, p = 6, 0.5
>>> rv = binom(n, p)
>>> ax.vlines(x, 0, rv.pmf(x), colors='k', linestyles='-', lw=1,
        label='Probablity')

>>> ax.legend(loc='best', frameon=False)
>>> plt.show()
```

The `binom` function in the SciPy package helps generate binomial distributions and the necessary statistics related to it. If you observe the preceding commands, there are parts of it that are from the matplotlib, which we'll use right now to plot the binomial distribution. The matplotlib library will be covered in detail in later chapters. The `plt.subplots` function helps in generating multiple plots on a screen. The `binom` function takes in the number of attempts and the probability of success. The `ax.vlines` function is used to plot vertical lines and `rv.pmf` within it helps in calculating the probability at various values of `x`. The `ax.legend` function adds a legend to the graph, and finally, `plt.show` displays the graph. The result is as follows:

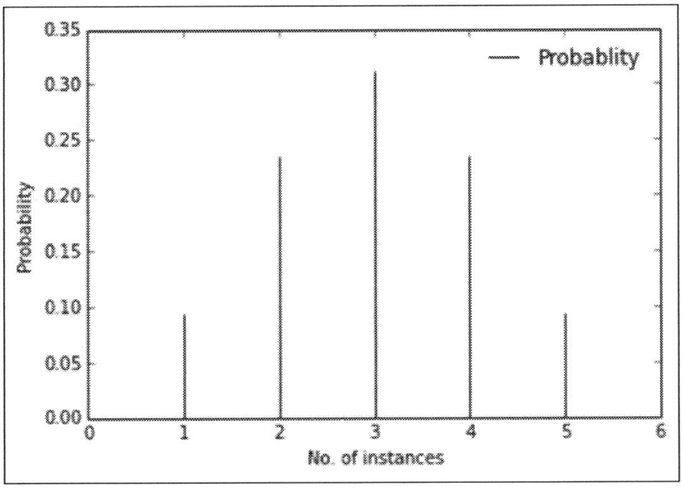

As you can see in the graph, if the coin is flipped six times, then getting three heads has the maximum probability, whereas getting a single head or five heads has the least probability.

Now, let's increase the number of attempts and see the distribution:

```
>>> fig, ax = plt.subplots(1, 1)
>>> x = range(101)
>>> n, p = 100, 0.5
>>> rv = binom(n, p)
>>> ax.vlines(x, 0, rv.pmf(x), colors='k', linestyles='-', lw=1,
          label='Probablity')

>>> ax.legend(loc='best', frameon=False)
>>> plt.show()
```

Here, we try to flip the coin 100 times and see the distribution:

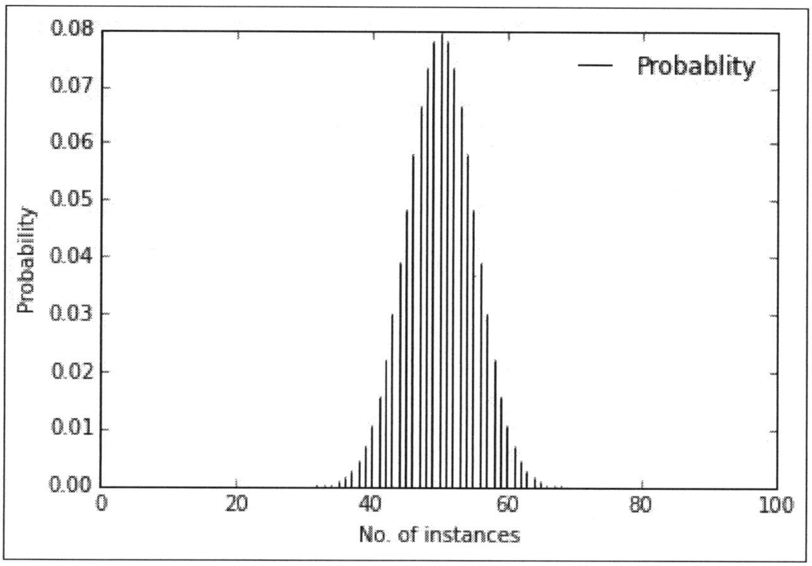

When the probability of success is changed to `0.4`, this is what you see:

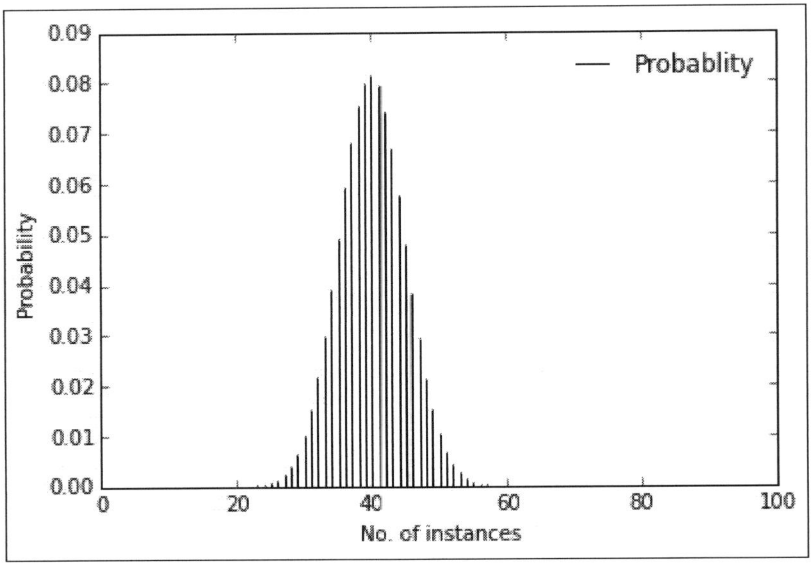

When the probability is `0.6`, this is what you see:

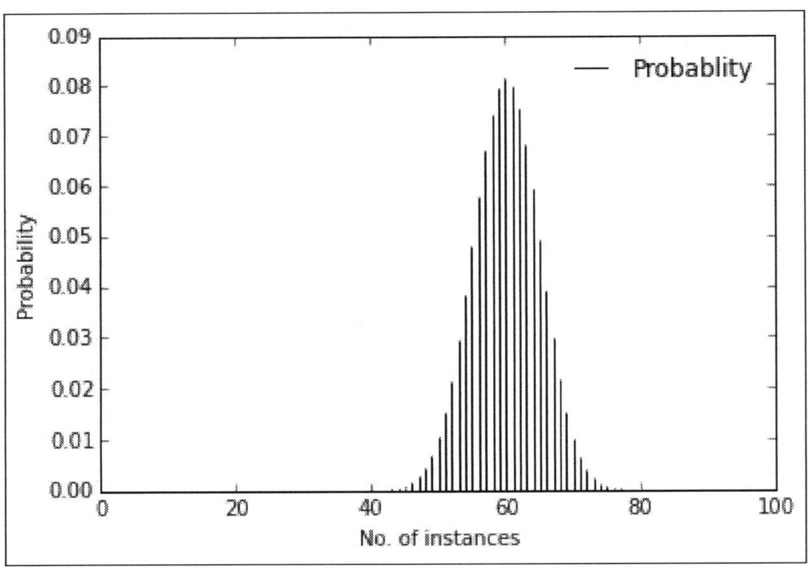

When you flip the coin 1000 times at `0.5` probability:

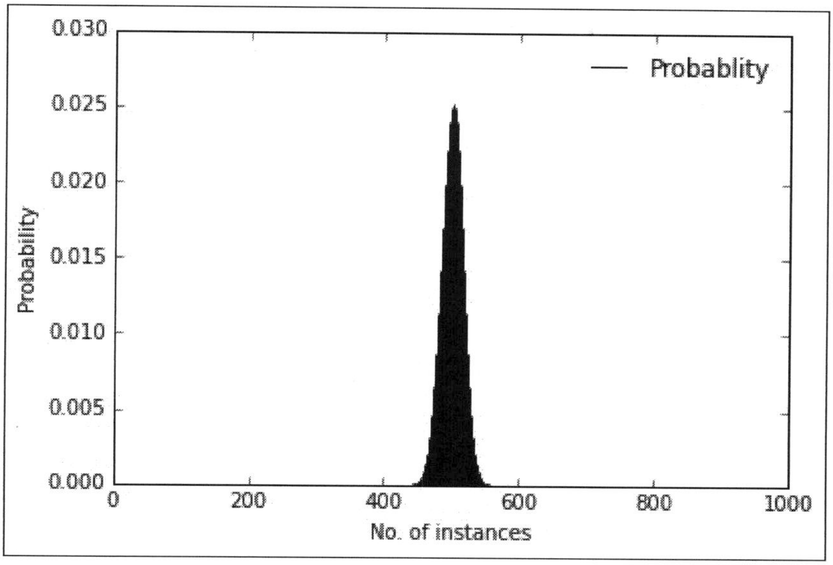

As you can see, the binomial distribution has started to resemble a normal distribution.

A Poisson distribution

A Poisson distribution is the probability distribution of independent interval occurrences in an interval. A binomial distribution is used to determine the probability of binary occurrences, whereas, a Poisson distribution is used for count-based distributions. If lambda is the mean occurrence of the events per interval, then the probability of having a *k* occurrence within a given interval is given by the following formula:

$$f(k;\lambda) = \Pr(X = k) = \frac{\lambda^k e^{-\lambda}}{k!}$$

Here, *e* is the Euler's number, *k* is the number of occurrences for which the probability is going to be determined, and lambda is the mean number of occurrences.

Let's understand this with an example. The number of cars that pass through a bridge in an hour is 20. What would be the probability of 23 cars passing through the bridge in an hour?

For this, we'll use the poisson function from SciPy:

```
>>> from scipy.stats import poisson
>>> rv = poisson(20)
>>> rv.pmf(23)

0.066881473662401172
```

With the Poisson function, we define the mean value, which is 20 cars. The `rv.pmf` function gives the probability, which is around 6%, that 23 cars will pass the bridge.

A Bernoulli distribution

You can perform an experiment with two possible outcomes: success or failure. Success has a probability of *p*, and failure has a probability of *1 - p*. A random variable that takes a *1* value in case of a success and *0* in case of failure is called a Bernoulli distribution. The probability distribution function can be written as:

$$P(n)=\begin{cases}1-p & \text{for } n=0\\ p & \text{for } n=1\end{cases}$$

It can also be written like this:

$$P(n)=p^{n}(1-p)^{1-n}$$

The distribution function can be written like this:

$$D(n)=\begin{cases}1-p & \text{for } n=0\\ 1 & \text{for } n=1\end{cases}$$

Following plot shows a Bernoulli distribution:

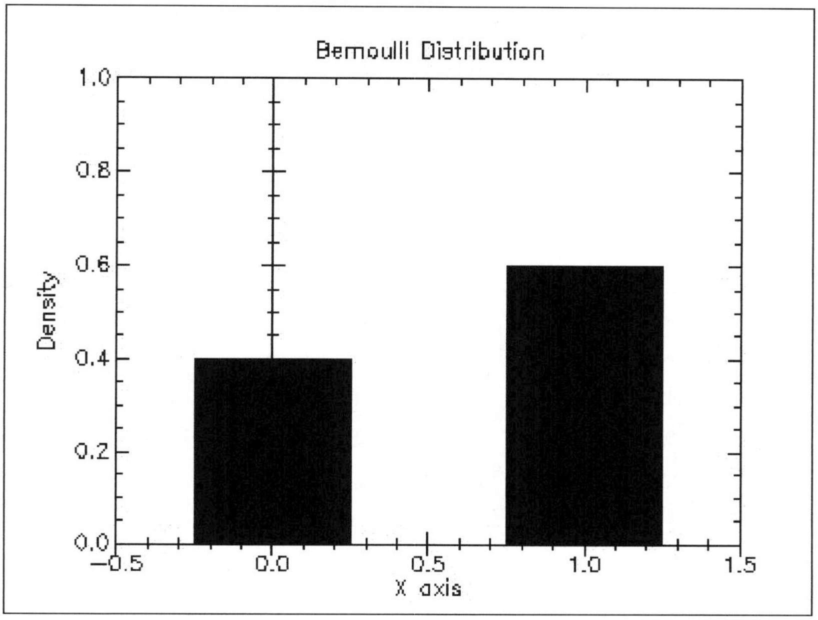

Voting in an election is a good example of the Bernoulli distribution.

A Bernoulli distribution can be generated using the `bernoulli.rvs()` function of the SciPy package. The following function generates a Bernoulli distribution with a probability of 0.7:

```
>>> from scipy import stats
>>> stats.bernoulli.rvs(0.7, size=100)
array([1, 1, 1, 1, 1, 0, 0, 1, 1, 0, 1, 1, 1, 0, 1, 1, 1, 1, 1, 1, 1,
         1, 0,
       1, 1, 1, 0, 1, 1, 0, 1, 0, 0, 1, 0, 0, 1, 0, 1, 0, 1, 1, 1, 1,
         1, 0,
       1, 1, 1, 1, 1, 0, 0, 1, 1, 1, 0, 1, 0, 1, 0, 0, 0, 0, 0, 1, 0,
         0, 0,
       1, 1, 1, 0, 1, 0, 1, 1, 1, 1, 1, 1, 0, 0, 1, 1, 1, 0, 0, 0, 1,
         1, 1,
       1, 0, 1, 1, 1, 0, 1, 1])])
```

If the preceding output is the number of votes for a candidate by people, then the candidate has 70% of the votes.

A z-score

A z-score, in simple terms, is a score that expresses the value of a distribution in standard deviation with respect to the mean. Let's take a look at the following formula that calculates the z-score:

$$z = (X - \mu) / \sigma$$

Here, X is the value in the distribution, μ is the mean of the distribution, and σ is the standard deviation of the distribution

Let's try to understand this concept from the perspective of a school classroom.

A classroom has 60 students in it and they have just got their mathematics examination score. We simulate the score of these 60 students with a normal distribution using the following command:

```
>>> classscore
>>> classscore = np.random.normal(50, 10, 60).round()


[ 56.  52.  60.  65.  39.  49.  41.  51.  48.  52.  47.  41.  60.
   54.  41.
  46.  37.  50.  50.  55.  47.  53.  38.  42.  42.  57.  40.  45.
   35.  39.
  67.  56.  35.  45.  47.  52.  48.  53.  53.  50.  61.  60.  57.
   53.  56.
  68.  43.  35.  45.  42.  33.  43.  49.  54.  45.  54.  48.  55.
   56.  30.]
```

The NumPy package has a random module that has a normal function, where 50 is given as the mean of the distribution, 10 is the standard deviation of the distribution, and 60 is the number of values to be generated. You can plot the normal distribution with the following commands:

```
>>> plt.hist(classscore, 30, normed=True) #Number of breaks is 30
>>> plt.show()
```

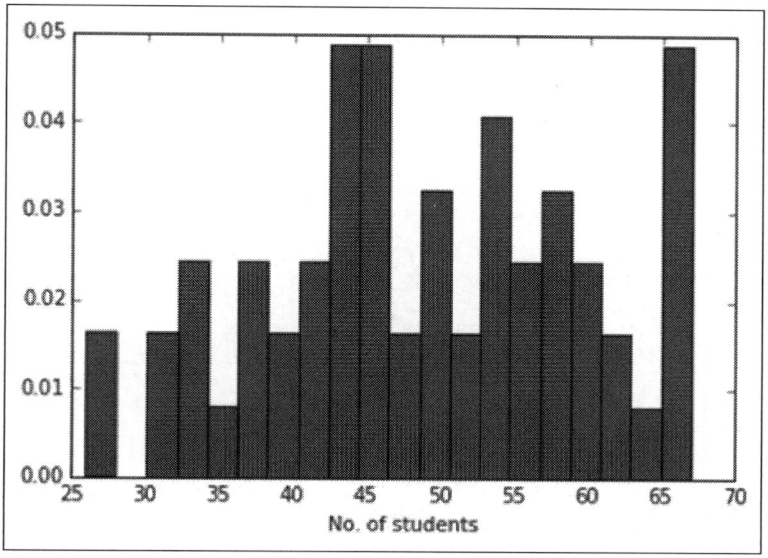

The score of each student can be converted to a z-score using the following functions:

```
>>> stats.zscore(classscore)


[ 0.86008868  0.38555699  1.33462036  1.92778497 -1.15667098
  0.02965823
 -0.91940514  0.26692407 -0.08897469  0.38555699 -0.20760761 -
  0.91940514
  1.33462036  0.62282284 -0.91940514 -0.32624053 -1.39393683
  0.14829115
  0.14829115  0.74145576 -0.20760761  0.50418992 -1.2753039  -
  0.80077222
 -0.80077222  0.9787216  -1.03803806 -0.44487345 -1.63120267 -
  1.15667098
  2.16505081  0.86008868 -1.63120267 -0.44487345 -0.20760761
  0.38555699
 -0.08897469  0.50418992  0.50418992  0.14829115  1.45325329
  1.33462036
  0.9787216   0.50418992  0.86008868  2.28368373 -0.6821393  -
  1.63120267
 -0.44487345 -0.80077222 -1.86846851 -0.6821393   0.02965823
  0.62282284
 -0.44487345  0.62282284 -0.08897469  0.74145576  0.86008868 -
  2.22436727]
```

So, a student with a score of 60 out of 100 has a z-score of 1.334. To make more sense of the z-score, we'll use the standard normal table.

This table helps in determining the probability of a score.

We would like to know what the probability of getting a score above 60 would be.

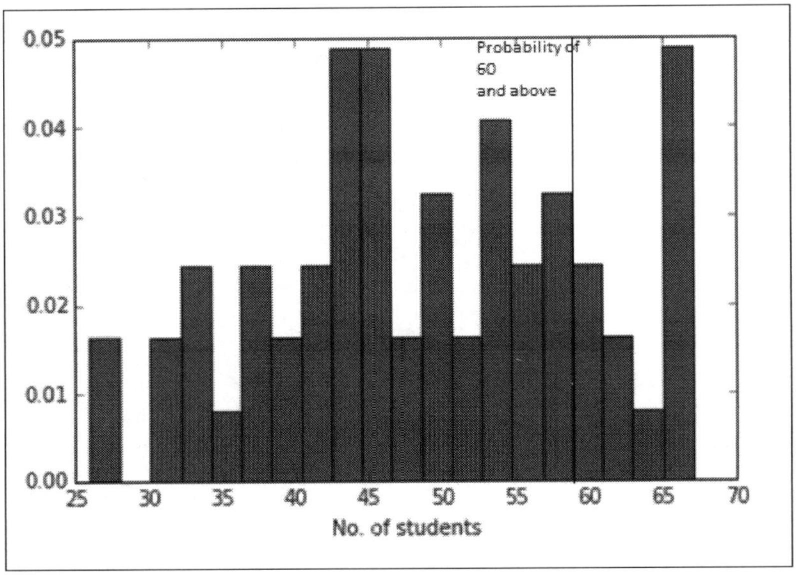

The standard normal table can help us in determining the probability of the occurrence of the score, but we do not have to perform the cumbersome task of finding the value by looking through the table and finding the probability. This task is made simple by the `cdf` function, which is the cumulative distribution function:

```
>>> prob = 1 - stats.norm.cdf(1.334)
>>> prob
```

```
0.091101928265359899
```

The `cdf` function gives the probability of getting values up to the z-score of `1.334`, and doing a minus one of it will give us the probability of getting a z-score, which is above it. In other words, 0.09 is the probability of getting marks above 60.

Let's ask another question, "how many students made it to the top 20% of the class?"

Here, we'll have to work backwards to determine the marks at which all the students above it are in the top 20% of the class:

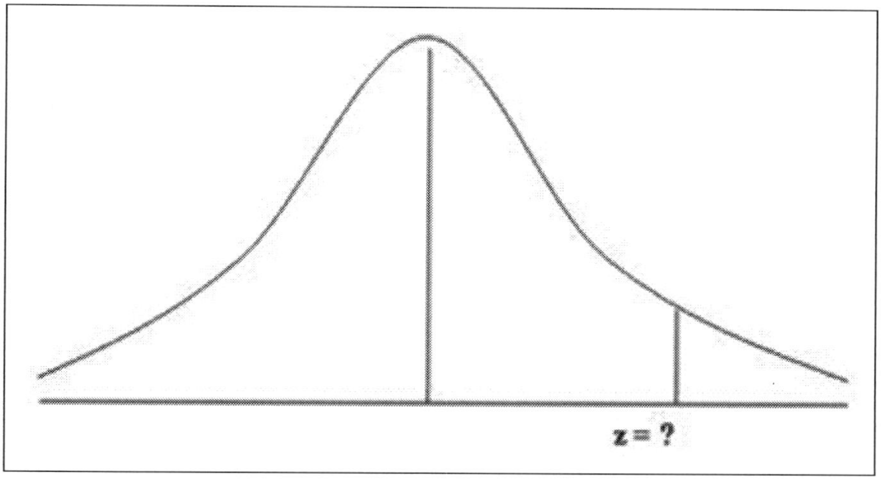

Now, to get the z-score at which the top 20% score marks, we can use the `ppf` function in SciPy:

```
>>> stats.norm.ppf(0.80)
```

```
0.8416212335729143
```

The z-score for the preceding output that determines whether the top 20% marks are at 0.84 is as follows:

```
>>> (0.84 * classscore.std()) + classscore.mean()
```

```
55.942594176524267
```

We multiply the z-score with the standard deviation and then add the result with the mean of the distribution. This helps in converting the z-score to a value in the distribution. The `55.83` marks means that students who have marks more than this are in the top 20% of the distribution.

The z-score is an essential concept in statistics, which is widely used. Now you can understand that it is basically used in standardizing any distribution so that it can be compared or inferences can be derived from it.

A p-value

A p-value is the probability of rejecting a null-hypothesis when the hypothesis is proven true. The null hypothesis is a statement that says that there is no difference between two measures. If the hypothesis is that people who clock in 4 hours of study everyday score more that 90 marks out of 100. The null hypothesis here would be that there is no relation between the number of hours clocked in and the marks scored.

If the p-value is equal to or less than the significance level (*a*), then the null hypothesis is inconsistent and it needs to be rejected.

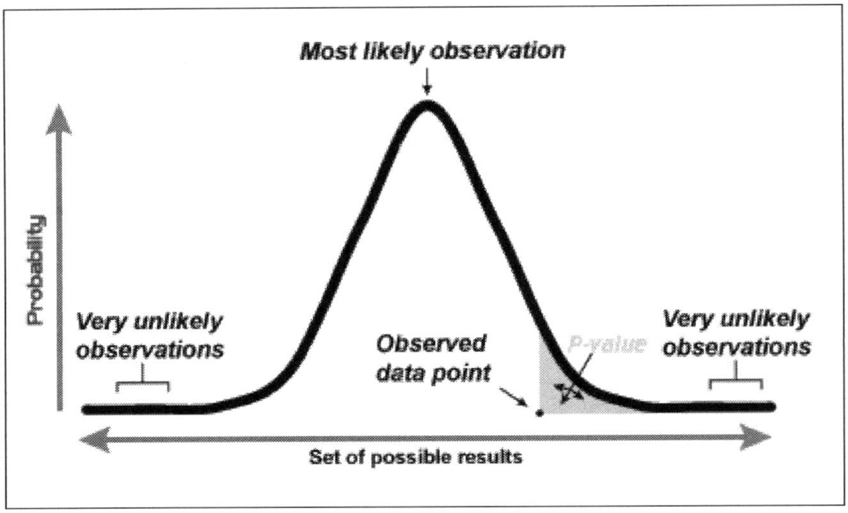

Let's understand this concept with an example where the **null hypothesis** is that it is common for students to score 68 marks in mathematics.

Let's define the significance level at 5%. If the p-value is less than 5%, then the null hypothesis is rejected and it is not common to score 68 marks in mathematics.

Let's get the z-score of 68 marks:

```
>>> zscore = ( 68 - classscore.mean() ) / classscore.std()

>>> zscore

2.283
```

Now, let's get the value:

```
>>> prob = 1 - stats.norm.cdf(zscore)
>>> prob
0.032835182628040638
```

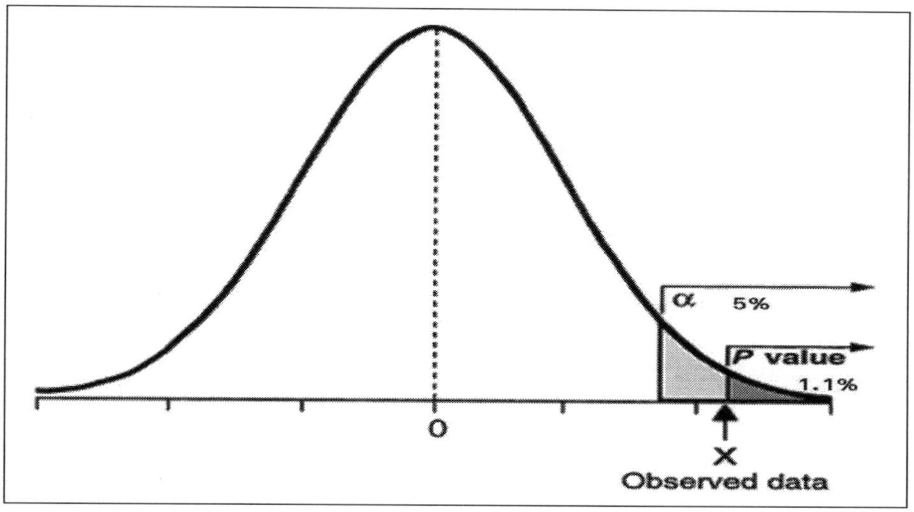

So, you can see that the p-value is at 3.2%, which is lower than the significance level. This means that the null hypothesis can be rejected, and it can be said that it's not common to get 68 marks in mathematics.

One-tailed and two-tailed tests

The example in the previous section was an instance of a one-tailed test where the null hypothesis is rejected or accepted based on one direction of the normal distribution.

In a two-tailed test, both the tails of the null hypothesis are used to test the hypothesis.

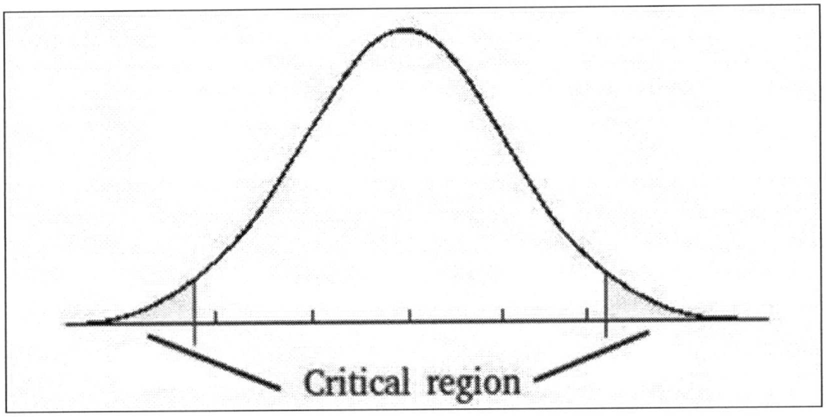

In a two-tailed test, when a significance level of 5% is used, then it is distributed equally in the both directions, that is, 2.5% of it in one direction and 2.5% in the other direction.

Let's understand this with an example. The mean score of the mathematics exam at a national level is 60 marks and the standard deviation is 3 marks.

The mean marks of a class are 53. The null hypothesis is that the mean marks of the class are similar to the national average. Let's test this hypothesis by first getting the z-score 60:

```
>>> zscore = ( 53 - 60 ) / 3.0
>>> zscore
-2.3333333333333335
```

The p-value would be:

```
>>> prob = stats.norm.cdf(zscore)
>>> prob

0.0098153286286453336
```

So, the p-value is 0.98%. The null hypothesis is to be rejected, and the p-value should be less than 2.5% in either direction of the bell curve. Since the p-value is less than 2.5%, we can reject the null hypothesis and clearly state that the average marks of the class are significantly different from the national average.

Type 1 and Type 2 errors

Type 1 error is a type of error that occurs when there is a rejection of the null hypothesis when it is actually true. This kind of error is also called an error of the first kind and is equivalent to false positives.

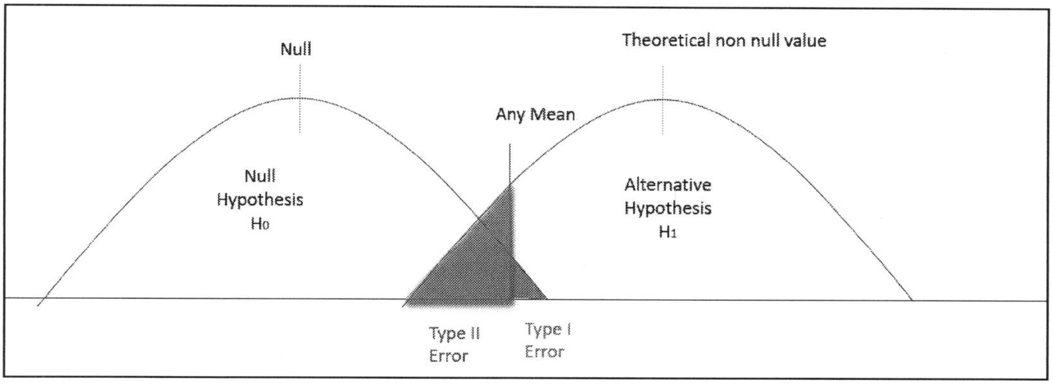

Let's understand this concept using an example. There is a new drug that is being developed and it needs to be tested on whether it is effective in combating diseases. The null hypothesis is that it is not effective in combating diseases.

The significance level is kept at 5% so that the null hypothesis can be accepted confidently 95% of the time. However, 5% of the time, we'll accept the rejecttion of the hypothesis although it had to be accepted, which means that even though the drug is ineffective, it is assumed to be effective.

The Type 1 error is controlled by controlling the significance level, which is alpha. Alpha is the highest probability to have a Type 1 error. The lower the alpha, the lower will be the Type 1 error.

The Type 2 error is the kind of error that occurs when we do not reject a null hypothesis that is false. This error is also called the error of the second kind and is equivalent to a false negative.

This kind of error occurs in a drug scenario when the drug is assumed to be ineffective but is actually it is effective.

These errors can be controlled one at a time. If one of the errors is lowered, then the other one increases. It depends on the use case and the problem statement that the analysis is trying to address, and depending on it, the appropriate error should reduce. In the case of this drug scenario, typically, a Type 1 error should be lowered because it is better to ship a drug that is confidently effective.

A confidence interval

A confidence interval is a type of interval statistics for a population parameter. The confidence interval helps in determining the interval at which the population mean can be defined.

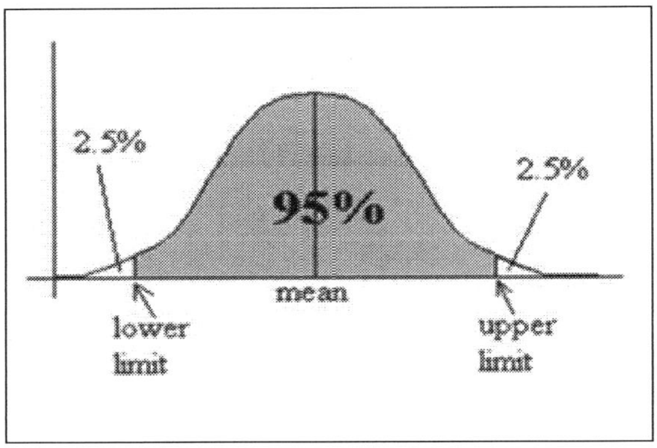

Let's try to understand this concept by using an example. Let's take the height of every man in Kenya and determine with 95% confidence interval the average of height of Kenyan men at a national level.

Let's take 50 men and their height in centimeters:

```
>>> height_data = np.array([ 186.0, 180.0, 195.0, 189.0, 191.0,
    177.0, 161.0, 177.0, 192.0, 182.0, 185.0, 192.0,

  173.0, 172.0, 191.0, 184.0, 193.0, 182.0, 190.0, 185.0, 181.0,
    188.0, 179.0, 188.0,

  170.0, 179.0, 180.0, 189.0, 188.0, 185.0, 170.0, 197.0, 187.0,
    182.0, 173.0, 179.0,

  184.0, 177.0, 190.0, 174.0, 203.0, 206.0, 173.0, 169.0, 178.0,
    201.0, 198.0, 166.0,

  171.0, 180.0])
```

Plotting the distribution, it has a normal distribution:

```
>>> plt.hist(height_data, 30, normed=True)
>>> plt.show()
```

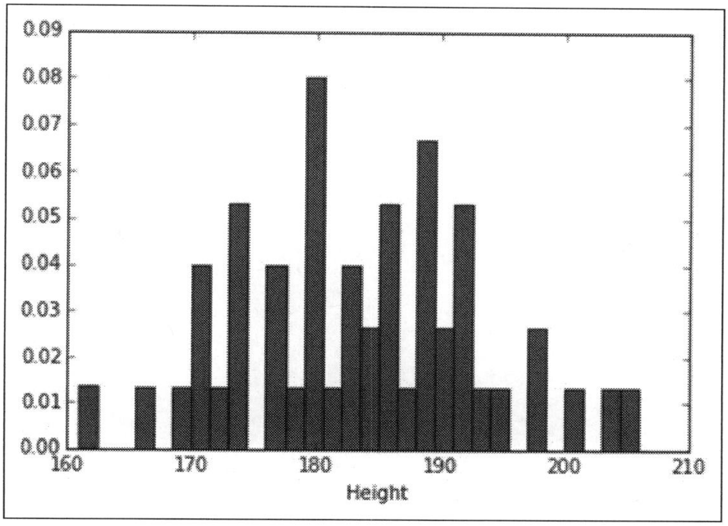

The mean of the distribution is as follows:

```
>>> height_data.mean()

183.24000000000001
```

So, the average height of a man from the sample is 183.4 cm.

To determine the confidence interval, we'll now define the standard error of the mean.

The standard error of the mean is the deviation of the sample mean from the population mean. It is defined using the following formula:

$$SE_{\bar{x}} = \frac{s}{\sqrt{n}}$$

Here, *s* is the standard deviation of the sample, and *n* is the number of elements of the sample.

This can be calculated using the `sem()` function of the SciPy package:

```
>>> stats.sem(height_data)

1.3787187190005252
```

So, there is a standard error of the mean of 1.38 cm. The lower and upper limit of the confidence interval can be determined by using the following formula:

$$Upper/Lower\ limit = mean(height) + / - sigma * SEmean(x)$$

For lower limit:

$$183.24 + (1.96 * 1.38) = 185.94$$

For upper limit:

$$183.24 - (1.96*1.38) = 180.53$$

A 1.96 standard deviation covers 95% of area in the normal distribution.

We can confidently say that the population mean lies between 180.53 cm and 185.94 cm of height.

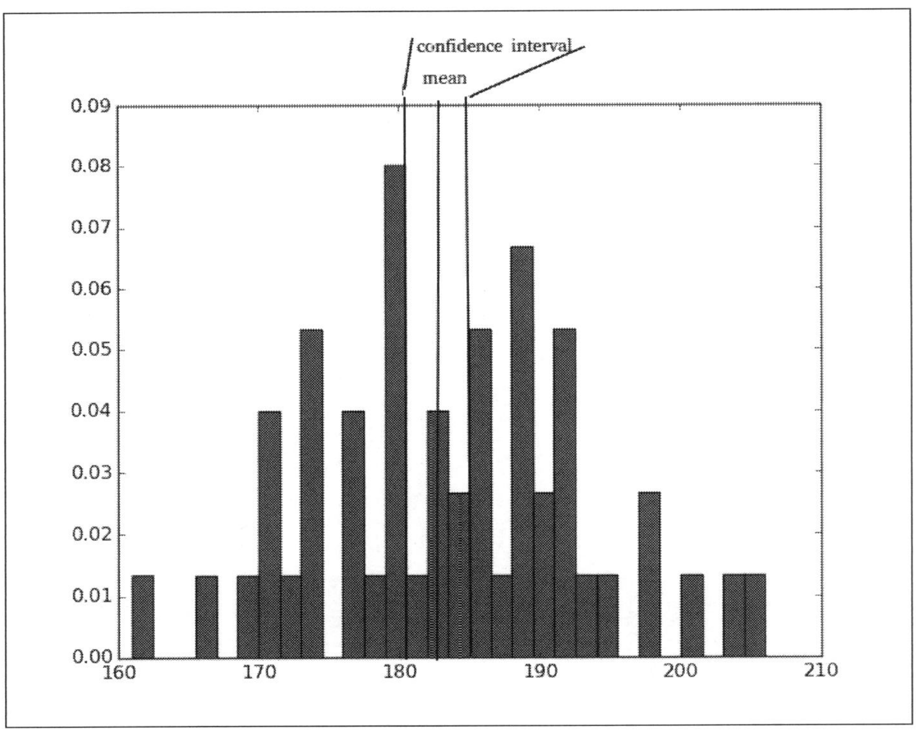

Let's assume we take a sample of 50 people, record their height, and then repeat this process 30 times. We can then plot the averages of each sample and observe the distribution.

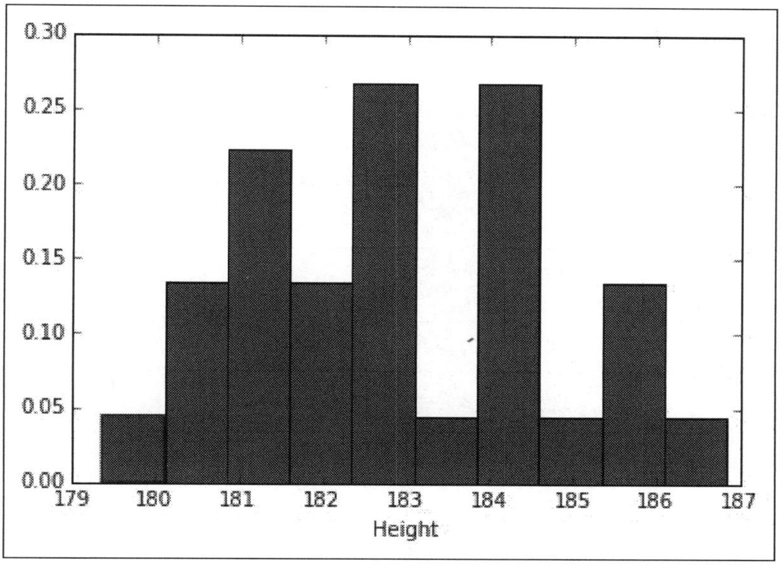

The commands that simulated the preceding plot is as follows:

```
>>> average_height = []
>>> for i in xrange(30):
>>>     sample50 = np.random.normal(183, 10, 50).round()
>>>     average_height.append(sample50.mean())

>>> plt.hist(average_height, 20, normed=True)
>>> plt.show()
```

You can observe that the mean ranges from 180 to 187 cm when we simulated the average height of 50 sample men, which was taken 30 times.

Let's see what happens when we sample 1000 men and repeat the process 30 times:

```
>>> average_height = []
>>> for i in xrange(30):
>>>     sample1000 = np.random.normal(183, 10, 1000).round()
```

```
>>>     average_height.append(sample1000.mean())


>>> plt.hist(average_height, 10, normed=True)
>>> plt.show()
```

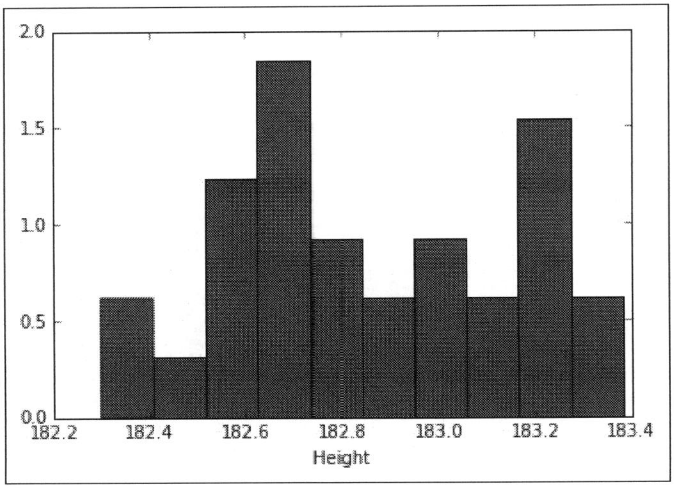

As you can see, the height varies from 182.4 cm and to 183.4 cm. What does this mean?

It means that as the sample size increases, the standard error of the mean decreases, which also means that the confidence interval becomes narrower, and we can tell with certainty the interval that the population mean would lie on.

Correlation

In statistics, correlation defines the similarity between two random variables. The most commonly used correlation is the Pearson correlation and it is defined by the following:

$$\rho_{X,Y} = \frac{\operatorname{cov}(X,Y)}{\sigma_X \sigma_Y} = \frac{E\left[(X-\mu_X)(Y-\mu_Y)\right]}{\sigma_X \sigma_Y}$$

The preceding formula defines the Pearson correlation as the covariance between *X* and *Y*, which is divided by the standard deviation of *X* and *Y*, or it can also be defined as the expected mean of the sum of multiplied difference of random variables with respect to the mean divided by the standard deviation of X and Y. Let's understand this with an example. Let's take the mileage and horsepower of various cars and see if there is a relation between the two. This can be achieved using the `pearsonr` function in the SciPy package:

```
>>> mpg = [21.0, 21.0, 22.8, 21.4, 18.7, 18.1, 14.3, 24.4, 22.8,
       19.2, 17.8, 16.4, 17.3, 15.2, 10.4, 10.4, 14.7, 32.4, 30.4,

       33.9, 21.5, 15.5, 15.2, 13.3, 19.2, 27.3, 26.0, 30.4, 15.8,
       19.7, 15.0, 21.4]
>>> hp = [110, 110, 93, 110, 175, 105, 245, 62, 95, 123, 123, 180,
      180, 180, 205, 215, 230, 66, 52, 65, 97, 150, 150, 245,

      175, 66, 91, 113, 264, 175, 335, 109]


>>> stats.pearsonr(mpg,hp)


(-0.77616837182658638, 1.7878352541210661e-07)
```

The first value of the output gives the correlation between the horsepower and the mileage and the second value gives the p-value.

So, the first value tells us that it is highly negatively correlated and the p-value tells us that there is significant correlation between them:

```
>>> plt.scatter(mpg, hp)
>>> plt.show()
```

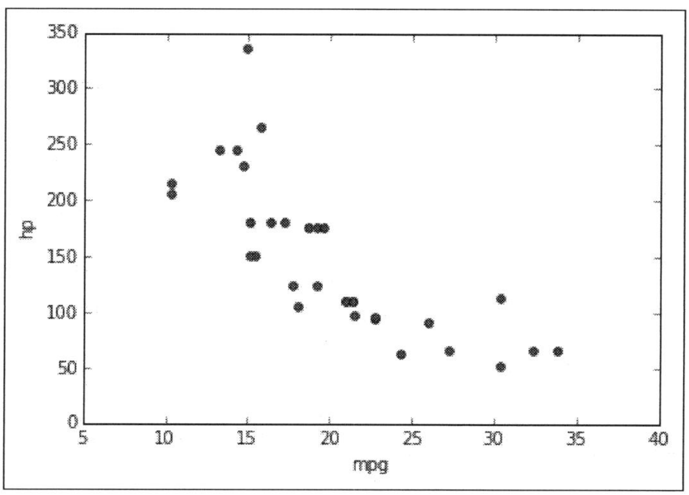

From the plot, we can see that as the mpg increases, the horsepower decreases.

Let's look into another correlation called the Spearman correlation. The Spearman correlation applies to the rank order of the values and so it provides a monotonic relation between the two distributions. It is useful for ordinal data (data that has an order, such as movie ratings or grades in class) and is not affected by outliers.

Let's get the Spearman correlation between the miles per gallon and horsepower. This can be achieved using the `spearmanr()` function in the SciPy package:

```
>>> stats.spearmanr(mpg,hp)


(-0.89466464574996252, 5.085969430924539e-12)
```

We can see that the Spearman correlation is -0.89 and the p-value is significant.

Let's do an experiment in which we introduce a few outlier values in the data and see how the Pearson and Spearman correlation gets affected:

```
>>> mpg = [21.0, 21.0, 22.8, 21.4, 18.7, 18.1, 14.3, 24.4, 22.8,
        19.2, 17.8, 16.4, 17.3, 15.2, 10.4, 10.4, 14.7, 32.4, 30.4,

        33.9, 21.5, 15.5, 15.2, 13.3, 19.2, 27.3, 26.0, 30.4, 15.8,
        19.7, 15.0, 21.4, 120, 3]
>>> hp = [110, 110, 93, 110, 175, 105, 245, 62, 95, 123, 123, 180,
       180, 180, 205, 215, 230, 66, 52, 65, 97, 150, 150, 245,

       175, 66, 91, 113, 264, 175, 335, 109, 30, 600]


>>> plt.scatter(mpg, hp)
>>> plt.show()
```

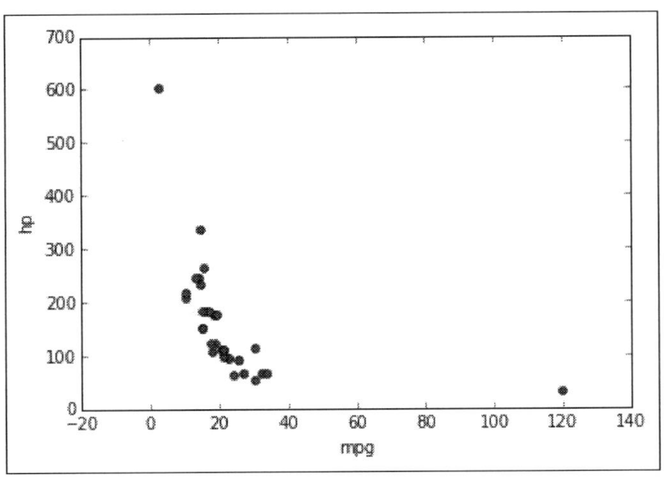

From the plot, you can clearly make out the outlier values. Lets see how the correlations get affected for both the Pearson and Spearman correlation

The following commands show you the Pearson correlation:

```
>>> stats.pearsonr(mpg, hp)
>>> (-0.47415304891435484, 0.0046122167947348462)
```

Here is the Spearman correlation:

```
>>> stats.spearmanr(mpg, hp)
>>> (-0.91222184337265655, 6.0551681657984803e-14)
```

We can clearly see that the Pearson correlation has been drastically affected due to the outliers, which are from a correlation of 0.89 to 0.47.

The Spearman correlation did not get affected much as it is based on the order rather than the actual value in the data.

Z-test vs T-test

We have already done a few Z-tests before where we validated our null hypothesis.

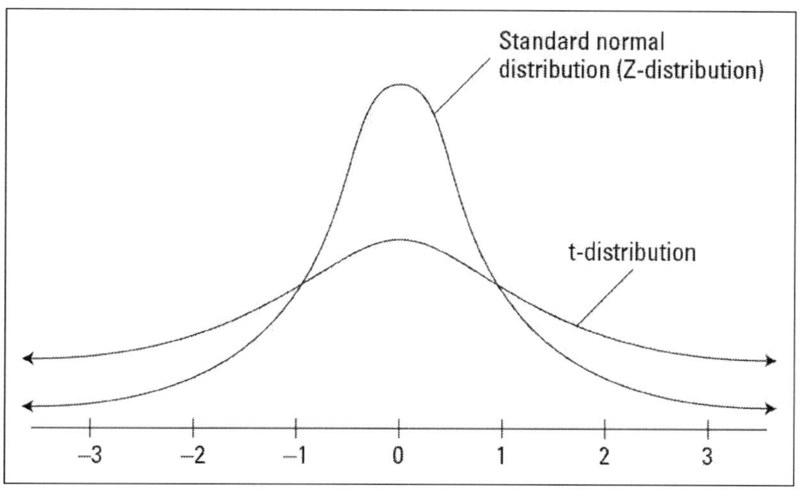

A T-distribution is similar to a Z-distribution—it is centered at zero and has a basic bell shape, but its shorter and flatter around the center than the Z-distribution.

The T-distributions' standard deviation is usually proportionally larger than the Z, because of which you see the fatter tails on each side.

The t distribution is usually used to analyze the population when the sample is small.

The Z-test is used to compare the population mean against a sample or compare the population mean of two distributions with a sample size greater than 30. An example of a Z-test would be comparing the heights of men from different ethnicity groups.

The T-test is used to compare the population mean against a sample, or compare the population mean of two distributions with a sample size less than 30, and when you don't know the population's standard deviation.

Let's do a T-test on two classes that are given a mathematics test and have 10 students in each class:

```
>>> class1_score = np.array([45.0, 40.0, 49.0, 52.0, 54.0, 64.0,
                    36.0, 41.0, 42.0, 34.0])


>>> class2_score = np.array([75.0, 85.0, 53.0, 70.0, 72.0, 93.0,
                    61.0, 65.0, 65.0, 72.0])
```

To perform the T-test, we can use the `ttest_ind()` function in the SciPy package:

```
>>> stats.ttest_ind(class1_score,class2_score)


(array(-5.458195056848407), 3.4820722850153292e-05)
```

The first value in the output is the calculated t-statistics, whereas the second value is the p-value and p-value shows that the two distributions are not identical.

The F distribution

The F distribution is also known as Snedecor's F distribution or the Fisher–Snedecor distribution.

An f statistic is given by the following formula:

$$f = \left[s_1^2 / \sigma_1^2 \right] / \left[s_2^2 / \sigma_2^2 \right]$$

Here, s_1 is the standard deviation of a sample 1 with an n_1 size, s_2 is the standard deviation of a sample 2, where the size $n_2\sigma_1$ is the population standard deviation of a sample $1\sigma_2$ is the population standard deviation of a sample 12.

The distribution of all the possible values of **f** statistics is called F distribution. The `d1` and `d2` represent the degrees of freedom in the following chart:

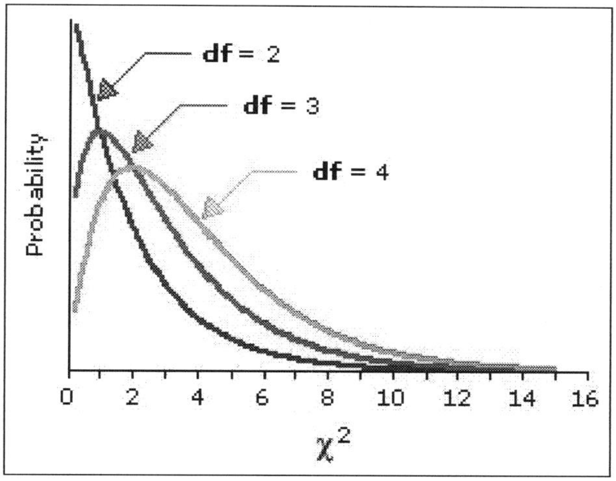

The chi-square distribution

The chi-square statistics are defined by the following formula:

$$X^2 = \left[(n-1)*s^2\right]/\sigma^2$$

Here, *n* is the size of the sample, *s* is the standard deviation of the sample, and *σ* is the standard deviation of the population.

If we repeatedly take samples and define the chi-square statistics, then we can form a chi-square distribution, which is defined by the following probability density function:

$$Y = Y_0 * \left(X^2\right)^{(v/2-1)} * e^{-X2/2}$$

Here, Y_0 is a constant that depends on the number of degrees of freedom, X_2 is the chi-square statistic, $v = n - 1$ is the number of degrees of freedom, and *e* is a constant equal to the base of the natural logarithm system.

Y_0 is defined so that the area under the chi-square curve is equal to one.

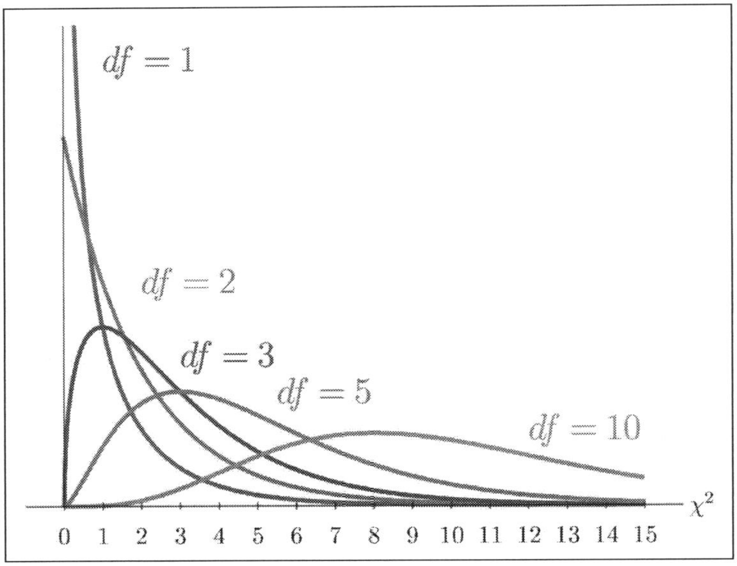

Chi-square for the goodness of fit

The Chi-square test can be used to test whether the observed data differs significantly from the expected data. Let's take the example of a dice. The dice is rolled 36 times and the probability that each face should turn upwards is 1/6. So, the expected distribution is as follows:

Expected Frequency	Outcome
6	1
6	2
6	3
6	4
6	5
6	6

```
>>> expected = np.array([6,6,6,6,6,6])
```

The observed distribution is as follows:

Observed Frequency	Outcome
7	1
5	2
3	3
9	4
6	5
6	6

```
>>> observed = observed = np.array([7, 5, 3, 9, 6, 6])
```

The null hypothesis in the chi-square test is that the observed value is similar to the expected value.

The chi-square can be performed using the `chisquare` function in the SciPy package:

```
>>> stats.chisquare(observed,expected)
(3.3333333333333333, 0.64874235866759344)
```

The first value is the chi-square value and the second value is the p-value, which is very high. This means that the null hypothesis is valid and the observed value is similar to the expected value.

The chi-square test of independence

The chi-square test of independence is a statistical test used to determine whether two categorical variables are independent of each other or not.

Let's take the following example to see whether there is a preference for a book based on the gender of people reading it:

Flavour				
Total	**Biography**	**Suspense**	**Romance**	**Gender**
280	60	120	100	Men
640	90	200	350	Women
920	150	320	450	

The Chi-Square test of independence can be performed using the `chi2_contingency` function in the SciPy package:

```
>>> men_women = np.array([[100, 120, 60],[350, 200, 90]])
>>> stats.chi2_contingency(men_women)
(28.362103174603167, 6.9382117170577439e-07, 2, array([[
        136.95652174,    97.39130435,    45.65217391],

        [ 313.04347826,   222.60869565,   104.34782609]]))
```

The first value is the chi-square value:

The second value is the p-value, which is very small, and means that there is an association between the gender of people and the genre of the book they read. The third value is the degrees of freedom. The fourth value, which is an array, is the expected frequencies.

ANOVA

Analysis of Variance (**ANOVA**) is a statistical method used to test differences between two or more means.

This test basically compares the means between groups and determines whether any of these means are significantly different from each other:

$$H_0 : \mu_1 = \mu_2 = \mu_3 = \cdots = \mu_k$$

ANOVA is a test that can tell you which group is significantly different from each other. Let's take the height of men who are from three different countries and see if their heights are significantly different from others:

```
>>> country1 = np.array([ 176.,  179.,  180.,  188.,  187.,  184.,  171.,
        201.,  172.,
        181.,  192.,  187.,  178.,  178.,  180.,  199.,  185.,  176.,
        207.,  177.,  160.,  174.,  176.,  192.,  189.,  187.,  183.,
        180.,  181.,  200.,  190.,  187.,  175.,  179.,  181.,  183.,
        171.,  181.,  190.,  186.,  185.,  188.,  201.,  192.,  188.,
        181.,  172.,  191.,  201.,  170.,  170.,  192.,  185.,  167.,
        178.,  179.,  167.,  183.,  200.,  185.])


>>> country2 = np.array([ 177.,  165.,  175.,  172.,  179.,  192.,  169.,
                185.,  187.,
```

```
        167.,  162.,  165.,  188.,  194.,  187.,  175.,  163.,  178.,
        197.,  172.,  175.,  185.,  176.,  171.,  172.,  186.,  168.,
        178.,  191.,  192.,  175.,  189.,  178.,  181.,  170.,  182.,
        166.,  189.,  196.,  192.,  189.,  171.,  185.,  198.,  181.,
        167.,  184.,  179.,  178.,  193.,  179.,  177.,  181.,  174.,
        171.,  184.,  156.,  180.,  181.,  187.])
```

```
>>> country3 = np.array([ 191.,  190.,  191.,  185.,  190.,  184.,
        173.,  175.,  200.,
        190.,  191.,  184.,  167.,  194.,  195.,  174.,  171.,  191.,
        174.,  177.,  182.,  184.,  176.,  180.,  181.,  186.,  179.,
        176.,  186.,  176.,  184.,  194.,  179.,  171.,  174.,  174.,
        182.,  198.,  180.,  178.,  200.,  200.,  174.,  202.,  176.,
        180.,  163.,  159.,  194.,  192.,  163.,  194.,  183.,  190.,
        186.,  178.,  182.,  174.,  178.,  182.])
```

To perform the one-way ANOVA, we can use the `f_oneway()` function of the SciPy package:

```
>>> stats.f_oneway(country1,country2,country3)
(2.9852039682631375, 0.053079678812747652)
```

The first value of the output gives the F-value and the second value gives the p-value. Since the p-value is greater than 5% by a small margin, we can tell that the mean of the heights in the three countries is not significantly different from each other.

Summary

In this chapter, you learned about the various probability distributions. You also learned about how to use z-score, p-value, Type 1, and Type 2 errors. You gained an insight into the Z-test and T-test followed by the chi-square distribution and saw how it can be used to test a hypothesis.

In the next chapter, you'll learn about data mining and how to execute it.

3
Finding a Needle in a Haystack

Analyzing a dataset to find patterns is an art as much as it is a science. There can be a lot of metrics associated with a dataset and you would like to find the needle in this haystack. For us, a needle is the insight that we look for within data that we weren't aware of earlier. Here, insight could refer to important information about people who buy milk of a particular brand and also buy cereals of another brand, for instance. The retail store can then stack the products near each other.

Whenever you try to analyze a dataset, you should have a detailed understanding of it and also of the domain that it is associated with. If it's a simple dataset that can be understood very easily, then the analysis can be performed directly, but if the dataset relates to the sensor data of a turbine, then domain understanding of how turbines work and what is critical to their functioning will add richness to your analysis.

The understanding of a domain is like the North Star: it helps you navigate your analysis.

In this chapter, you'll learn the following topics:

- How to structure your analysis for data mining
- How to present your analysis
- How to perform data mining on a Titanic survivors dataset

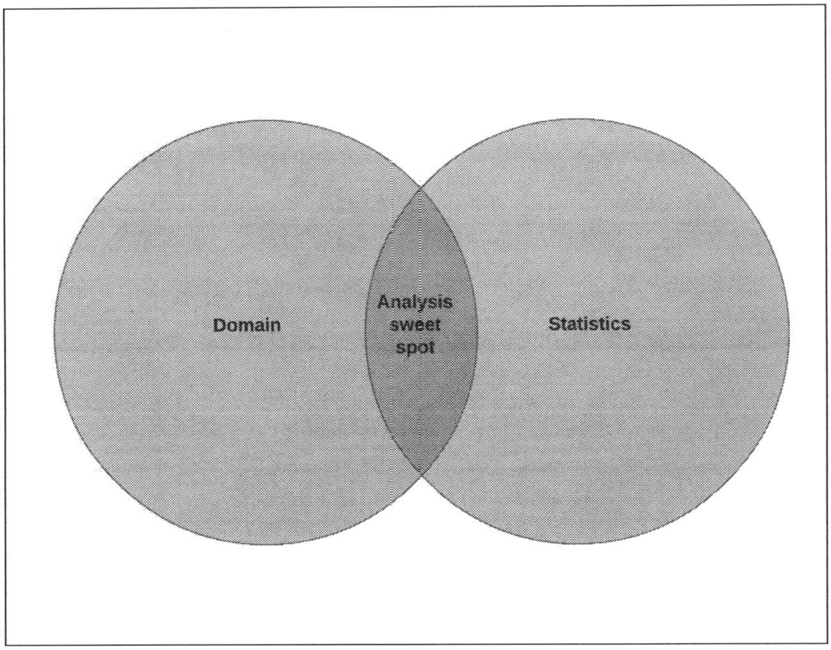

What is data mining?

Data mining is the process of exploring data and finding patterns in it using machine learning, statistics, and database systems. The end goal of data mining is to derive useful information from data, which can be utilized to increase revenue, reduce costs, or even save lives through some of its applications.

When you have a dataset that needs to be mined, it is not feasible to use all the data-mining techniques that are available on every column field of the data to derive insights. This will be a cumbersome task and will take a long time to derive any useful insights.

To speed up the process of mining data, knowledge of domains is a great help. With this knowledge, one can understand what the data represents and how to analyze it to gain insights.

The best way to start data mining is to derive themes on which the data needs to be mined. If you have the sales data of a **Fast Moving Consumer Goods** (**FMCG**) company, then themes could be as follows:

- Brand behavior
- Outlet behavior
- Growth of products
- Seasonal effect on products

The themes help by giving a direction to explore data and finding patterns in it.

Once you have the themes, you need to put questions under them to streamline the analysis:

- **Brand behavior**: The following are the questions used to streamline the analysis:
    - Which are the top brands?
    - Which brands have the maximum coverage?
    - Which brands are cannibalizing the sales of the other brands?
- **Outlet behavior**: The following are the questions used to streamline the analysis:
    - What percentage of outlets takes up 80% of revenue?
    - What kind of outlets have the highest number of sales?
    - What kind of outlets sell primarily premium products?
- **Growth of products**: The following are the questions used to streamline the analysis:
    - Which are the fastest growing brands in terms of sale?
    - Which are the fastest growing brands in terms of volume?
    - Which brand's growth has flattened out?
- **Seasonal effect of the products**: The following are the questions used to streamline the analysis:
    - How many brands are seasonal?
    - What is the difference in terms of sales during seasonal and nonseasonal periods?
    - Which holiday brings in the maximum amount of sales for a particular brand?

The preceding questions under these themes give pinpointed directions to find patterns and perform an analysis that gives some quality results.

The process of exploring data can be summarized by the following flow chart:

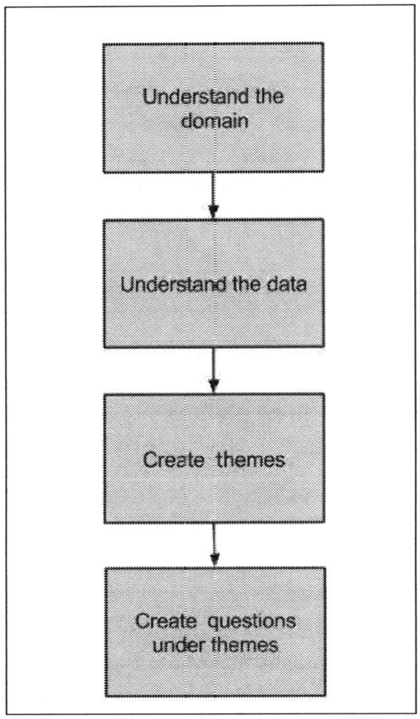

Presenting an analysis

After performing the analysis, you would need to present some observations. The most commonly used medium for doing this is through Microsoft PowerPoint presentations. The result of your analysis could be a construct in the form of a chart or table. When presenting these constructs, there is certain information that should be added to your slides. This is one of the most common templates used:

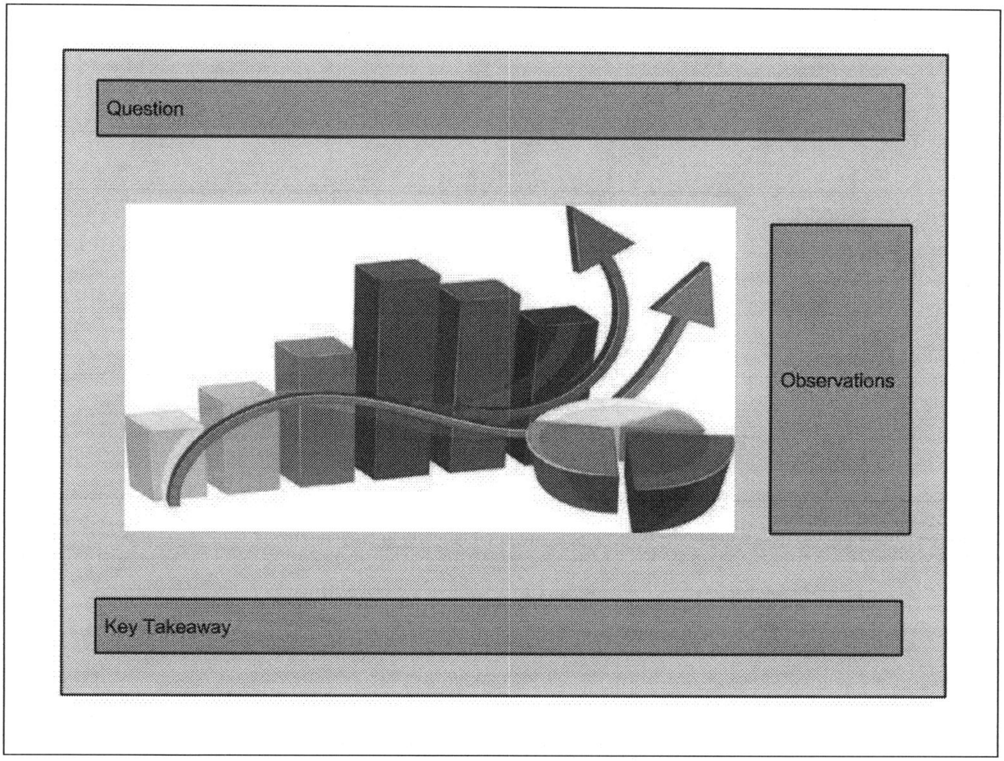

Here are the different sections of the preceding image:

- **Question**: The topmost part of the template should describe the problem statement that the particular analysis is trying to address.
- **Observation**: Here, the observations from the construct are listed in a vertical column. Sometimes, the observations can be marked over the construct using arrow marks or dialog boxes.
- **Key Takeaway**: Toward the bottom of the image, you can describe what is concluded from the chart.

Studying the Titanic

To perform the data analysis, we'll be using the Titanic dataset from Kaggle.

This dataset is simple to understand and does not require any domain understanding to derive insights.

This dataset contains the details of each passenger on the Titanic and also whether they survived or not.

The following are the field descriptions:

Field	Descriptions
`survival`	Survival(`0` = No, `1` = Yes)
`pclass`	Passenger class(`1` = 1st, `2` = 2nd, `3` = 3rd)
`name`	Name of the passenger
`sex`	Gender of the passenger
`age`	Age of the passenger
`sibsp`	Number of siblings/spouses aboard
`parch`	Number of parents/children aboard
`ticket`	Ticket number
`fare`	Passenger fare
`cabin`	Cabin
`embarked`	Port of embarkation (`C` = Cherbourg, `Q` = Queenstown, `S` = Southampton)

Since the data is quite simple to understand, we'll keep the survival analysis as the main theme that can be used for the analysis of the data. We'll attach questions to these themes.

These are the questions that we'll answer:

- Which passenger class has the maximum number of survivors?
- What is the distribution, based on gender, of the survivors among the different classes?
- What is the distribution of the nonsurvivors among classes that have relatives aboard the ship?
- What is the survival percentage among different age groups?

Which passenger class has the maximum number of survivors?

To answer this question, we'll construct a simple bar plot of the number of survivors and the percentage of survivors in each class, respectively. You can do this using the following command:

```
>>> import pandas as pd
>>> import pylab as plt
>>> import numpy as np

>>> df = pd.read_csv('Data/titanic data.csv')

>>> df['Pclass'].isnull().value_counts()
>>> False    891
>>> dtype: int64

>>> df['Survived'].isnull().value_counts()
>>> False    891
>>> dtype: int64

>>> #Passengers survived in each class
>>> survivors = df.groupby('Pclass')['Survived'].agg(sum)

>>> #Total Passengers in each class
>>> total_passengers = df.groupby('Pclass')['PassengerId'].count()
>>> survivor_percentage = survivors / total_passengers

>>> #Plotting the Total number of survivors
>>> fig = plt.figure()
>>> ax = fig.add_subplot(111)
>>> rect = ax.bar(survivors.index.values.tolist(),
          survivors, color='blue', width=0.5)
>>> ax.set_ylabel('No. of survivors')
>>> ax.set_title('Total number of survivors based on class')
>>> xTickMarks = survivors.index.values.tolist()
>>> ax.set_xticks(survivors.index.values.tolist())
```

```
>>> xtickNames = ax.set_xticklabels(xTickMarks)
>>> plt.setp(xtickNames, fontsize=20)
>>> plt.show()
```

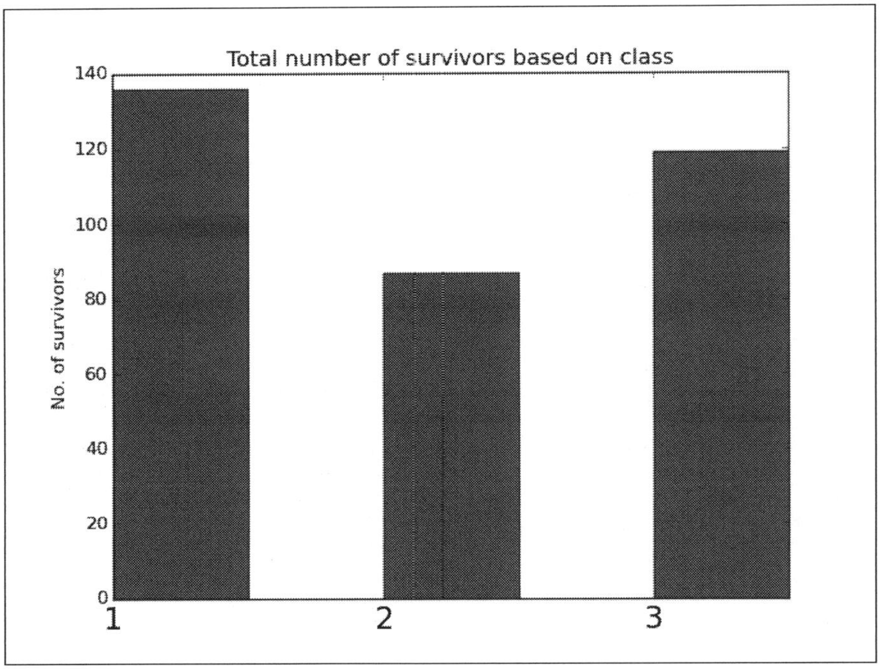


```
>>> #Plotting the percentage of survivors in each class

>>> fig = plt.figure()
>>> ax = fig.add_subplot(111)

>>> rect = ax.bar(survivor_percentage.index.values.tolist(),
        survivor_percentage, color='blue', width=0.5)
>>> ax.set_ylabel('Survivor Percentage')
>>> ax.set_title('Percentage of survivors based on class')
>>> xTickMarks = survivors.index.values.tolist()
>>> ax.set_xticks(survivors.index.values.tolist())
>>> xtickNames = ax.set_xticklabels(xTickMarks)
>>> plt.setp(xtickNames, fontsize=20)
>>> plt.show()
```

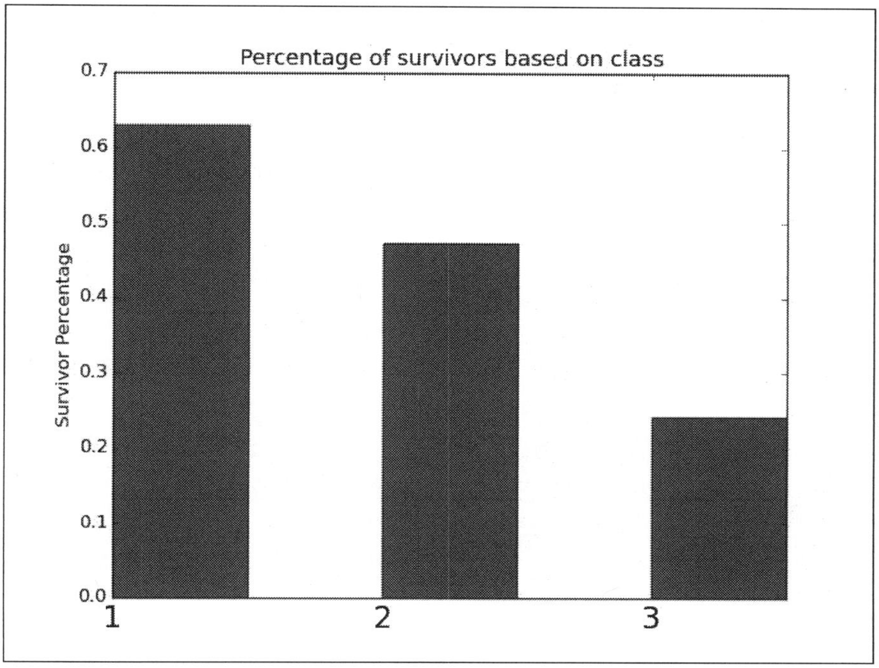

In the preceding code, we performed a preliminary check for null values on the fields that are utilized. After this, we calculated the number of survivors and the percentage of survivors in each class. Then, we plotted two bar charts for the total number of survivors and the percentage of survivors.

These are our observations:

- The maximum number of survivors are in the first and third class, respectively
- With respect to the total number of passengers in each class, first class has the maximum survivors at around 61%
- With respect to the total number of passengers in each class, third class has the minimum number of survivors at around 25%

This is our key takeaway:

- There was clearly a preference toward saving those from the first class as the ship was drowning. It also had the maximum percentage of survivors

What is the distribution of survivors based on gender among the various classes?

To answer this question, we'll use the following code to plot a side-by-side bar chart to compare the survival rate and percentage among men and women with respect to the class they were in.

```
>>> #Checking for any null values
>>> df['Sex'].isnull().value_counts()
>>> False    891
>>> dtype: int64

>>> # Male Passengers survived in each class
>>> male_survivors = df[df['Sex'] == 'male']
                .groupby('Pclass')['Survived'].agg(sum)

>>> #Total Male Passengers in each class
>>> male_total_passengers = df[df['Sex'] == 'male']
                        .groupby('Pclass')['PassengerId'].count()
>>> male_survivor_percentage = male_survivors / male_total_passengers

>>> # Female Passengers survived in each class
>>> female_survivors = df[df['Sex'] == 'female']
                .groupby('Pclass')['Survived'].agg(sum)

>>> #Total Female Passengers in each class
>>> female_total_passengers = df[df['Sex'] == 'female']
                        .groupby('Pclass')['PassengerId'].count()
>>> female_survivor_percentage = female_survivors /
                        female_total_passengers

>>> #Plotting the total passengers who survived based on Gender
>>> fig = plt.figure()
>>> ax = fig.add_subplot(111)
>>> index = np.arange(male_survivors.count())
>>> bar_width = 0.35
>>> rect1 = ax.bar(index, male_survivors, bar_width, color='blue',
    label='Men')
>>> rect2 = ax.bar(index + bar_width, female_survivors, bar_width,
    color='y', label='Women')
```

```
>>> ax.set_ylabel('Survivor Numbers')
>>> ax.set_title('Male and Female survivors based on class')
>>> xTickMarks = male_survivors.index.values.tolist()
>>> ax.set_xticks(index + bar_width)
>>> xtickNames = ax.set_xticklabels(xTickMarks)
>>> plt.setp(xtickNames, fontsize=20)
>>> plt.legend()
>>> plt.tight_layout()
>>> plt.show()
```

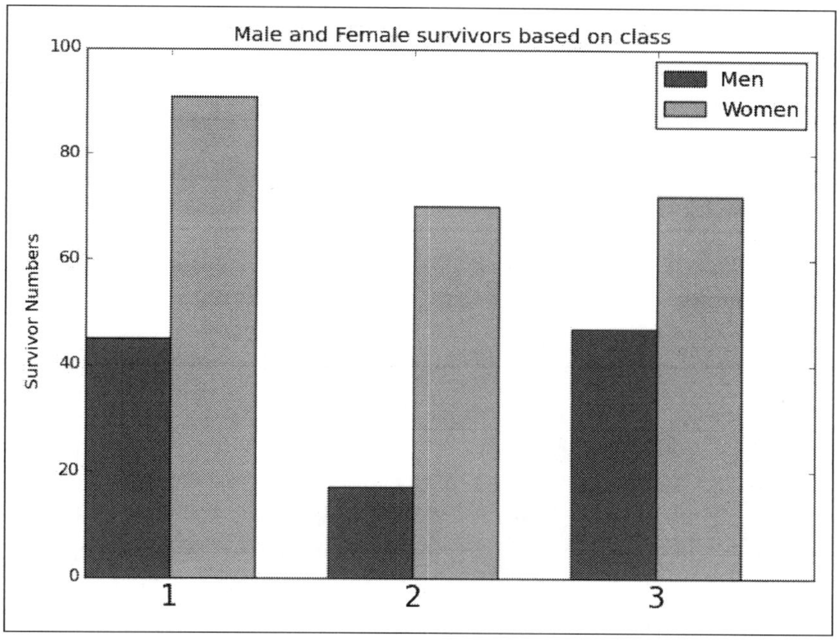


```
>>> #Plotting the percentage of passengers who survived based on Gender
>>> fig = plt.figure()
>>> ax = fig.add_subplot(111)
>>> index = np.arange(male_survivor_percentage.count())
>>> bar_width = 0.35
>>> rect1 = ax.bar(index, male_survivor_percentage, bar_width,
     color='blue', label='Men')
>>> rect2 = ax.bar(index + bar_width, female_survivor_percentage,
     bar_width, color='y', label='Women')
>>> ax.set_ylabel('Survivor Percentage')
```

```
>>> ax.set_title('Percentage Male and Female of
     survivors based on class')
>>> xTickMarks = male_survivor_percentage.index.values.tolist()
>>> ax.set_xticks(index + bar_width)
>>> xtickNames = ax.set_xticklabels(xTickMarks)
>>> plt.setp(xtickNames, fontsize=20)
>>> plt.legend()
>>> plt.tight_layout()
>>> plt.show()
```

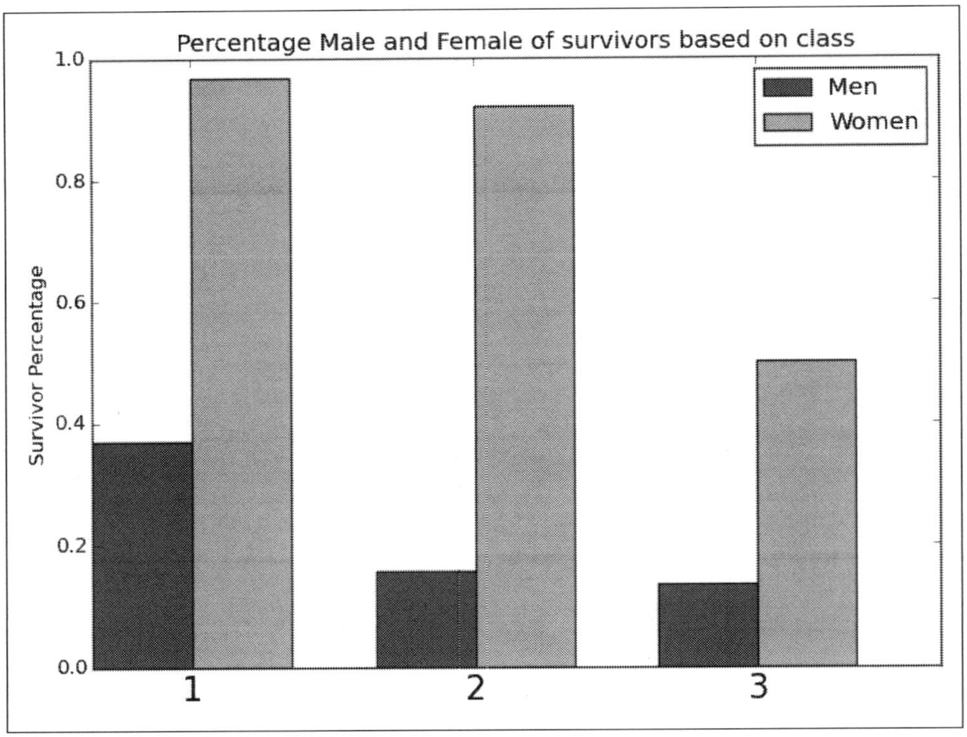

In the preceding code, the number of male and female survivors is calculated and then a side-by-side bar plot is plotted. After this, the percentage of male and female survivors with respect to the total number of males and females in their respective classes are taken and then plotted.

These are our observations:

- The majority of survivors are females in all the classes
- More than 90% of female passengers in first and second class survived
- The percentage of male passengers who survived in first and third class, respectively, are comparable

This is our key takeaway:

- Female passengers were given preference for lifeboats and the majority were saved.

What is the distribution of nonsurvivors among the various classes who have family aboard the ship?

To answer this question, we'll use the following code to plot bar charts again using the total number of nonsurvivors in each class who each had family aboard, and the percentage with respect to the total number of passengers:

```
>>> #Checking for the null values
>>> df['SibSp'].isnull().value_counts()
>>> False     891
>>> dtype: int64

>>> #Checking for the null values
>>> df['Parch'].isnull().value_counts()
>>> False     891
>>> dtype: int64


>>> #Total number of non-survivors in each class
>>> non_survivors = df[(df['SibSp'] > 0) | (df['Parch'] > 0) &
       (df['Survived'] == 0)].groupby('Pclass')['Survived'].agg('count')
>>> #Total passengers in each class
>>> total_passengers = df.groupby('Pclass')['PassengerId'].count()
>>> non_survivor_percentage = non_survivors / total_passengers
>>> #Total number of non survivors with family based on class
>>> fig = plt.figure()
```

```
>>> ax = fig.add_subplot(111)
>>> rect = ax.bar(non_survivors.index.values.tolist(), non_survivors,
       color='blue', width=0.5)
>>> ax.set_ylabel('No. of non survivors')
>>> ax.set_title('Total number of non survivors with
                 family based on class')
>>> xTickMarks = non_survivors.index.values.tolist()
>>> ax.set_xticks(non_survivors.index.values.tolist())
>>> xtickNames = ax.set_xticklabels(xTickMarks)
>>> plt.setp(xtickNames, fontsize=20)
>>> plt.show()
```

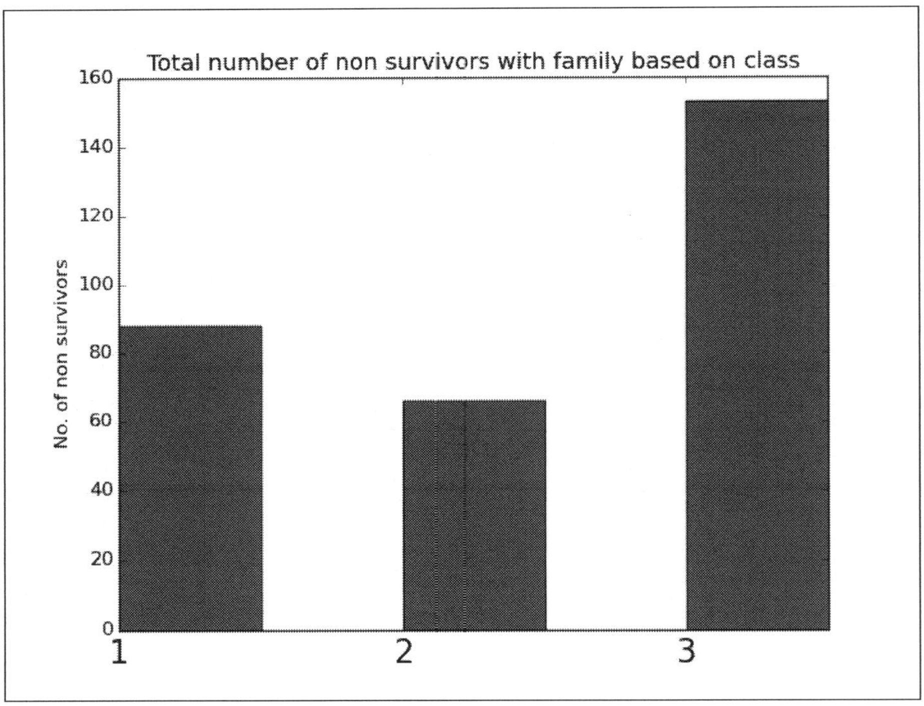


```
>>> #Plot of percentage of non survivors with family based on class
>>> fig = plt.figure()
>>> ax = fig.add_subplot(111)
>>> rect = ax.bar(non_survivor_percentage.index.values.tolist(),
     non_survivor_percentage, color='blue', width=0.5)
>>> ax.set_ylabel('Non Survivor Percentage')
```

```
>>> ax.set_title('Percentage of non survivors with
                family based on class')
>>> xTickMarks = non_survivor_percentage.index.values.tolist()
>>> ax.set_xticks(non_survivor_percentage.index.values.tolist())
>>> xtickNames = ax.set_xticklabels(xTickMarks)
>>> plt.setp(xtickNames, fontsize=20)
>>> plt.show()
```

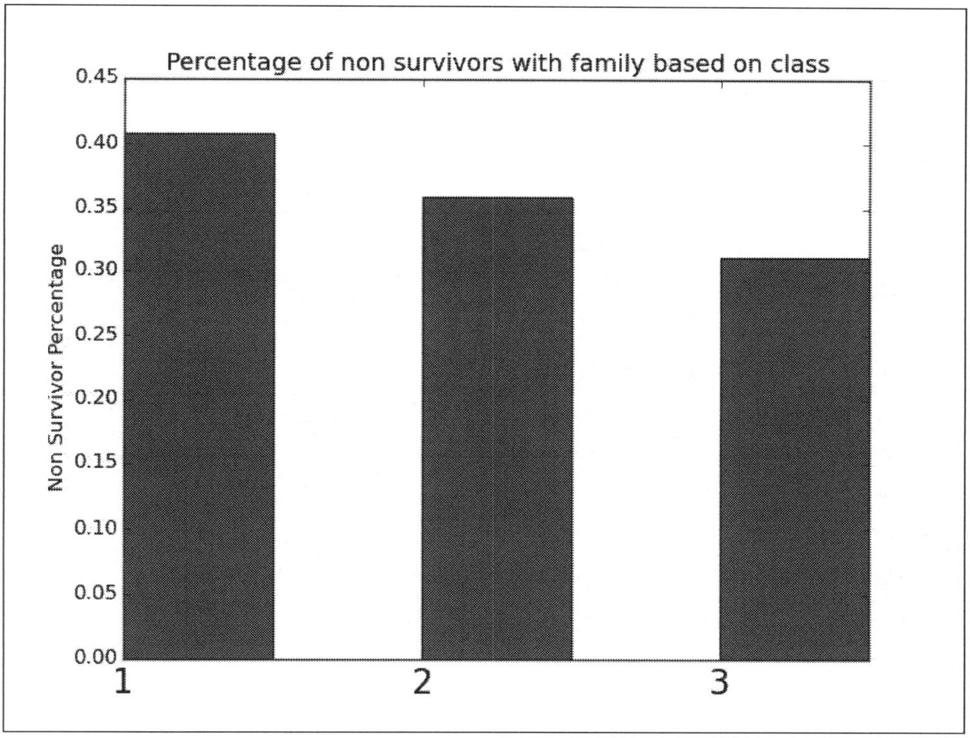

The code here is pretty similar to the code used in the previous questions. Here, we can get the number of the nonsurvivors who have a family and then perform the usual bar plots.

These are our observations:

- There are lot of nonsurvivors in the third class
- Second class has the least number of nonsurvivors with relatives
- With respect to the total number of passengers, the first class, who had relatives aboard, has the maximum nonsurvivor percentage and the third class has the least

This is our key takeaway:

- Even though third class has the highest number of nonsurvivors with relatives aboard, it primarily had passengers who did not have relatives on the ship, whereas in first class, most of the people had relatives aboard the ship

What was the survival percentage among different age groups?

For this question, we'll use the following code to plot pie charts to compare the proportion of survivors in terms of number and percentage with respect to the different age groups:

```
>>> #Checking for null values
>>> df['Age'].isnull().value_counts()
>>> False    714
>>> True     177
>>> dtype: int64


>>> #Defining the age binning interval
>>> age_bin = [0, 18, 25, 40, 60, 100]
>>> #Creating the bins
>>> df['AgeBin'] = pd.cut(df.Age, bins=age_bin)
>>> #Removing the null rows
>>> d_temp = df[np.isfinite(df['Age'])]  # removing all na instances
>>> #Number of survivors based on Age bin
>>> survivors = d_temp.groupby('AgeBin')['Survived'].agg(sum)
>>> #Total passengers in each bin
>>> total_passengers = d_temp.groupby('AgeBin')['Survived'].agg('count')
>>> #Plotting the pie chart of total passengers in each bin
>>> plt.pie(total_passengers,
     labels=total_passengers.index.values.tolist(),
     autopct='%1.1f%%', shadow=True, startangle=90)
>>> plt.title('Total Passengers in different age groups')
>>> plt.show()
```

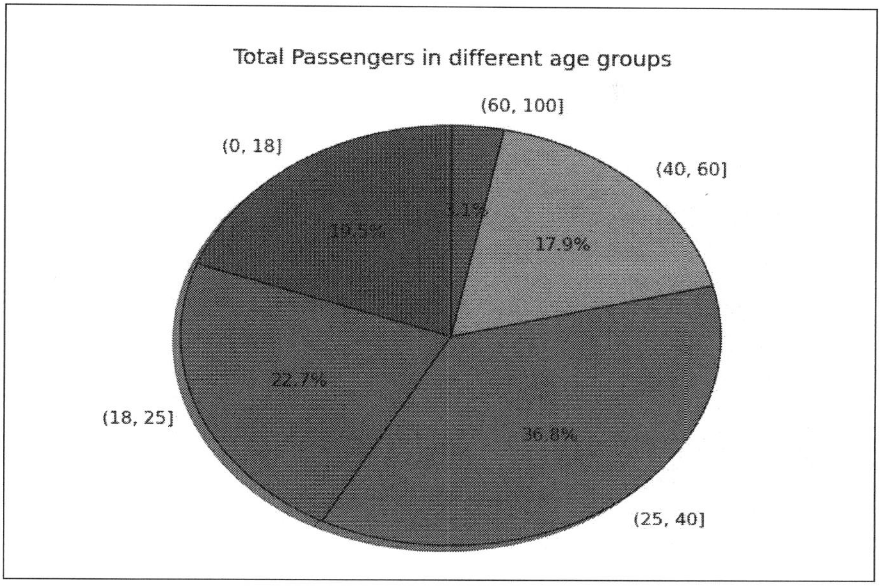


```
>>> #Plotting the pie chart of percentage passengers in each bin
>>> plt.pie(survivors, labels=survivors.index.values.tolist(),
     autopct='%1.1f%%', shadow=True, startangle=90)
>>> plt.title('Survivors in different age groups')
>>> plt.show()
```

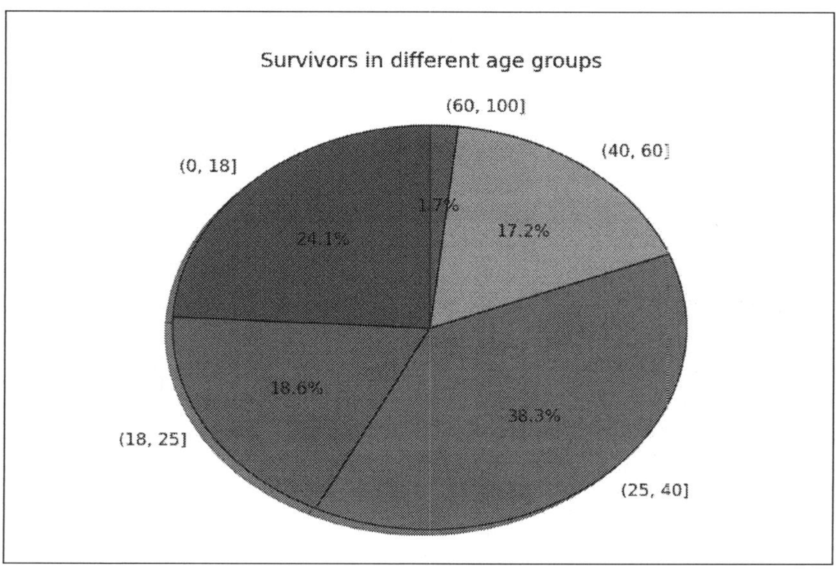

In the code, we defined the bin with the age_bin variable and then added a column called AgeBin, where bin values are filled using the cut function. After this, we filtered out all the rows with the age set as null. After this, we created two pie charts: one for the total number of passengers in each age group and another for the number of survivors in each age group.

These are our observations:

- The 25-40 age group has the maximum number of passengers, and 0-18 has the second highest number of passengers
- Among the people who survived, the 18-25 age group has the second highest number of survivors
- The 60-100 age group has a lower proportion among the survivors

This is our key takeaway:

- The 25-40 age group had the maximum number of survivors compared to any other age group, and people who were old were either not lucky enough or made way for the younger people to the lifeboats.

Summary

In this chapter, we learned the meaning of data mining. We learned the importance of domain knowledge in performing analysis and how to perform data mining in a systematic manner. We also learned how to present the results of data mining. Toward the end, we took an example and performed a few analyses to extract useful information.

In the next chapter, you'll learn about how to create visualizations on data and where to apply different kinds of visualizations.

> **Downloading the example code**
>
> You can download the example code files for all Packt books you have purchased from your account at `http://www.packtpub.com`. If you purchased this book elsewhere, you can visit `http://www.packtpub.com/support` and register to have the files e-mailed directly to you.
>
> The codes provided in the code bundle are for both IPython notebook and Python 2.7. In the chapters, Python conventions have been followed.

4

Making Sense of Data through Advanced Visualization

Visualization is a very integral part of data science. It helps in communicating a pattern or a relationship that cannot be seen by looking at raw data. It's easier for a person to remember a picture and recollect it as compared to lines of text. This holds true for data too.

In this chapter, we'll cover the following topics:

- Controlling the properties of a plot
- Combining multiple plots
- Styling your plots
- Creating various advanced visualizations

Controlling the line properties of a chart

There are many properties of a line that can be set, such as the color, dashes, and several others. There are essentially three ways of doing this. Let's take a simple line chart as an example:

```
>>> plt.plot([1,2,3,4], [1,4,9,16])
>>> plt.show()
```

After the preceding code is executed we'll get the following output:

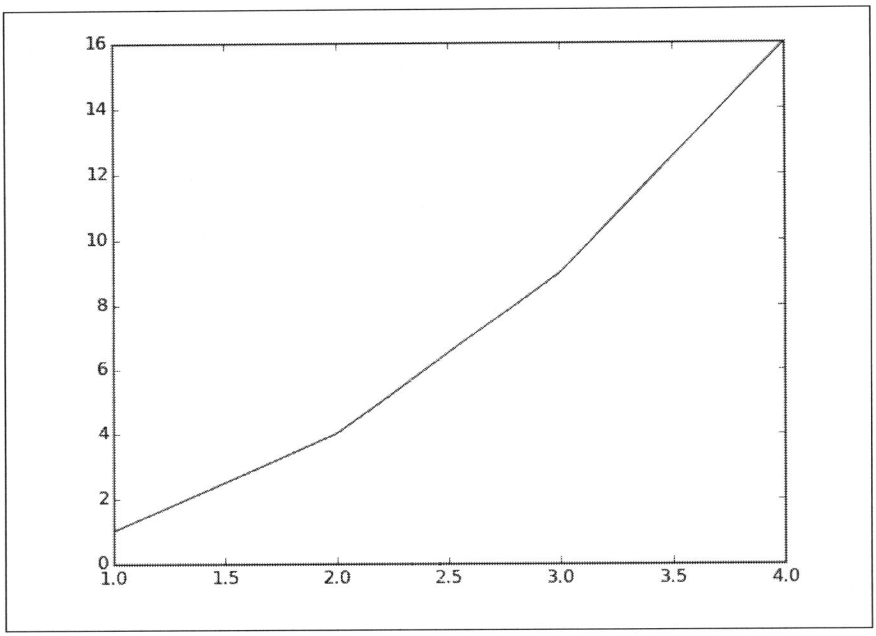

Using keyword arguments

We can use arguments within the plot function to set the property of the line:

```
>>> import numpy as np
>>> import pandas as pd
>>> import matplotlib.pyplot as plt
>>> import pandas.tools.rplot as rplot


>>> plt.plot([1, 2, 3, 4], [1, 4, 9, 16], linewidth=4.0)  # increasing
        # the line width
>>> plt.show()
```

After the preceding code is executed we'll get the following output:

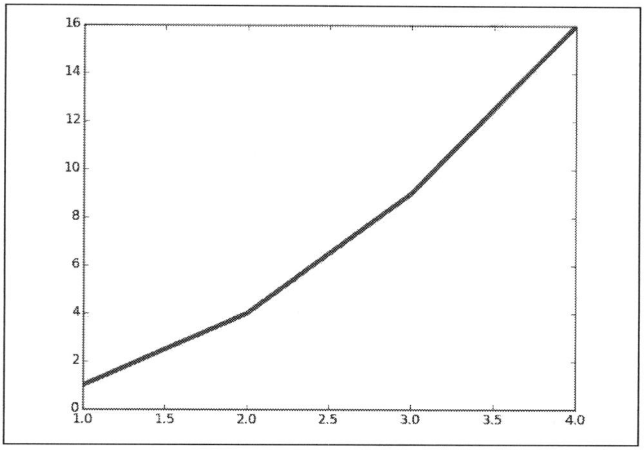

Using the setter methods

The plot function returns the list of line objects, for example `line1, line2 = plot(x1,y1,x2,y2)`. Using the line setter method of line objects we can define the property that needs to be set:

```
>>> line, = plt.plot([1, 2, 3, 4], [1, 4, 9, 16])
>>> line.set_linestyle('--') # Setting dashed lines
>>> plt.show()
```

After the preceding code is executed we'll get the following output:

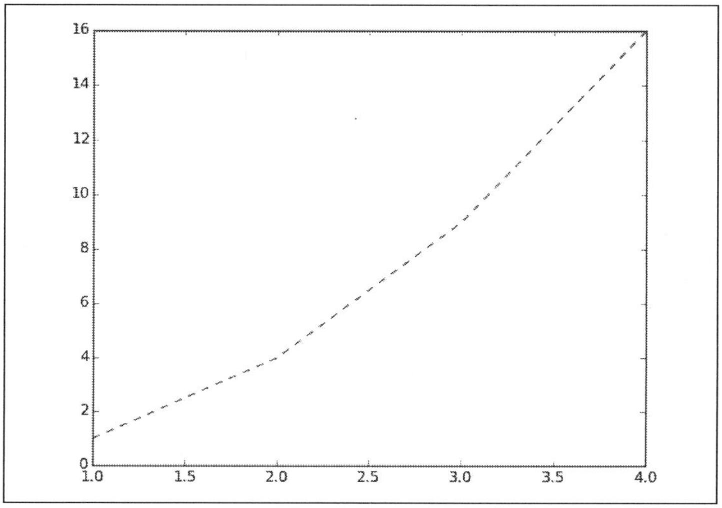

You can view the acceptable line style at http://matplotlib.org/api/lines_api.html.

Using the setp() command

The `setp()` command can be used to set multiple properties of a line:

```
>>> line, = plt.plot([1, 2, 3, 4], [1, 4, 9, 16])
>>> plt.setp(line, color='r', linewidth=2.0)  # setting the color
        # and width of the line
>>> plt.show()
```

After the preceding code is executed we'll get the following output:

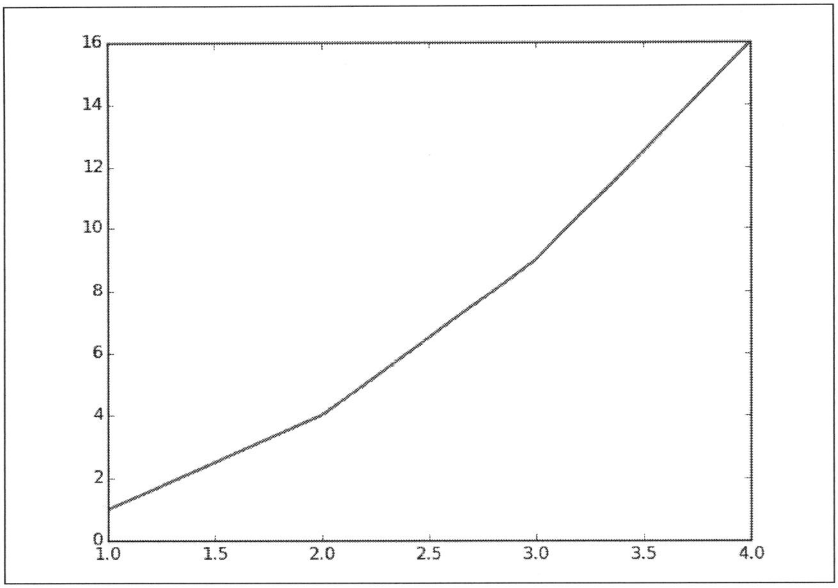

Creating multiple plots

One very useful feature of matplotlib is that it makes it easy to plot multiple plots, which can be compared to each other:

```
>>> p1 = np.arange(0.0, 30.0, 0.1)

>>> plt.subplot(211)
```

```
>>> plt.plot(p1, np.sin(p1)/p1, 'b--')


>>> plt.subplot(212)
>>> plt.plot(p1, np.cos(p1), 'r--')
>>> plt.show()
```

In the preceding code, we use a subplot function is used to plot multiple plots that need to be compared. A subplot with a value of `211` means that there will be two rows, one column, and one figure:

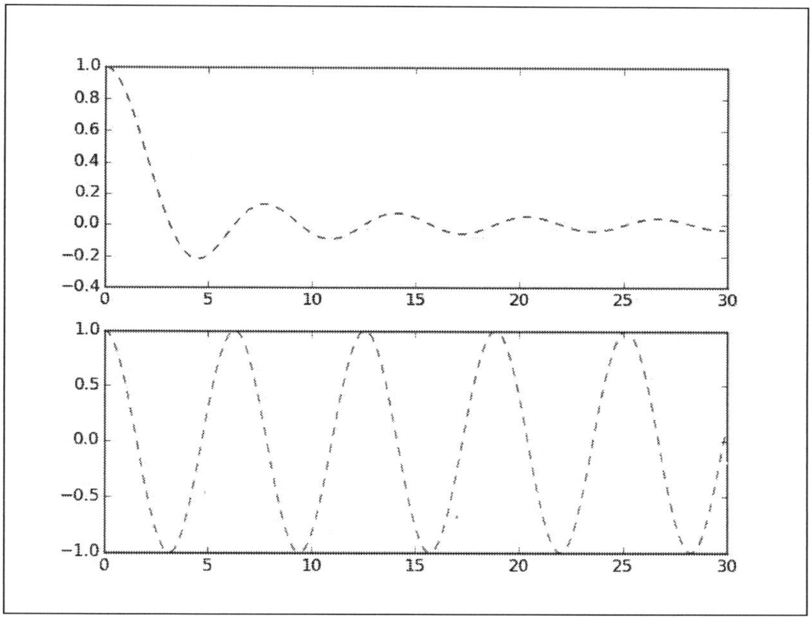

Playing with text

Adding text to your chart can be done by using a simple matplotlib function. You only have to use the `text()` command to add it to the chart:

```
>>> # Playing with text
>>> n = np.random.random_sample((5,))


>>> plt.bar(np.arange(len(n)), n)
>>> plt.xlabel('Indices')
>>> plt.ylabel('Value')
```

```
>>> plt.text(1, .7, r'$\mu=' + str(np.round(np.mean(n), 2)) + ' $')

>>> plt.show()
```

In the preceding code, the `text()` command is used to add text within the plot:

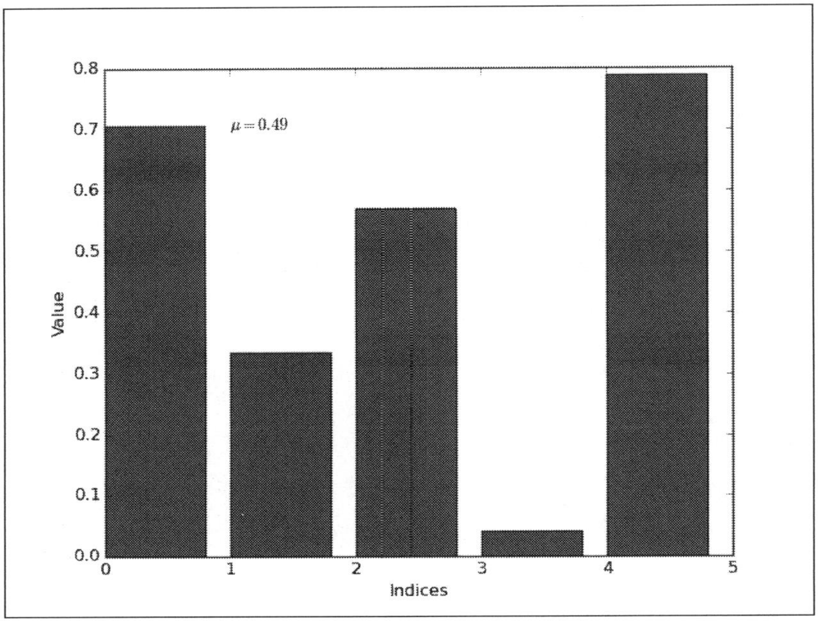

The first parameter takes the *x* axis value and the second parameter takes the *y* axis value. The third parameter is the text that needs to be added to the plot. The latex expression has been used to plot the `mu` mean within the plot.

A certain section of the chart can be annotated by using the annotate command. The annotate command will take the text, the position of the section of plot that needs to be pointed at, and the position of the text:

```
>>> ax = plt.subplot(111)
>>> t = np.arange(0.0, 5.0, 0.01)
>>> s = np.cos(2*np.pi*t)
>>> line, = plt.plot(t, s, lw=2)
>>> plt.annotate('local max', xy=(2, 1), xytext=(3, 1.5),
            arrowprops=dict(facecolor='black', shrink=0.05),
            )
>>> plt.ylim(-2,2)
>>> plt.show()
```

After the preceding code is executed we'll get the following output:

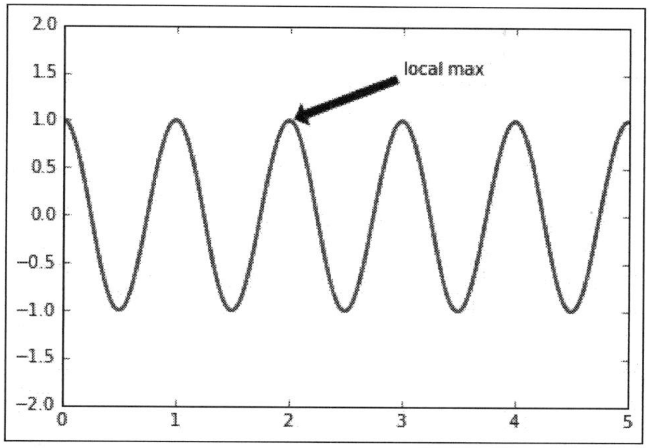

Styling your plots

The style package within the matplotlib library makes it easier to change the style of the plots that are being plotted. It is very easy to change to the famous `ggplot` style of the R language or use the Nate Silver's website `http://fivethirtyeight.com/` for `fivethirtyeight` style. The following example shows the plotting of a simple line chart with the `ggplot` style:

```
>>> plt.style.use('ggplot')
>>> plt.plot([1, 2, 3, 4], [1, 4, 9, 16])
>>> plt.show()
```

After the preceding code is executed we'll get the following output:

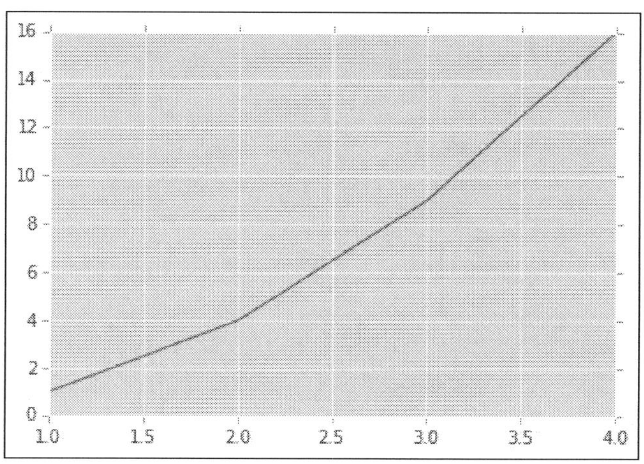

In the preceding code, `plt.style.use()` is used to set the style of the plot. It is a global set, so after it is executed, all the plots that follow will have the same style.

The following code gives the popular `fivethirtyeight` style, which is Nate Silver's website on **data journalism**, where his team write articles on various topics by applying data science:

```
>>> plt.style.use('fivethirtyeight')
>>> plt.plot([1, 2, 3, 4], [1, 4, 9, 16])
>>> plt.show()
```

After the preceding code is executed we'll get the following output:

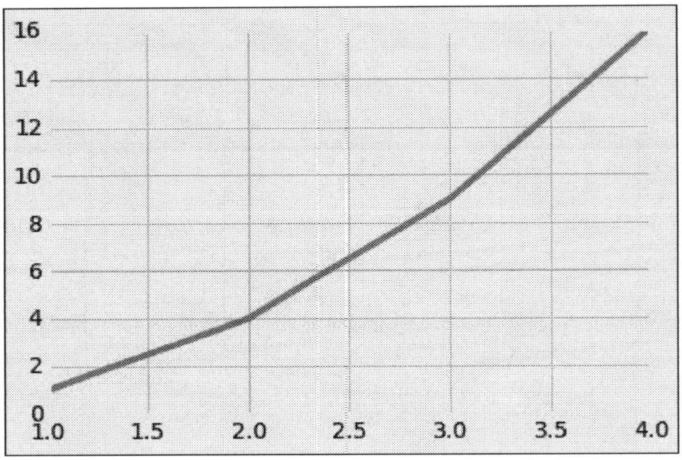

Sometimes, you just want a specific block of code to have a particular style and the rest of the plots in the code to have the default style. This can be achieved using the `plt.style.context` function and the style can be specified within it. Once the following code is executed, only the plot that is specified within it is plotted with the given style:

```
>>> with plt.style.context(('dark_background')):
        plt.plot([1, 2, 3, 4], [1, 4, 9, 16])
>>> plt.show()
```

After the preceding code is executed we'll get the following output:

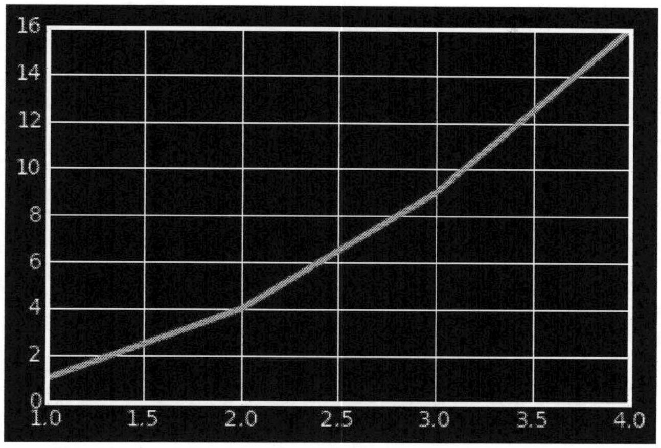

Box plots

A box plot is a very good plot to understand the spread, median, and outliers of data:

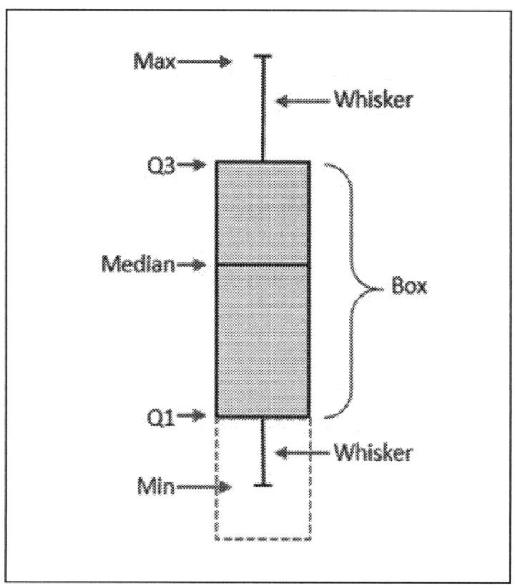

The various parts of the preceding figure are explained as follows:

- **Q3**: This is the 75th percentile value of the data. It's also called the upper hinge.
- **Q1**: This is the 25th percentile value of the data. It's also called the lower hinge.
- **Box**: This is also called a step. It's the difference between the upper hinge and the lower hinge.

- **Median**: This is the midpoint of the data.
- **Max**: This is the upper inner fence. It is 1.5 times the step above **Q3**.
- **Min**: This is the lower inner fence. It is 1.5 times the step below **Q1**.

Any value that is greater than **Max** or lesser than **Min** is called an outlier, which is also known as a flier.

The following code will create some data, and by using the `boxplot` function we'll create box plots:

```
>>> ## Creating some data
>>> np.random.seed(10)
>>> box_data_1 = np.random.normal(100, 10, 200)
>>> box_data_2 = np.random.normal(80, 30, 200)
>>> box_data_3 = np.random.normal(90, 20, 200)

>>> ## Combining the different data in a list
>>> data_to_plot = [box_data_1, box_data_2, box_data_3]

>>> # Create the boxplot
>>> bp = plt.boxplot(data_to_plot)
```

After the preceding code is executed we'll get the following output:

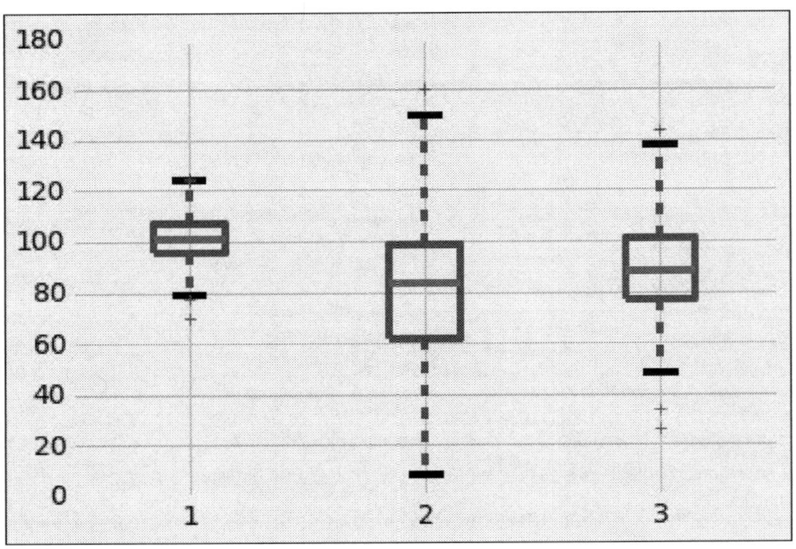

The bp variable in the boxplot function is a Python dictionary with key values such as boxes, whiskers, fliers, caps, and median. The values in the keys represent the different components of the box plot and their properties. The properties can be accessed and altered appropriately to style the box plot to your liking. The following code gives you an example of how to style your boxplot:

```
>>> ## add patch_artist=True option to ax.boxplot()
>>> ## to get fill color
>>> bp = plt.boxplot(data_to_plot, patch_artist=True)


>>> ## change outline color, fill color and linewidth of the boxes
>>> for box in bp['boxes']:
       # change outline color
       box.set( color='#7570b3', linewidth=2)
       # change fill color
       box.set( facecolor = '#1b9e77' )


>>> ## change color and linewidth of the whiskers
>>> for whisker in bp['whiskers']:
       whisker.set(color='#7570b3', linewidth=2)


>>> ## change color and linewidth of the caps
>>> for cap in bp['caps']:
        cap.set(color='#7570b3', linewidth=2)


>>> ## change color and linewidth of the medians
>>> for median in bp['medians']:
       median.set(color='#b2df8a', linewidth=2)


>>> ## change the style of fliers and their fill
>>> for flier in bp['fliers']:
       flier.set(marker='o', color='#e7298a', alpha=0.5)
```

In the preceding code, we take the key values of boxplots and set their properties in terms of color, line width, and face color. Similarly, we perform the same task for the other components, such as whiskers, caps, medians, and fliers.

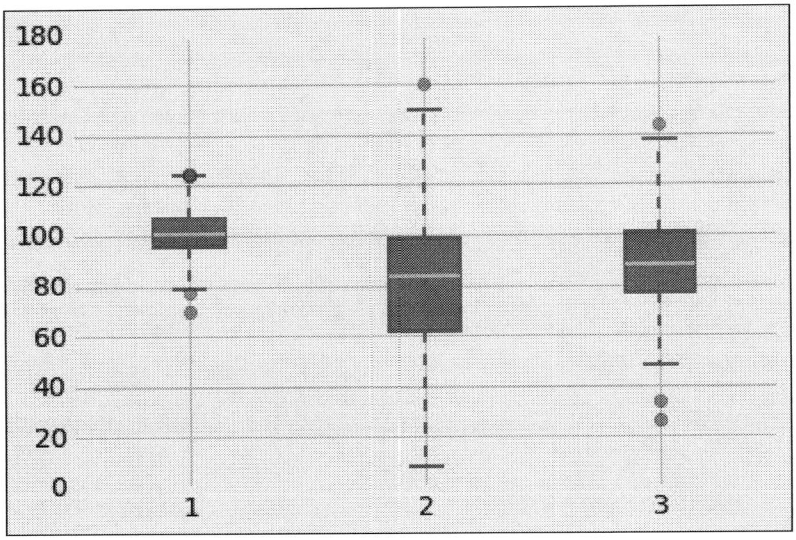

Heatmaps

A heatmap is a graphical representation where individual values of a matrix are represented as colors. A heatmap is very useful in visualizing the concentration of values between two dimensions of a matrix. This helps in finding patterns and gives a perspective of depth.

Let's start off by creating a basic heatmap between two dimensions. We'll create a 10 x 6 matrix of random values and visualize it as a heatmap:

```
>>> # Generate Data
>>> data = np.random.rand(10,6)
>>> rows = list('ZYXWVUTSRQ')  #Ylabel
>>> columns = list('ABCDEF')  #Xlabel


>>> #Basic Heat Map plot
>>> plt.pcolor(data)
>>> plt.show()
```

After the preceding code is executed we'll get the following output:

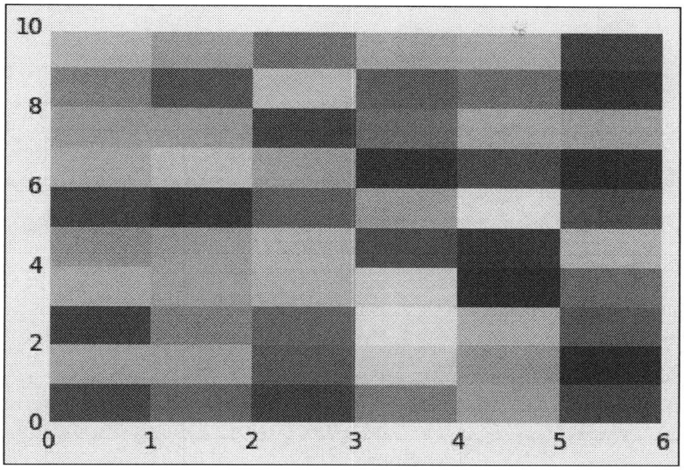

In the preceding code, we used the `pcolor()` function to create the heatmap colors. We'll now add labels to the heatmap:

```
>>> # Add Row/Column Labels
>>> plt.pcolor(data)
>>> plt.xticks(np.arange(0,6)+0.5,columns)
>>> plt.yticks(np.arange(0,10)+0.5,rows)
>>> plt.show()
```

After the preceding code is executed we'll get the following output:

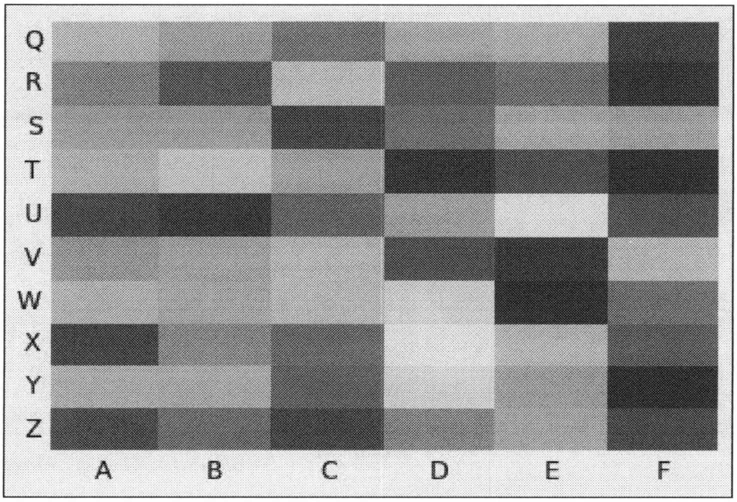

We'll now adjust the color of the heatmap to make it more visually representative. This will help us to understand the data:

```
>>> # Change color map
>>> plt.pcolor(data,cmap=plt.cm.Reds,edgecolors='k')
>>> plt.xticks(np.arange(0,6)+0.5,columns)
>>> plt.yticks(np.arange(0,10)+0.5,rows)
>>> plt.show()
```

After the preceding code is executed we'll get the following output:

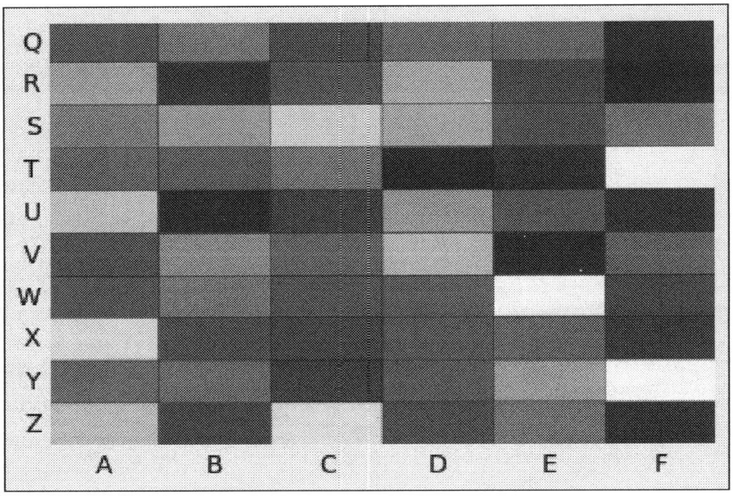

In some instances, there might be a huge number of values that need to be plotted on the heatmap. This can be done by binning the values first and then using the following code to plot it:

```
>>> # Generate some test data
>>> x = np.random.randn(8873)
>>> y = np.random.randn(8873)

>>> heatmap, xedges, yedges = np.histogram2d(x, y, bins=50)
>>> extent = [xedges[0], xedges[-1], yedges[0], yedges[-1]]

>>> plt.imshow(heatmap, extent=extent)
>>> plt.show()
```

After the preceding code is executed we'll get the following output:

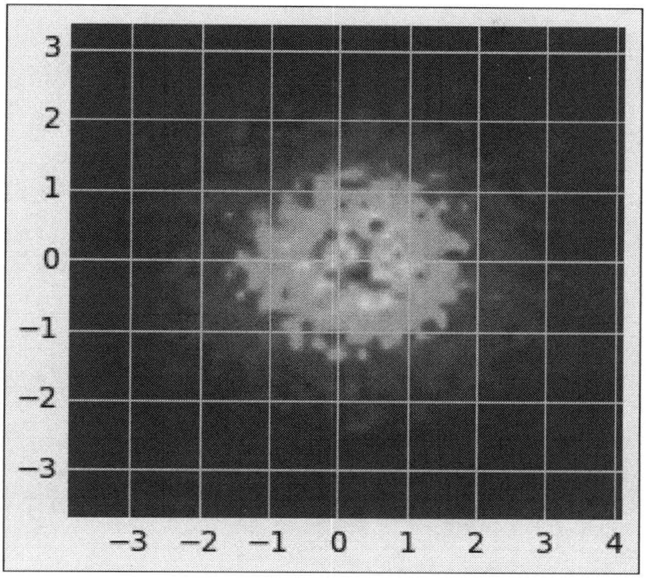

In the preceding code, the `histogram2d` function helped in binning the the 2D values. Post this, we feed the values to the heatmap to get the preceding plot. Since we used the `randn()`, the values generated were random normally distributed numbers, which means that the concentration of numbers will be more toward the mean. This can be seen in the preceding plot, which shows the center to be red and the exterior area to be blue.

Scatter plots with histograms

We can combine a simple scatter plot with histograms for each axis. These kinds of plots help us see the distribution of the values of each axis.

Let's generate some randomly distributed data for the two axes:

```
>>> from matplotlib.ticker import NullFormatter
>>> # the random data
>>> x = np.random.randn(1000)
>>> y = np.random.randn(1000)
```

A `NullFormatter` object is created, which will be used for eliminating the *x* and *y* labels of the histograms:

```
>>> nullfmt   = NullFormatter()         # no labels
```

The following code defines the size, height, and width of the scatter and histogram plots:

```
>>> # definitions for the axes
>>> left, width = 0.1, 0.65
>>> bottom, height = 0.1, 0.65
>>> bottom_h = left_h = left+width+0.02

>>> rect_scatter = [left, bottom, width, height]
>>> rect_histx = [left, bottom_h, width, 0.2]
>>> rect_histy = [left_h, bottom, 0.2, height]
```

Once the size and height are defined, the axes are plotted for the scatter plot as well as both the histograms:

```
>>> # start with a rectangular Figure
>>> plt.figure(1, figsize=(8,8))

>>> axScatter = plt.axes(rect_scatter)
>>> axHistx = plt.axes(rect_histx)
>>> axHisty = plt.axes(rect_histy)
```

The histograms' x and y axis labels are eliminated by using the `set_major_formatter` method, and by assigning the `NullFormatter` object to it, the scatter plot is plotted:

```
>>> # no labels
>>> axHistx.xaxis.set_major_formatter(nullfmt)
>>> axHisty.yaxis.set_major_formatter(nullfmt)

>>> # the scatter plot:
>>> axScatter.scatter(x, y)
```

The limits of the x and y axes are computed using the following code, where the max of the x and y values are taken. The max value is then divided by the bin, then one is added to it before it is again multiplied with the bin value. This is done so there is some space ahead of the `max` value:

```
>>> # now determine nice limits by hand:
>>> binwidth = 0.25
>>> xymax = np.max( [np.max(np.fabs(x)), np.max(np.fabs(y))] )
>>> lim = ( int(xymax/binwidth) + 1) * binwidth
```

The limit value that is calculated is then assigned to the `set_xlim` method of the `axScatter` object:

```
>>> axScatter.set_xlim( (-lim, lim) )
>>> axScatter.set_ylim( (-lim, lim) )
```

The `bins` variable creates a list of interval values, which will be used with the histograms:

```
>>> bins = np.arange(-lim, lim + binwidth, binwidth)
```

The histograms are plotted and the one that is horizontal is set using the orientation parameter:

```
>>> axHistx.hist(x, bins=bins)
>>> axHisty.hist(y, bins=bins, orientation='horizontal')
```

The limit value of the scatter plot is fetched and then assigned to the limit methods of the histogram:

```
>>> axHistx.set_xlim( axScatter.get_xlim() )
>>> axHisty.set_ylim( axScatter.get_ylim() )

>>> plt.show()
```

After the preceding code is executed we'll get the following output:

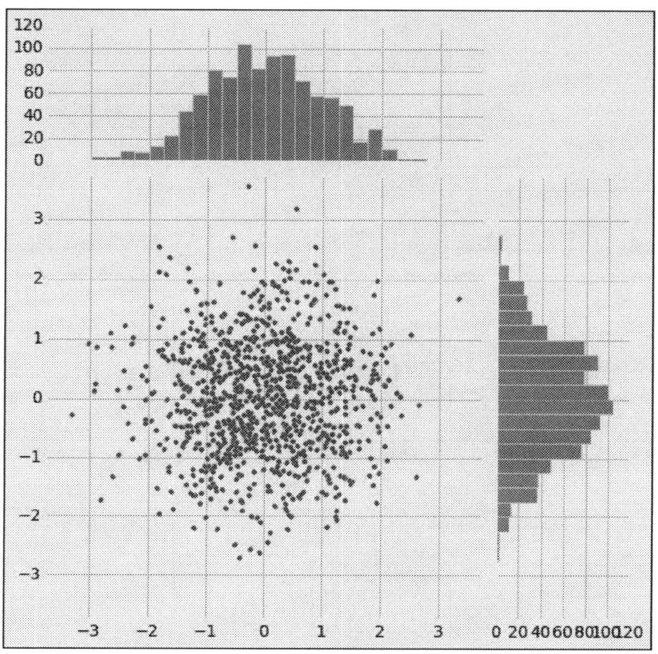

A scatter plot matrix

A scatter plot matrix can be formed for a collection of variables where each of the variables will be plotted against each other. The following code generates a DataFrame `df`, which consists of four columns with normally distributed random values and column names named from `a` to `d`:

```
>>> df = pd.DataFrame(np.random.randn(1000, 4),
        columns=['a', 'b', 'c', 'd'])


>>> spm = pd.tools.plotting.scatter_matrix(df, alpha=0.2,
       figsize=(6, 6), diagonal='hist')
```

After the preceding code is executed we'll get the following output:

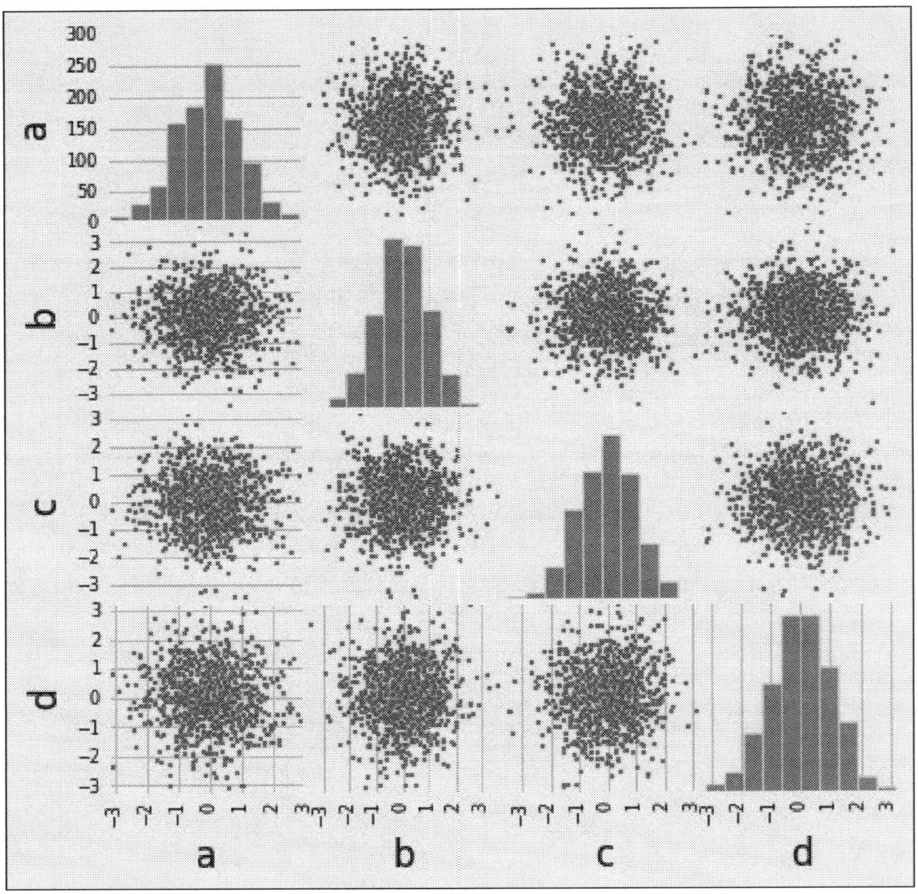

The `scatter_matrix()` function helps in plotting the preceding figure. It takes in the data frame object and the required parameters that are defined to customize the plot. You would have observed that the diagonal graph is defined as a histogram, which means that in the section of the plot matrix where the variable is against itself, a histogram is plotted.

Instead of the histogram, we can also use the kernel density estimation for the diagonal:

```
>>> spm = pd.tools.plotting.scatter_matrix(df, alpha=0.2,
        figsize=(6, 6), diagonal='kde')
```

After the preceding code is executed we'll get the following output:

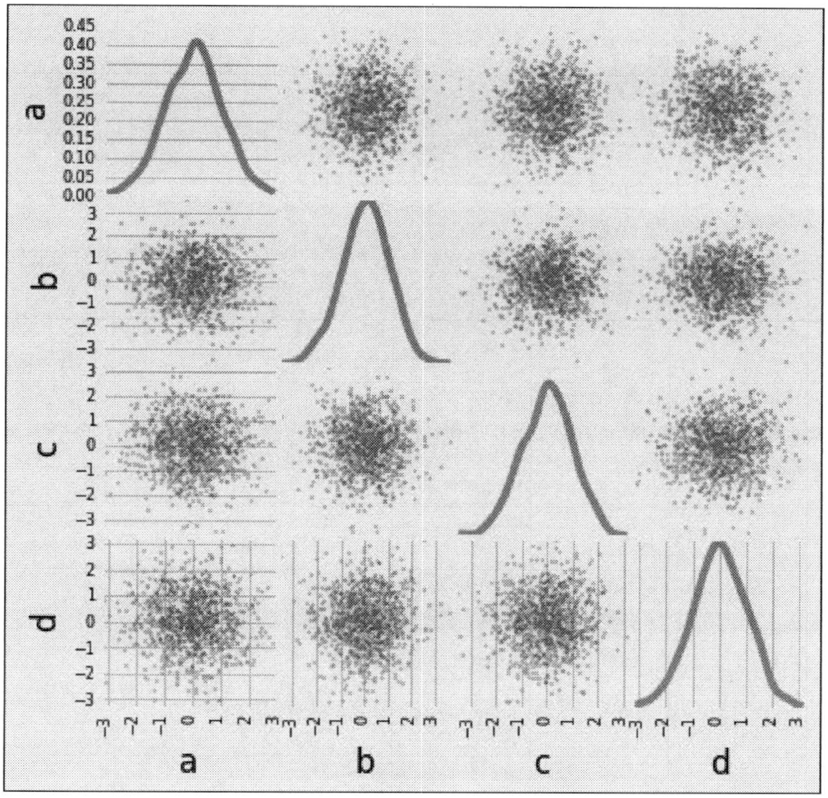

The kernel density estimation is a nonparametric way of estimating the probability density function of a random variable. It basically helps in understanding whether the data is normally distributed and the side toward which it is skewed.

Area plots

An area plot is useful for comparing the values of different factors across a range. The area plot can be stacked in nature, where the areas of the different factors are stacked on top of each other. The following code gives an example of a stacked area plot:

```
>>> df = pd.DataFrame(np.random.rand(10, 4),
        columns=['p', 'q', 'r', 's'])


>>> df.plot(kind='area');
```

After the preceding code is executed we'll get the following output:

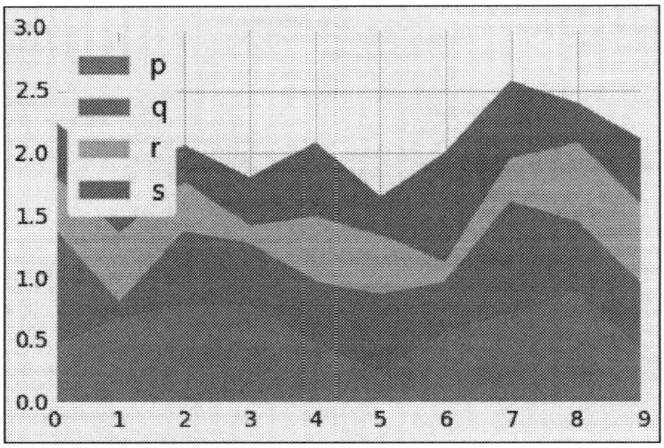

To remove the stack of area plot, you can use the following code:

```
>>> df.plot(kind='area', stacked=False);
```

After the preceding code is executed we'll get the following output:

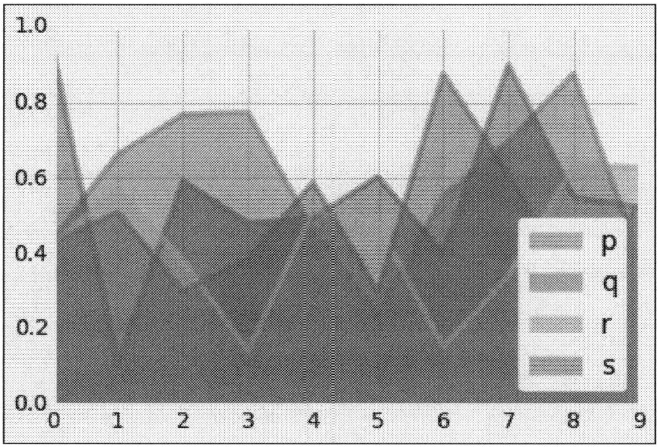

Bubble charts

A bubble chart is basically a scatter plot with an additional dimension. The additional dimension helps in setting the size of the bubble, which means that the greater the size of the bubble, the larger the value that represents the bubble. This kind of a chart helps in analyzing the data of three dimensions.

The following code creates a sample data of three variables and this data is then fed to the `plot()` method where its kind is mentioned as a scatter and s is the size of the bubble:

```
>>> plt.style.use('ggplot')
>>> df = pd.DataFrame(np.random.rand(50, 3), columns=['a', 'b', 'c'])
>>> df.plot(kind='scatter', x='a', y='b', s=df['c']*400);
```

After the preceding code is executed we'll get the following output:

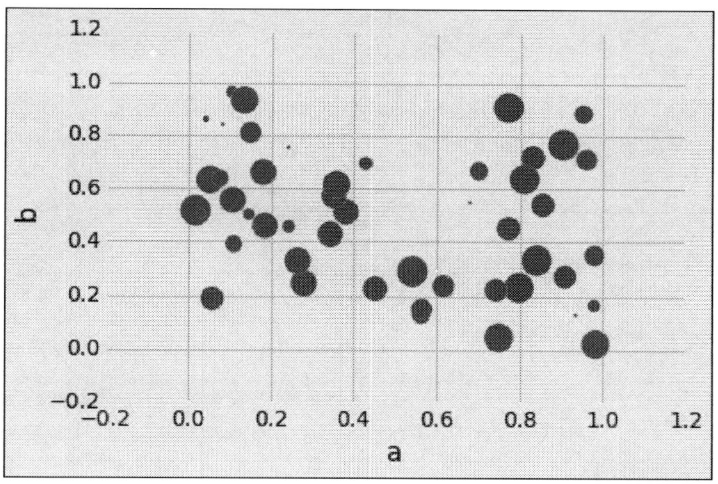

Hexagon bin plots

A hexagon bin plot can be created using the `DataFrame.plot()` function and `kind = 'hexbin'`. This kind of plot is really useful if your scatter plot is too dense to interpret. It helps in binning the spatial area of the chart and the intensity of the color that a hexagon can be interpreted as points being more concentrated in this area.

The following code helps in plotting the hexagon bin plot, and the structure of the code is similar to the previously discussed plots:

```
>>> df = pd.DataFrame(np.random.randn(1000, 2), columns=['a', 'b'])

>>> df['b'] = df['b'] + np.arange(1000)

>>> df.plot(kind='hexbin', x='a', y='b', gridsize=25)
```

After the preceding code is executed we'll get the following output:

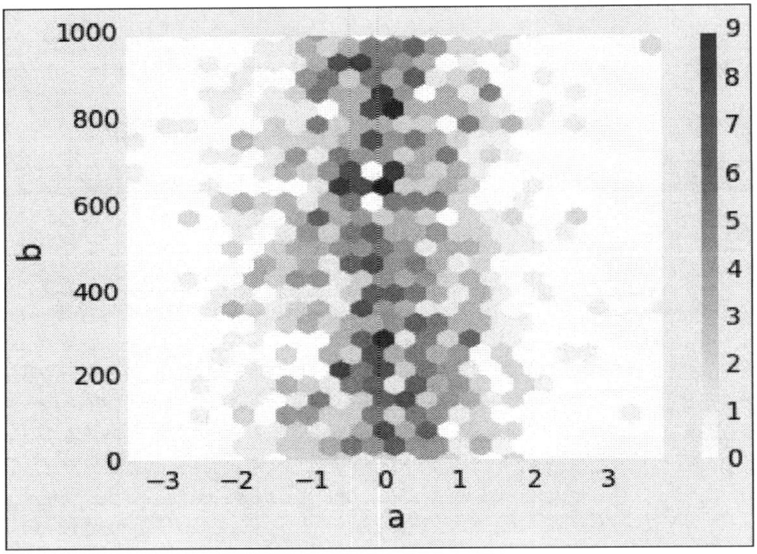

Trellis plots

A Trellis plot is a layout of smaller charts in a grid with consistent scales. Each smaller chart represents an item in a category, named conditions. The data displayed on each smaller chart is conditional for the items in the category.

Trellis plots are useful for finding structures and patterns in complex data. The grid layout looks similar to a garden trellis, hence the name Trellis plots.

The following code helps in plotting a trellis chart where for each combination of sex and smoker/nonsmoker:

```
>>> tips_data = pd.read_csv('Data/tips.csv')
>>> plt.figure()
>>> plot = rplot.RPlot(tips_data, x='total_bill', y='tip')
>>> plot.add(rplot.TrellisGrid(['sex', 'smoker']))
>>> plot.add(rplot.GeomHistogram())
>>> plot.render(plt.gcf())
```

After the preceding code is executed we'll get the following output:

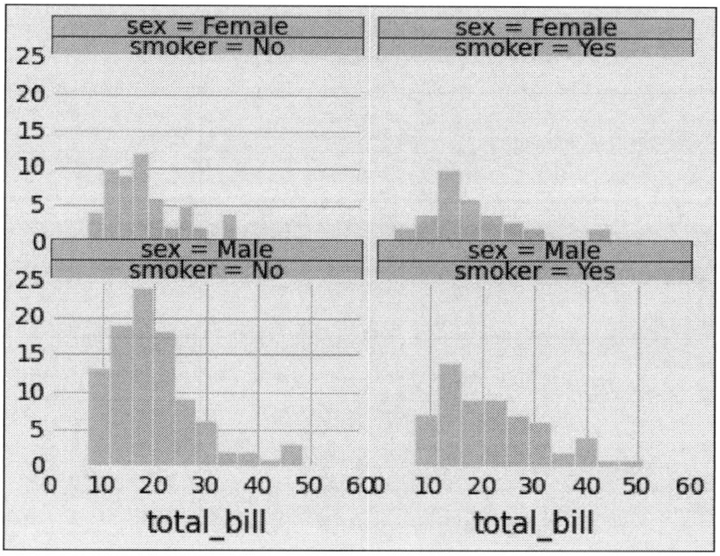

In the preceding code, `rplot.RPlot` takes the `tips_data` object. Also, the *x* and *y* axis values are defined. After this, the Trellis grid is defined based on the smoker and sex. In the end, we use `GeomHistogram()` to plot a histogram.

To change the Trellis plot to a kernel density estimate, we can use the following code:

```
>>> plt.figure()
>>> plot = rplot.RPlot(tips_data, x='total_bill', y='tip')
>>> plot.add(rplot.TrellisGrid(['sex', 'smoker']))
>>> plot.add(rplot.GeomDensity())
>>> plot.render(plt.gcf())
```

After the preceding code is executed we'll get the following output:

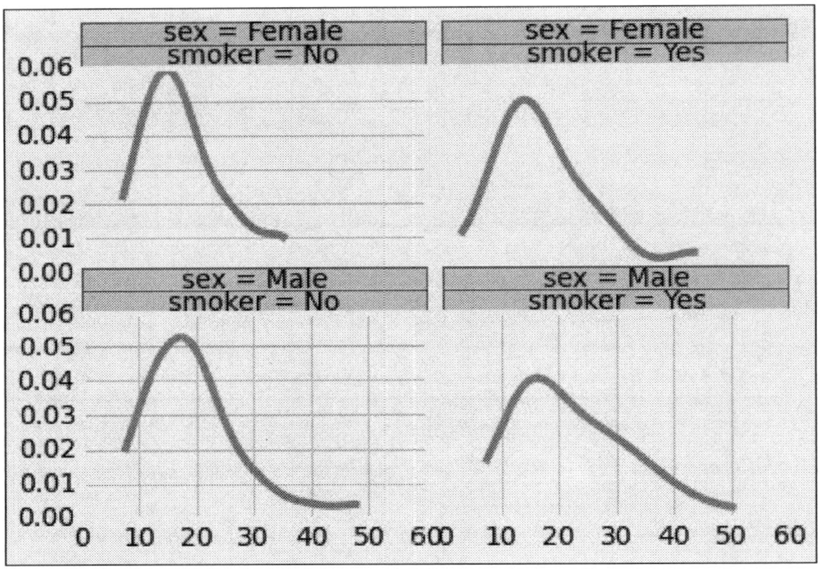

We could also have a scatter plot with a poly fit line on it:

```
>>> plt.figure()
>>> plot = rplot.RPlot(tips_data, x='total_bill', y='tip')
>>> plot.add(rplot.TrellisGrid(['sex', 'smoker']))
>>> plot.add(rplot.GeomScatter())
>>> plot.add(rplot.GeomPolyFit(degree=2))
>>> plot.render(plt.gcf())
```

After the preceding code is executed we'll get the following output:

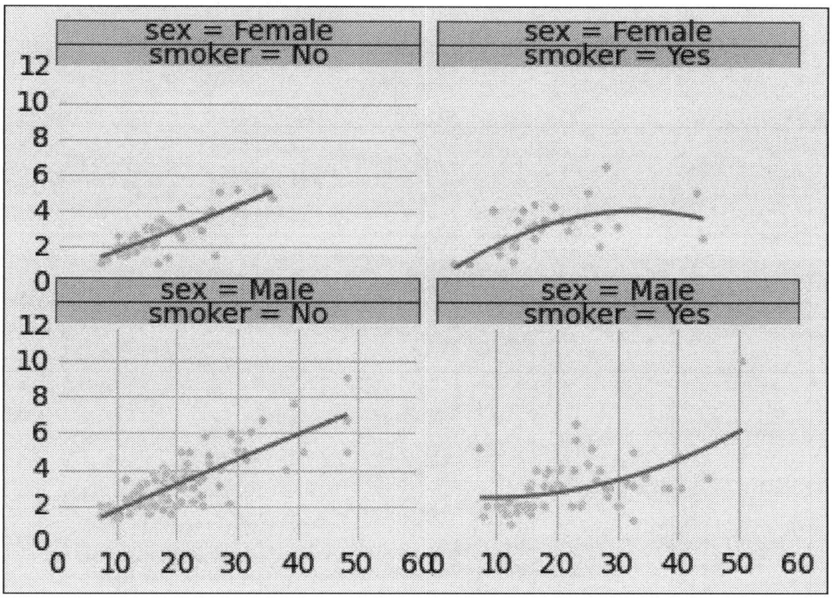

The code is similar to the previous example. The only difference is that `GeomScatter()` and `GeomPolyFit` are used to get the fit line on the plot.

The scatter plot can be combined with a 2D kernel density plot by using the following code:

```
>>> plt.figure()
>>> plot = rplot.RPlot(tips_data, x='total_bill', y='tip')
>>> plot.add(rplot.TrellisGrid(['sex', 'smoker']))
>>> plot.add(rplot.GeomScatter())
>>> plot.add(rplot.GeomDensity2D())
>>> plot.render(plt.gcf())
```

After the preceding code is executed we'll get the following output:

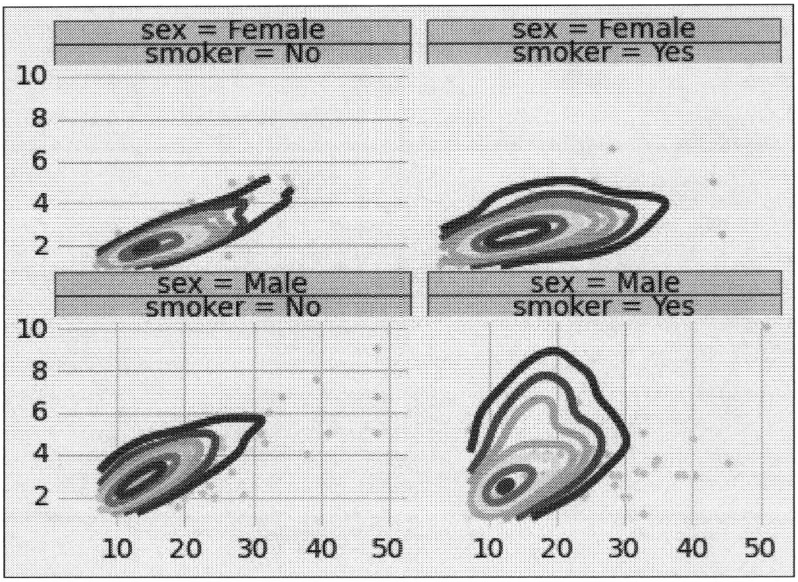

A 3D plot of a surface

We'll now plot a 3D plot, where the `Sin` function is plotted against the sum of the square values of the two axes:

```
>>> from mpl_toolkits.mplot3d import Axes3D
>>> fig = plt.figure()
>>> ax = Axes3D(fig)
>>> X = np.arange(-4, 4, 0.25)
>>> Y = np.arange(-4, 4, 0.25)
>>> X, Y = np.meshgrid(X, Y)
>>> R = np.sqrt(X**2 + Y**2)
>>> Z = np.sin(R)
>>> ax.plot_surface(X, Y, Z, rstride=1, cstride=1, cmap='hot')
```

After the preceding code is executed we'll get the following output:

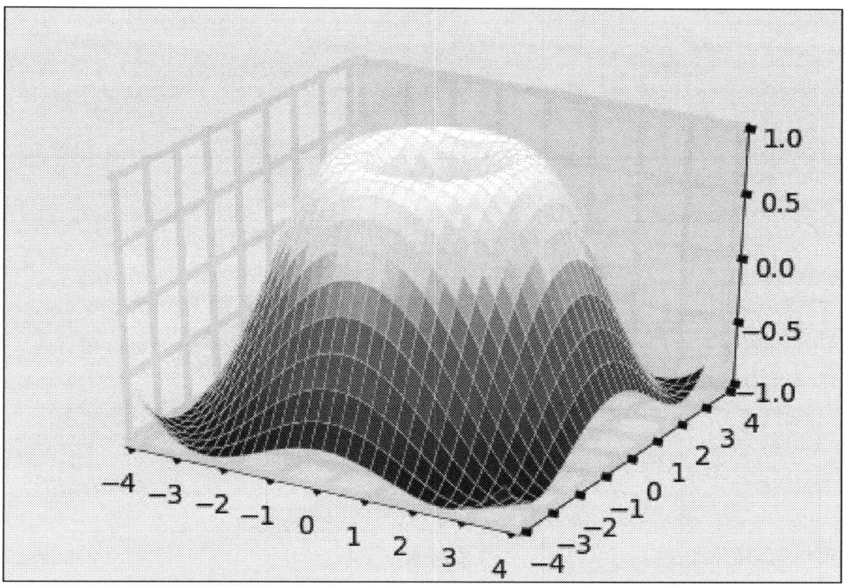

In the preceding code, we defined the *x* and *y* axes with values ranging from -4 to 4. We created a coordinate matrix with `meshgrid()`, then squared the values of *x* and *y*, and finally, summed them up. This was then fed to the `plot_surface` function. The `rstride` and `cstride` parameters in simple terms help in sizing the cell on the surface.

Let's adjust the view using `view_int`. The following is the view at `0` degree elevation and `0` degree angle:

```
>>> fig = plt.figure()
>>> ax = Axes3D(fig)
>>> ax.view_init(elev=0., azim=0)
>>> ax.plot_surface(X, Y, Z, rstride=1, cstride=1, cmap='hot')
```

After the preceding code is executed we'll get the following output:

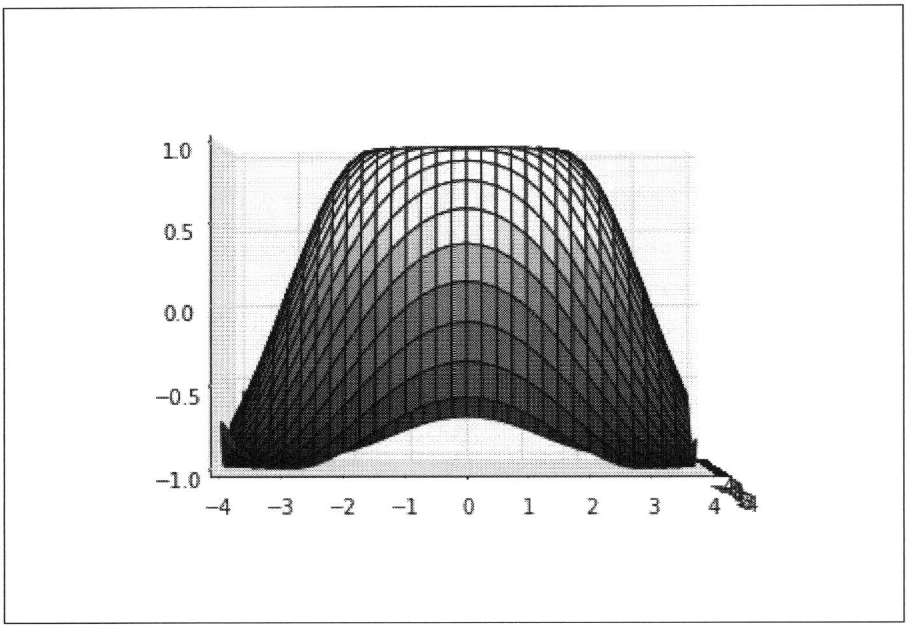

The following is the view at `50` degrees elevation:

```
>>> fig = plt.figure()
>>> ax = Axes3D(fig)
>>> ax.view_init(elev=50., azim=0)
>>> ax.plot_surface(X, Y, Z, rstride=1, cstride=1, cmap='hot')
```

After the preceding code is executed we'll get the following output:

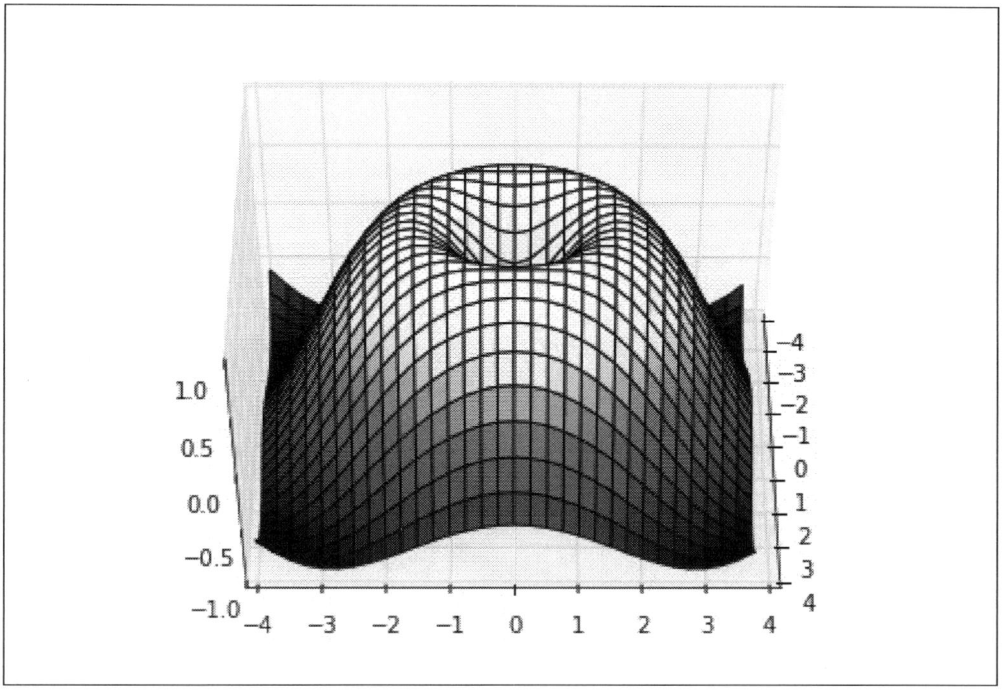

The following is the view at `50` degrees elevation and `30` degrees angle:

```
>>> fig = plt.figure()
>>> ax = Axes3D(fig)
>>> ax.view_init(elev=50., azim=30)
>>> ax.plot_surface(X, Y, Z, rstride=1, cstride=1, cmap='hot')
```

After the preceding code is executed we'll get the following output:

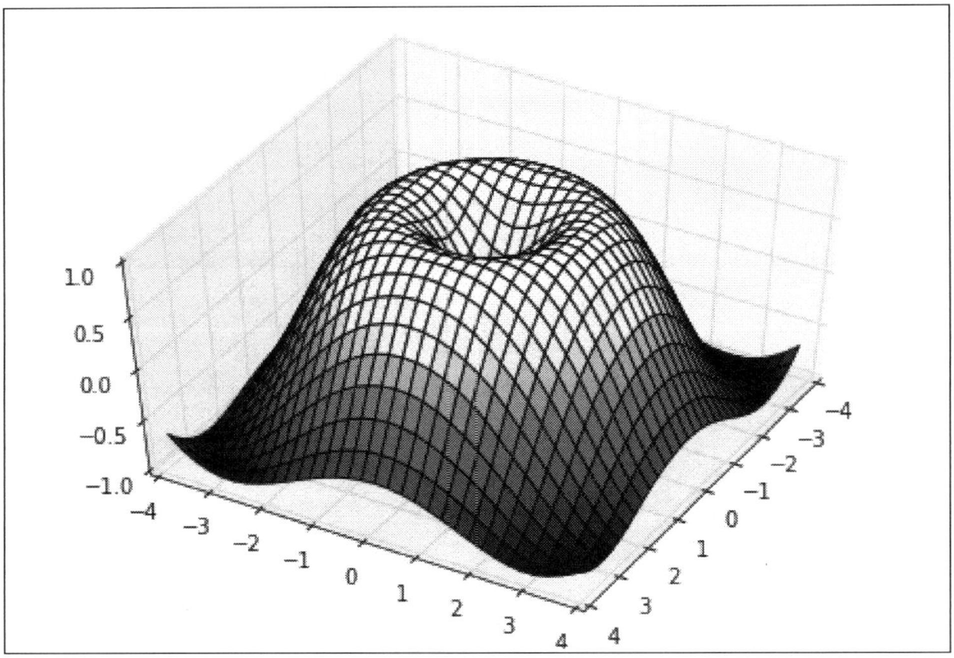

Summary

In this chapter, you learned how to use the various properties of a chart. You also learned how to combine multiple charts and style them. There were multiple advanced visualizations that you have gained knowledge of through this chapter.

In the next chapter, we will understand what machine learning is and also explore a few machine learning techniques.

5
Uncovering Machine Learning

Machine learning is a technique to teach programs that use data, to generate algorithms instead of explicitly programming an algorithm from scratch.

It is a field of computer science that originates from the research into artificial intelligence. It is closely associated to statistics and mathematical optimization, which give methods, theories, and application domains to the field. Machine learning is used in various computing tasks where programming explicitly rule-based algorithms is infeasible. Example applications include; e-mail spam filters, search engines, language translation, and computer visions. Machine learning can be sometimes confused with data mining, although it focuses mainly on exploratory data analysis.

Here are some of the terminologies that will be used in this chapter henceforth:

- **Features**: This refers to distinctive traits that help define the outcome
- **Samples**: A sample is an item to process. It could be a document, image, audio, or a CSV file
- **Feature vector**: This refers to numerical features, such as an n-dimensional vector, that represents some object
- **Feature extraction**: This refers to the processing of a feature vector where data is transformed from a high-dimensional space to a lower-dimensional space
- **Training set**: This refers to a set of data that discovers potentially predictive relationships
- **Testing set**: This refers to a set of data that tests out predications

Different types of machine learning

Machine learning is divided into mainly three types depending on the nature of the learning target or the feedback available to the learning system:

1. **Supervised learning**: The computer is presented with a given set of inputs and their respective outputs. The goal of the program is to learn from the inputs in order to reproduce the outputs.
2. **Unsupervised learning**: There is no target variable in the case of unsupervised learning. The computer is left on its own to find patterns within the data.
3. **Reinforcement learning**: A program has to interact with its environment in a dynamic manner, such as a driving a car.

Supervised learning

As described earlier, a supervised learning algorithm studies the training data and generates a function, which can be used for predicting new instances.

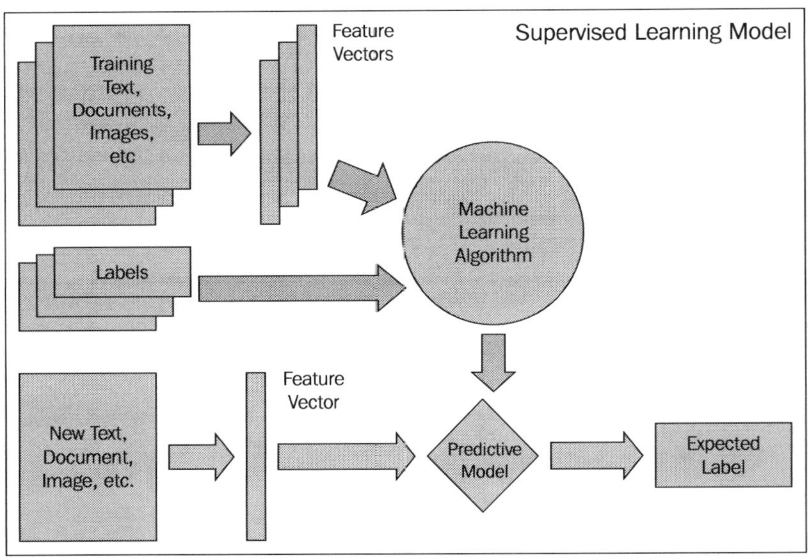

As you can see from the preceding diagram, there is training data, which the machine learning model will learn from.

Let's assume that the training data is a set of text that represents different news articles. These news articles can be related to sports, international, national, and various other categories of news. These categories will act us as our labels. From this training data, we'll derive feature vectors where each word could be a vector or certain vectors could be derived from the text. For example, the number of instances of the word "Football" could be a vector, or the number of instances of the word "Prime Minister" could be a vector as well.

These feature vectors and labels are fed to the Machine Learning Algorithm, which learns from the data. Once the model is trained, it is then used on the new data where the features are again extracted and then inputted to the model, which generates the target data.

Here are few examples of supervised machine learning algorithms, which will be introduced in this chapter, and some of them will be explained in detail in the following chapters:

1. Decision tree
2. Linear regression
3. Logistic regression
4. The naive Bayes classifier

Unsupervised learning

As described earlier, unsupervised learning tries to find hidden structures in unlabeled data. As you can see in the following diagram, there is no label that is inputted to the algorithm:

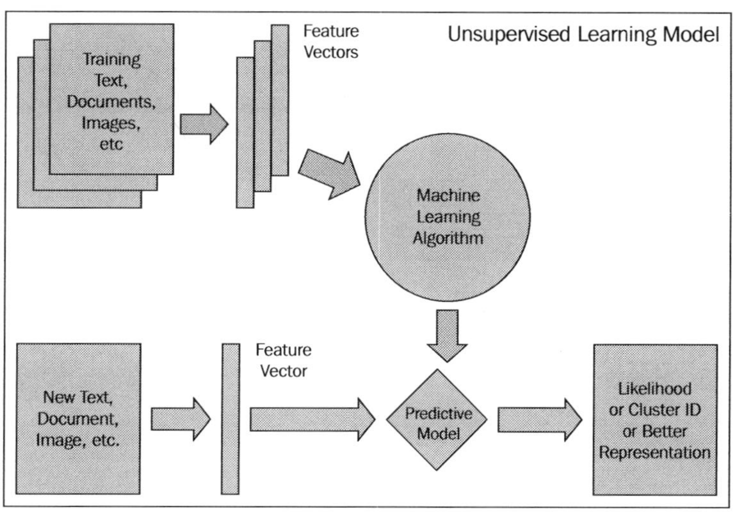

Let's take the example of images that will act as our training and input datasets. The images contain the faces of a human being, horses, and insects. From these images, features are extracted, which will help identify the group that the images belong to. These features are then inputted to the unsupervised machine learning algorithm. The algorithm will find patterns within the data and help in bucketing these images to the respective group.

This same algorithm can then be used for new images and helps in bucketing the images into the required buckets.

Here are a few examples of unsupervised machine learning algorithms, which will be introduced in this chapter, and some of it will be covered in detail in the following chapters:

1. The k-means clustering
2. Hierarchical clustering

Reinforcement learning

In reinforcement learning, the data to be inputted is provided as a stimulus to the model from the environment to which the machine learning model must respond and react. Feedback is provided not like a teaching process as in the case of supervised learning, but as punishments and rewards in the environment.

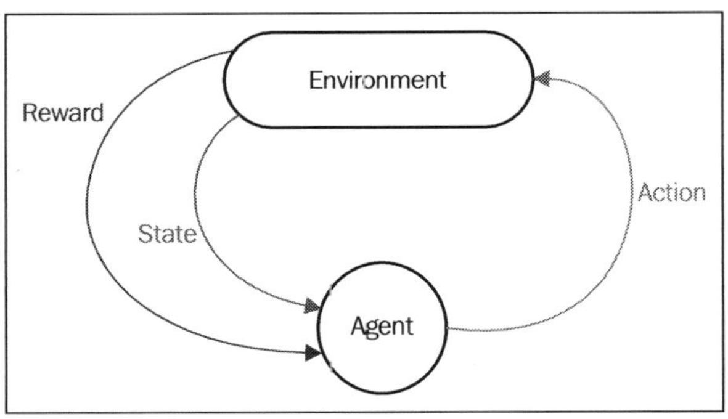

The actions taken by the agent results in it learning from its outcome, instead of being explicitly taught, and the action it selects is based on its past experience and also by the fresh choices made by it, which basically means it is learning from trial and error. The agent receives the reinforcement signal in the form of a numerical reward that encodes the success and the agent seeks to teach itself to take actions that will increase the accumulated reward over time.

Reinforcement learning is used heavily in robotics and not much in data science. The following are the algorithms that come under reinforcement learning:

1. Temporal difference learning
2. Q learning

Decision trees

A simple predictive model maps the outcomes of an item to the input data. It is a popular predictive modeling technique, which is used commonly in the industry:

Decision tree models are basically of two types:

- **Classification trees**: These refer to dependent variables that take a finite value. In these tree structures, branches represent the rules of the features that lead to the class labels, and leaves represent the class labels of the outcome.
- **Regression trees**: When dependent variables takes continuous values, then they're called regression trees.

Let's take an example. The following data represents whether you should play tennis or not, based on the overall outlook of weather, humidity, and wind intensity:

Play	Wind	Humidity	Outlook
`No`	`Low`	`High`	`Sunny`
`No`	`High`	`Normal`	`Rain`
`Yes`	`Low`	`High`	`Overcast`
`Yes`	`Weak`	`Normal`	`Rain`
`Yes`	`Low`	`Normal`	`Sunny`
`Yes`	`Low`	`Normal`	`Overcast`
`Yes`	`High`	`Normal`	`Sunny`

If you take this data, use `Play` as the target variable, and the remaining as the independent variable, then you'll get a decision tree model that will have the following structure as the rules.

So, when new data comes in, it will traverse this tree to come to this conclusion, which will be the outcome:

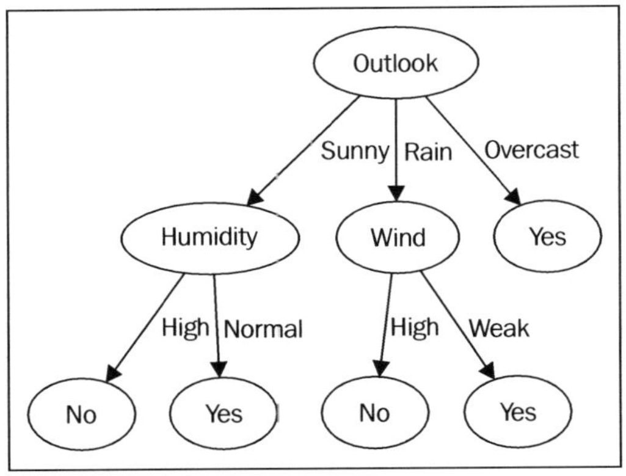

Decision trees are the simplest of the predictive models and here are a few of their advantages:

1. It's easy to communicate and visualize decision trees.
2. It is possible to find odd patterns. Suppose you are trying to find the voting pattern between two parties for an election and you have data on the education, income, sex, and age. You might observe a pattern where highly educated people have a very low income and vote for a particular party.
3. Decision trees make minimal assumptions on the data.

Here are the disadvantages of a decision tree:

1. There is a high classification error rate, while the training set is small in comparison to the number of classes.
2. There is an exponential growth in computing when the data and the number of dependent variables increase in size.
3. There is a need for discrete data for a particular construction algorithm.

Linear regression

Linear regression is an approach in modeling that helps model the scalar linear relationship between a scalar dependent variable, *Y*, and an independent variable, *X*, which can be one or more in value:

$$y = X\beta + \varepsilon$$

Let's try to understand this using an example. The following table shows the list of height and weight of students in a class:

Height (inches)	Weight (pounds)
50	125
58	135
63	145
68	144
70	170
79	165
84	171
75	166
65	160

If we run this through a simple linear regression function, which will be covered in a later chapter, with the weight as a dependent variable, y, and the independent variable, x, which is the height, we get the following equation:

$$y = 1.405405405\,x + 57.87687688$$

If you plot the preceding equation as a line with `57.88` as the intercept and the slope of the line being `1.4` on top of a scatter plot with `Weight` in the y axis and `Height` in the x axis, then the following plot is obtained:

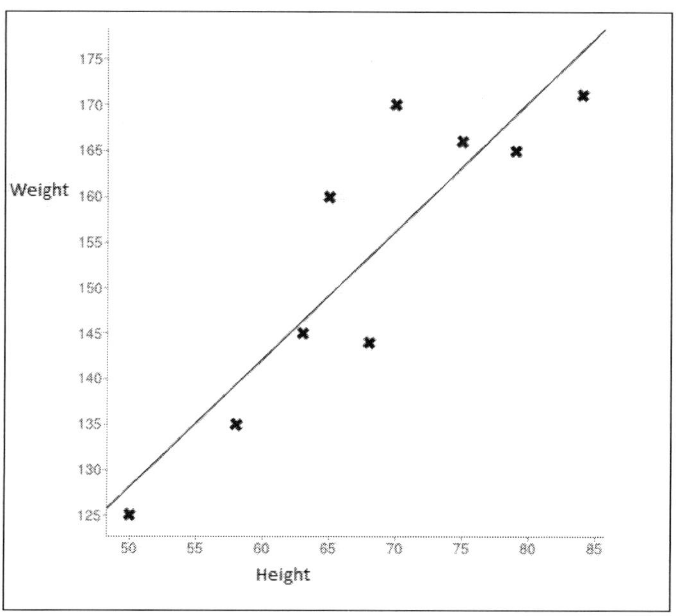

In this example, the regression algorithm tries to create the preceding equation, which has the least error when predicting the weight of the student. This was an example of a simple linear regression. In *Chapter 6, Performing Predictions with a Linear Regression*, we'll dwell on the concept of linear regression further with multiple variables.

Logistic regression

Logistic regression is another supervised learning technique, which is basically a probabilistic classification model. It is mainly used in predicting a binary predictor, such as whether a customer is going to churn or if a credit card transaction is fraudulent.

Logistic regression uses logistics. A logistic function is a very useful function that can take any value from a negative infinity to a positive infinity, and output values from `0` to `1`. Hence, it is interpretable as a probability. The following is the logistic function that generates predicted values from `0` to `1` based on the dependent `x` variable:

$$F(x) = \frac{1}{1 + e^{-(\beta_0 + \beta_1 x)}}$$

Here, x will be the independent variable and $F(x)$ will be the dependent variable.

If you try to plot the logistic function from a negative infinity to a positive infinity, then you'll get the following *S* shaped graph:

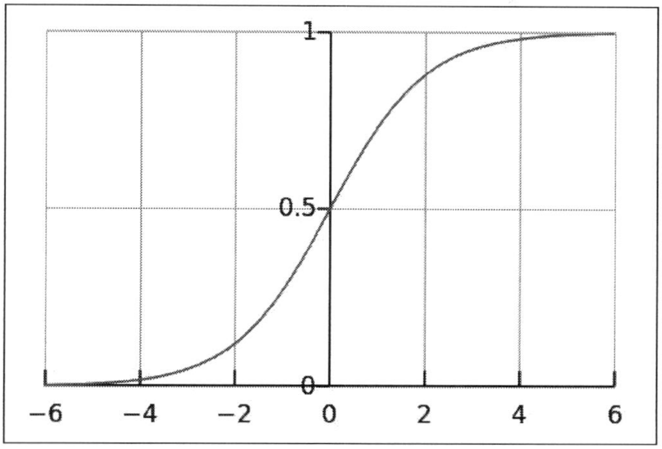

Logistic regression can be applied in the following scenarios:

1. Deriving a propensity score for a customer in a retail store of buying a new product that has been launched.
2. The likelihood of a transformer failing using the sensor data associated with it.
3. The likelihood of a user clicking on an ad that is shown on a website based on their behavior.

Logistic regression has many more applications, and it will be covered in the following chapters in greater detail with examples.

The naive Bayes classifier

The naive Bayes classifier is a simple probabilistic classifier, which is based on the Bayes theorem. The assumption made is that there is strong interdependence between the features, because of which it is called naive. The following is the Bayes theorem:

$$P(A|B)=\frac{P(B|A)P(A)}{P(B)}$$

Here in the preceding formula, *A* and *B* are events, *P(A)* and *P(B)* are the probabilities of *A* and *B* and are interdependent of each other. *P(A | B)* is the probability of *A*, given that *B* is `True`, which is a conditional probability. *P(B | A)* is the probability of *B*, given that *A* is `True`. The naive Bayes formula is as follows:

$$P(A_k \mid B) = P(A_k \cap B) / P(A_1 \cap B) + P(A_2 \cap B) + \ldots + P(A_n \cap B)$$

Let's try solving this equation to understand the naive Bayes formula with the following example:

Stacy has her engagement tomorrow in Austin at an outdoor ceremony. In the past few years, Austin has had only six rainy days in a year. Unfortunately, there has been rain forecast for tomorrow by the weatherman. 80% of the time, the weatherman accurately forecasts the rain. However, he incorrectly forecasts the weather 20% of the time when it does not rain. Determine the probability that it will rain on the day of Stacy's engagement. The following are some events based on which the probability can be calculated:

- *AI*: This event states that it rains on Stacy's engagement
- *A2*: This event states that it does not rain on Stacy's engagement
- *B*: This event states that the weatherman predicts rain

The following are the probabilities based on the preceding events:

- *P(AI) = 6/365 = 0.016438*: This means that it rains six days out of the year
- *P(AII) = 359/365 = 0.98356*: This means that it does not rain 359 days out of the year
- *P(B | AI) = 0.8*: This means that 80% of the time, it rains as predicted by the weatherman
- *P(B | AII) = 0.2*: This means that 20% of the time, it does not rain as predicted by the weatherman

The following formula helps us in calculating the naive Bayes probability:

$$P(AI \mid B) = P(AI)P(B \mid AI) / (P(AI)\, P(B \mid AI) + P(AII)\, P(B \mid AII))$$

$$P(AI \mid B) = (0.0164 * 0.8) / (0.0164*0.8 + 0.9834 * 0.2)$$

$$P(AI \mid B) = 0.065$$

So, the preceding calculation says that even though the weatherman predicted rain, there is only a 6.5% chance that it will actually rain according to the Bayes theorem

The naive Bayes is used heavily in e-mail filtering. It takes the instance of each word in an e-mail and computes the probability whether the e-mail is spam is not. The naive Bayes model learns from the previous history of e-mails and marks mails as spam, which helps it come to a conclusion on whether an e-mail is spam or not.

The k-means clustering

The k-means clustering is an unsupervised learning technique that helps in partitioning data of *n* observations into *K* buckets of similar observations.

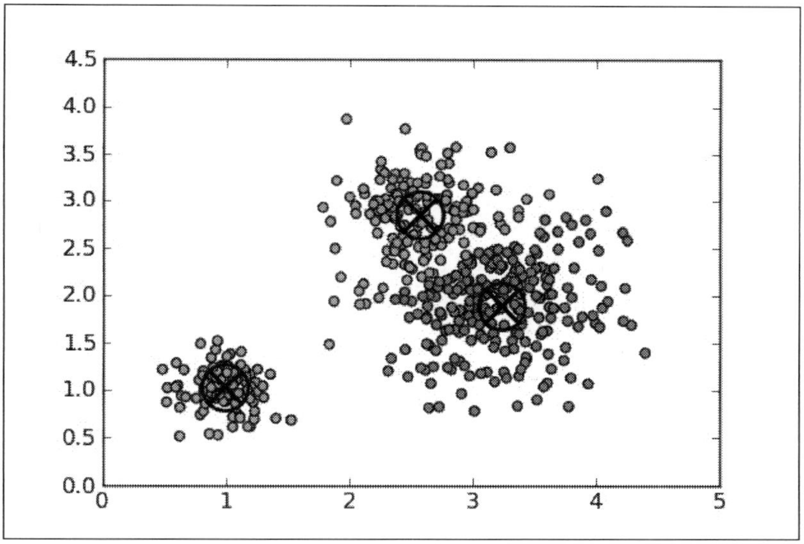

The clustering algorithm is called so because it operates by computing the mean of the features which refer to the dependent variables based on which we cluster things, such as segmenting of customers based on an average transaction amount and the average number of products purchased in a quarter of a year. This mean value then becomes the center of a cluster. The number *K* refers to the number of clusters, that is, the technique consisting of computing a *K* number of means, leading to the *clustering* of the data around these k-means.

How do we choose this K? If we have some idea of what we are looking for or how many clusters we expect or want, then we set *K* to be this number before we start the engines and let the algorithm compute along.

If we don't know how many there are, then our exploration will take a little longer and involve some trial and error, say, as we try $K=3$, 4, and 5 until we see that the clusters are making some sense to us in our domain.

$$J(V)=\sum_{i=1}^{c}\sum_{j=1}^{c_i}\left(\left\|x_i-v_j\right\|\right)^2$$

Here, $||x_i - v_j||$ is the Euclidean distance between *xi* and *vj*, c_i is in the ith cluster, the number of data points, *c* is the number of cluster centers.

The k-means clustering is widely used in computer visions, market segmentations, astronomy, geostatistics, and agriculture.

The k-means clustering will be covered in much more detail and with real-life examples in a later chapter.

Hierarchical clustering

Hierarchical clustering is an unsupervised learning technique where a hierarchy of clusters is built out of observations.

This clustering groups data at various levels of a cluster tree or dendrogram. It is not a single set of clusters, but a hierarchy of multiple levels where clusters at a particular level are joined as clusters on the next level. This allows you to decide the level of clustering that is most suitable.

The hierarchical clusters essentially are of two types:

- **Agglomerative hierarchical clustering**: This is a bottom-up method where each observation starts in its own cluster and two other clusters as they go up a hierarchy
- **Divisive hierarchical clustering**: This is a top-down approach where observations start off in a single cluster and then they are split into two as they go down a hierarchy

The following image shows **Agglomerative** and **Divisive** hierarchical clustering:

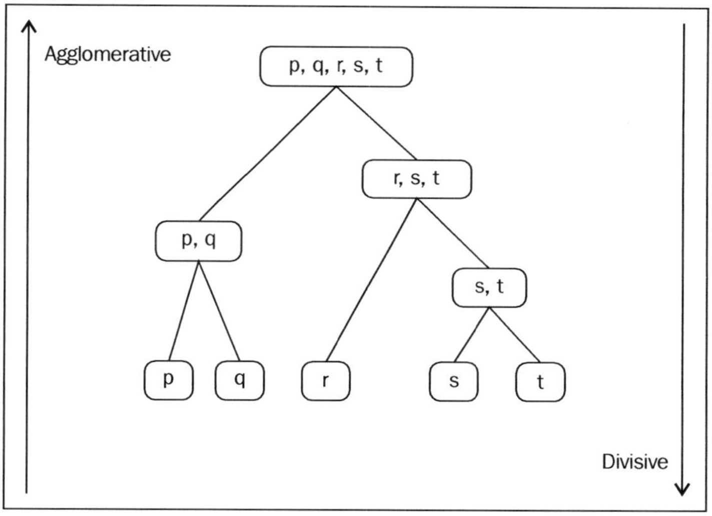

Hierarchical clustering will be explained in more detail in later chapters.

Summary

In this chapter, you understood the meaning of machine learning and its different types. You were introduced to commonly used machine learning algorithms as well.

In the next chapter, you'll learn how to create linear regression models.

6

Performing Predictions with a Linear Regression

Linear regression analysis is the most widely used of all statistical techniques: it is the study of linear, additive relationships between variables. It's widely used in various industries to create models, which will help in a business. For example, in the retail industry, there are various factors affecting the sale of a product. These factors could be the price, promotions, or seasonal factors, to name a few. A linear regression model helps in understanding the influence of each of these factors on the sales of a product as well as to calculate the baseline sales, which is basically the number of sales of this product in the event that there were no external factors, such as price, promotions, and so on.

In the preceding chapter, you were introduced to linear regression along with an example of a simple linear regression. In this chapter, you'll learn how to create the following:

- A simple linear regression model
- A multiple linear regression model

Simple linear regression

A simple linear regression has a single variable, and it can be described using the following formula:

$$y= A + Bx$$

Here, y is the dependent variable, x is the independent variable, A is the intercept (where x is to the power of zero) and B is the co-efficient

The dataset that we'll be using contains the height (cm) and weight (kg) of a sample of men.

The following code ingests the data and creates a simple scatter plot in order to understand the distribution of the weight versus the height:

```
>>> import numpy as np
>>> import pandas as pd
>>> from scipy import stats
>>> import matplotlib.pyplot as plt
>>> sl_data = pd.read_csv('Data/Mens_height_weight.csv')
>>> fig, ax = plt.subplots(1, 1)
>>> ax.scatter(sl_data['Height'],sl_data['Weight'])
>>> ax.set_xlabel('Height')
>>> ax.set_ylabel('Weight')
>>> plt.show()
```

The following is the output of the preceding code:

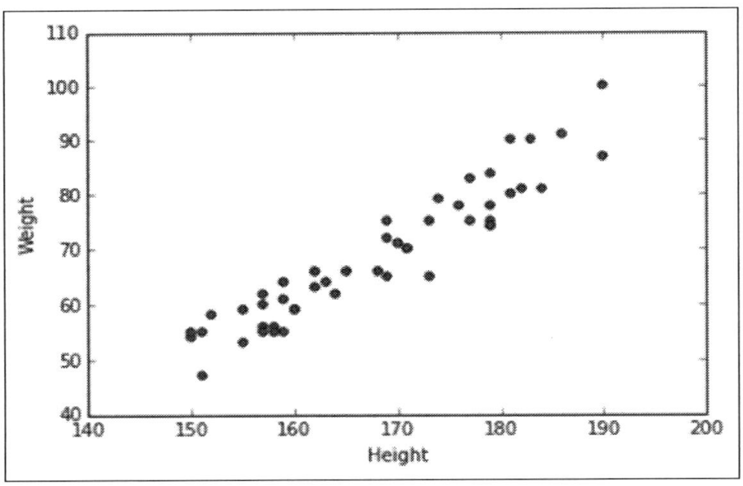

From the plot, you can see that there is a linear relationship between the weight and height of the individual.

Let's see how the variables are correlated to each other as follows:

```
>>> sl_data.corr()
```

The preceding code helps in generating the following correlation matrix:

	Height	Weight
Height	1.000000	0.942603
Weight	0.942603	1.000000

We can clearly see that the height and weight are clearly correlated to each other based on a Pearson correlation value coefficient of 0. 94. A Pearson correlation ranges from -1 to +1, so when the number is more positive, the relation between the two variables is much stronger if they increase or decrease together. If the correlation value is negative, then the relation between the two variables is strong, but is in the opposite direction.

Let's generate a linear regression model with the weight as the dependent variable and x as the independent variable:

```
>>># Create linear regression object
>>> lm = linear_model.LinearRegression()


>>># Train the model using the training sets
>>> lm.fit(sl_data.Height[:,np.newaxis], sl_data.Weight)



>>> print 'Intercept is ' + str(lm.intercept_) + '\n'
Intercept is -99.2772096063

>>> print 'Coefficient value of the height is ' + str(lm.coef_) + '\n'
Coefficient value of the height is [ 1.00092142]


>>> print pd.DataFrame(zip(sl_data.columns,lm.coef_),
        columns = ['features', 'estimatedCoefficients'])
```

This is the output of preceding code:

	features	estimatedCoefficients
0	Height	1.000921

In the preceding code, we use `linear_model.LinearRegression()` to create a linear regression object, lm. We then use the `fit()` method of `lm` to define the dependent and independent variable, where in our case, the `weight` is the dependent variable and the `height` is the independent variable.

To get the intercept value, we use `lm.intercept_`, and to get the coefficient, we use the `lm.coef`.

The last line of the code helps in creating a DataFrame of the independent variable and its corresponding coefficients. This will be useful when we explore multiple regression in detail.

We'll now plot the scatter chart again with a trend line:

```
>>> fig, ax = plt.subplots(1, 1)
>>> ax.scatter(sl_data.Height,sl_data.Weight)
>>> ax.plot(sl_data.Height,lm.predict(sl_data.Height[:, np.newaxis]),
                    color = 'red')
>>> ax.set_xlabel('Height')
>>> ax.set_ylabel('Weight')
>>> plt.show()
```

Here is the output of the preceding code:

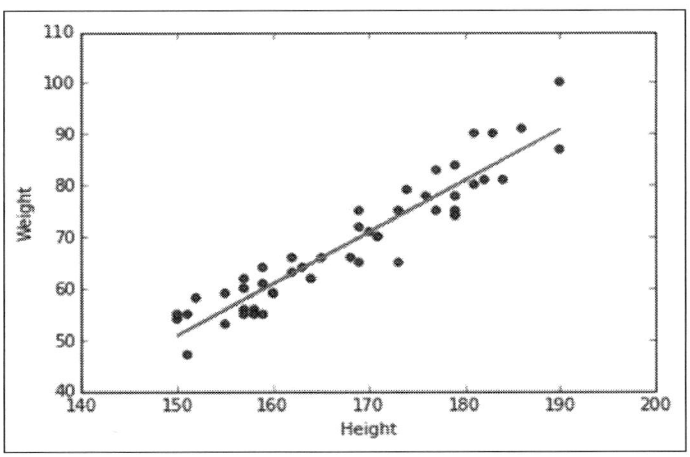

Multiple regression

Multiple linear regression occurs when more than one independent variable is used to predict a dependent variable:

$$Y' = a + b_1x_1 + b_2x_2 + \ldots\ldots + b_nx_n$$

Where, *Y* is the dependent variable, *a* is the intercept, *b1* and *b2* are the coefficients, and *x1* and *x2* are the independent variables

Also, note that squaring the dependent variable still makes it linear, but if the coefficient is squared, then it is nonlinear.

To build the multiple linear regression model, we'll utilize the NBA's basketball data to predict the average points scored per game

The following are the column descriptions of the data:

- `height`: This refers to the height in feet
- `weight`: This refers to the weight in pounds
- `success_field_goals`: This refers to the percentage of successful field goals (out of 100 that were attempted)
- `success_free_throws`: This refers tot the percentage of successful free throws (out of 100 that were attempted)
- `avg_points_scored`: This refers to the average points scored per game

The following code ingests this data and then we use the `descibe()` method of the DataFrame to get the univariate metrics on each of the fields:

```
>>> b_data = pd.read_csv('Data/basketball.csv')
>>> b_data.describe()
```

Here is the output of the preceding code:

	height	weight	success_field_goals	success_free_throws	avg_points_scored
count	54.000000	54.000000	54.000000	54.000000	54.000000
mean	6.587037	209.907407	0.449111	0.741852	11.790741
std	0.458894	30.265036	0.056551	0.100146	5.899257
min	5.700000	105.000000	0.291000	0.244000	2.800000
25%	6.225000	185.000000	0.415250	0.713000	8.150000
50%	6.650000	212.500000	0.443500	0.753500	10.750000
75%	6.900000	235.000000	0.483500	0.795250	13.600000
max	7.600000	263.000000	0.599000	0.900000	27.400000

From the preceding table, we get an understanding of the data. The following observations can be made:

1. The average height of a basketball player is around 6.5 feet.
2. The shortest player is 5.7 feet.
3. The tallest player is 7.7 feet (Shaquille O'Neal stands at 7.1 feet).
4. The player with the least weight is at 105 pounds, which is quite obscure.
5. The heaviest player is 263 pounds.
6. The best field goal percentage for a player is 60%.
7. The worst field goal percentage for a player is 29%.
8. The average field goal attempt for a player is 45 %, but from the small standard deviation, we can see that a majority of the players have a field goal percentage between 40 and 50%.
9. Among free throws, there is a player who misses 3/4th of the time.
10. The best free throw player has a 90% success rate.
11. Most of the players have a success percentage for free throws of around 70 to 80%.
12. The highest score scored per game by a player is 27.
13. The least scored is 3.
14. On an average, the players score 12 points.

Let's see the correlation between the variables:

```
>>> b_data.corr()
```

The following is the output of the preceding code:

	height	weight	success_field_goals	success_free_throws	avg_points_scored
height	1.000000	0.834324	0.495546	-0.259271	-0.068906
weight	0.834324	1.000000	0.516051	-0.290159	-0.009844
success_field_goals	0.495546	0.516051	1.000000	-0.018570	0.338760
success_free_throws	-0.259271	-0.290159	-0.018570	1.000000	0.244852
avg_points_scored	-0.068906	-0.009844	0.338760	0.244852	1.000000

From the preceding table, we can see the following:

1. There is a high correlation between height and weight.
2. There is a weak positive correlation between successful field goals in terms of height and weight.
3. The average points scored seem to have the maximum correlation with `success_field_goals`, but they're not highly correlated.

Let's see the distribution of each of the independent variables with respect to the dependent variable:

```
>>> fig, ax = plt.subplots(1, 1)
>>> ax.scatter(b_data.height, b_data.avg_points_scored)
>>> ax.set_xlabel('height')
>>> ax.set_ylabel('Average points scored per game')
>>> plt.show()
```

Here is the output of the preceding code:

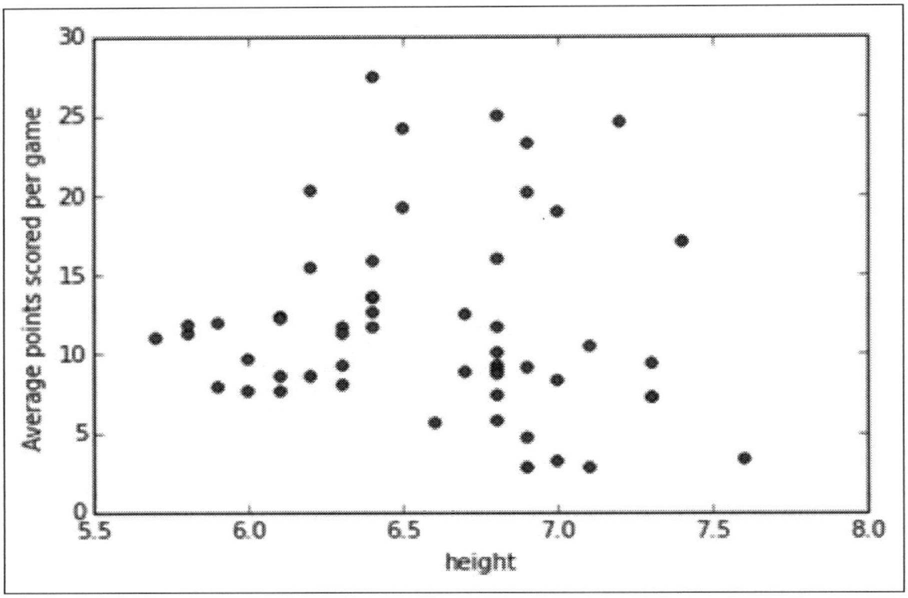

In the preceding scatter plot, we can see that there is no clear pattern between the average points scored and the height. The distribution looks quite random.

Let's look at the distribution between average points scored and the weight:

```
>>> fig, ax = plt.subplots(1, 1)
>>> ax.scatter(b_data.weight, b_data.avg_points_scored)
>>> ax.set_xlabel('weight')
>>> ax.set_ylabel('Average points scored per game')
>>> plt.show()
```

Here is the output of the preceding code:

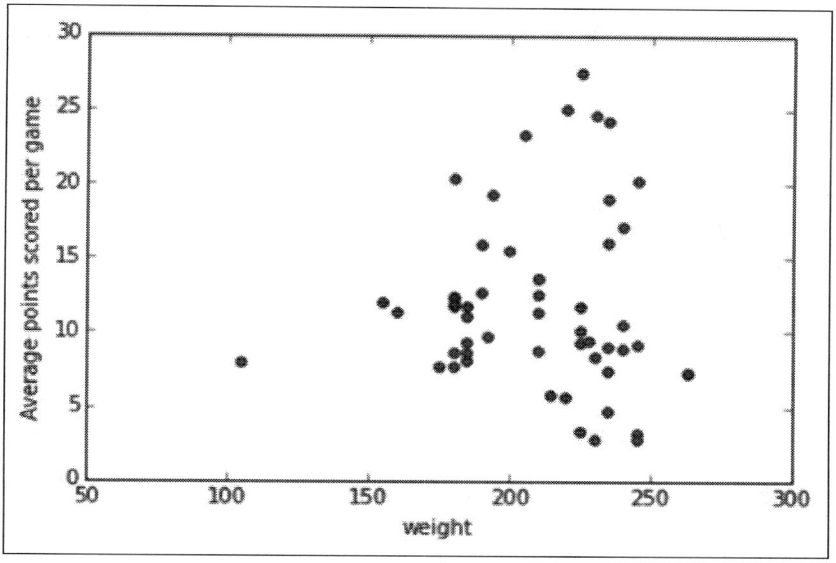

We can see that 105 pounds seems like an outlier and also has a relatively lower average point score. We can also see that the players who are almost 240 pounds have the maximum variations in terms of score, so a hypothesis can be made that the taller and heavier players have a greater score, while the shorter and heavier players have a lower score.

Now, let's look at the distribution between successful field goals and the average points scored:

```
>>> fig, ax = plt.subplots(1, 1)
>>> ax.scatter(b_data.success_field_goals, b_data.avg_points_scored)
>>> ax.set_xlabel('success_field_goals')
>>> ax.set_ylabel('Average points scored per game')
>>> plt.show()
```

Here is the output of the preceding code:

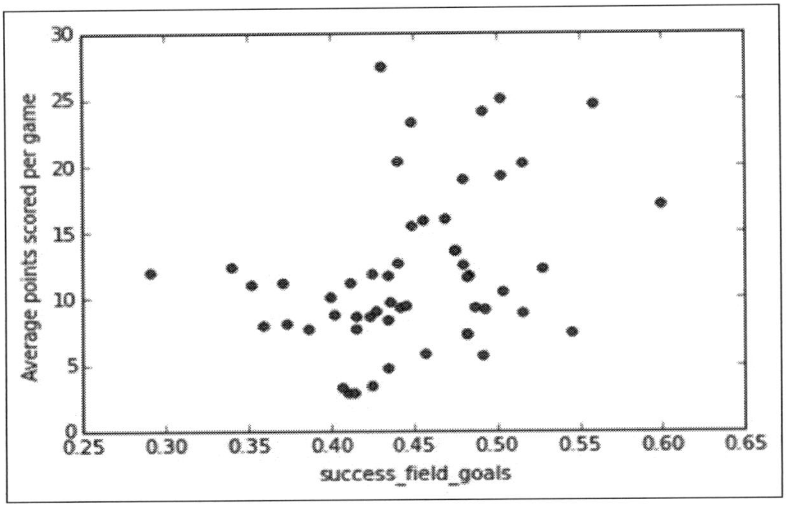

The `success_field_goals` variable has some linear relationship with the average points scored, but the distribution is still quite scattered.

Let's finally look at the distribution between successful free throws and the average points scored per game:

```
>>> fig, ax = plt.subplots(1, 1)
>>> ax.scatter(b_data.success_free_throws, b_data.avg_points_scored)
>>> x.set_xlabel('success_free_throws')
>>> ax.set_ylabel('Average points scored per game')
>>> plt.show()
```

Here is the output of the preceding code:

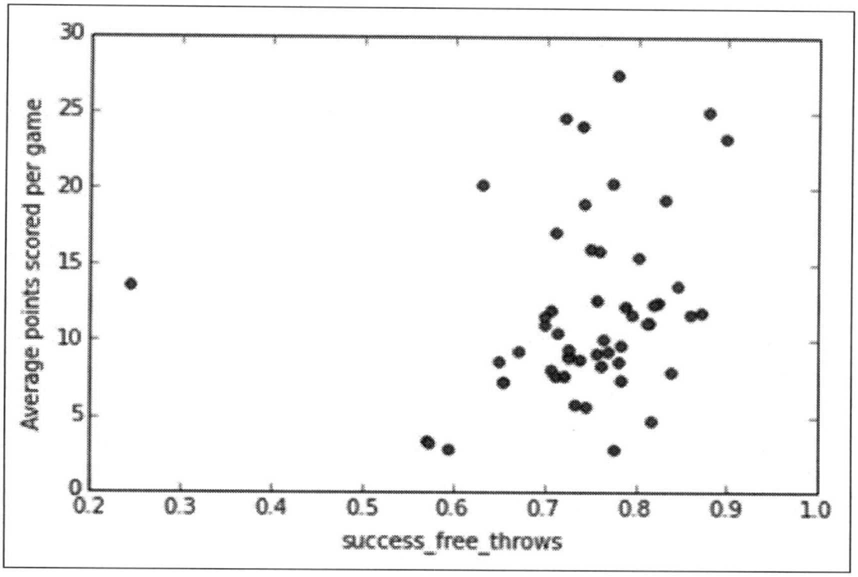

We can see that there is a player whose free throws are quite bad, but the average points scored seem to be close to average as compared to other players, which means that he would be better at half field goals or he would make a lot of attempts to score. The overall distribution here is also quite scattered.

From the preceding analysis of the correlation and distribution, we can see that there are no clear-cut patterns between the average points scored and the independent variables. It can be expected that the model that will be built with the existing data won't be highly accurate.

Training and testing a model

Let's take the data and divide it into training and test sets:

```
>>> from sklearn import linear_model,cross_validation,
                  feature_selection,preprocessing
>>> import statsmodels.formula.api as sm
>>> from statsmodels.tools.eval_measures import mse
>>> from statsmodels.tools.tools import add_constant
>>> from sklearn.metrics import mean_squared_error


>>> X = b_data.values.copy()
>>> X_train, X_valid, y_train, y_valid =
                    cross_validation.train_test_split( X[:, :-1],
                                                        X[:, -1],

                    train_size=0.80)
```

We first convert the data frame into an array structure using `values.copy()` of `b_data`. We then use the `train_test_split` function of `cross_validation` from SciKit to divide the data into training and test set for 80% of the data.

We'll learn how to build the linear regression models using the following packages:

- The statsmodels module
- The SciKit package

Even pandas provides an **Ordinary Least Square** (**OLS**) regression, which you can experiment with after you've completed this chapter. The ordinary least square is a method to estimate unknown coefficients and intercepts for a regression equation. We'll start off the with the statsmodels package. The **statsmodels** is a Python module that allows users to explore data, estimate statistical models, and perform statistical tests. An extensive list of descriptive statistics, statistical tests, plotting functions, and result statistics is available for different types of data and each estimator:

```
>>> result = sm.OLS( y_train, add_constant(X_train) ).fit()
>>> result.summary()
```

The OLS function helps in creating the linear regression object with a dependent and independent variable. The `fit()` method helps in fitting the model. Note that there is a `add_constant()` function, which is used to calculate the intercept while creating the model. By default, the `OLS()` function won't calculate the intercept, and it has to be explicitly mentioned with the the help of the `add_constant` function. The following image shows the summary of the regression model that we trained earlier, which shows the various metrics associated with the model:

OLS Regression Results

Dep. Variable:	y	**R-squared:**	0.265
Model:	OLS	**Adj. R-squared:**	0.187
Method:	Least Squares	**F-statistic:**	3.423
Date:	Sun, 22 Mar 2015	**Prob (F-statistic):**	0.0174
Time:	05:11:41	**Log-Likelihood:**	-130.25
No. Observations:	43	**AIC:**	270.5
Df Residuals:	38	**BIC:**	279.3
Df Model:	4		
Covariance Type:	nonrobust		

	coef	**std err**	**t**	**P>|t|**	**[95.0% Conf. Int.]**
const	15.5129	16.147	0.961	0.343	-17.175 48.200
x1	-5.9277	3.066	-1.933	0.061	-12.135 0.279
x2	0.0162	0.049	0.332	0.742	-0.082 0.115
x3	55.1647	19.044	2.897	0.006	16.612 93.717

Omnibus:	6.717	**Durbin-Watson:**	1.637
Prob(Omnibus):	0.035	**Jarque-Bera (JB):**	5.457
Skew:	0.786	**Prob(JB):**	0.0653
Kurtosis:	3.759	**Cond. No.**	5.20e+03

The preceding summary gives quite a lot of information about the model. The main parameter to look for is the *r* square value, which tells you how much of the variance of the dependent variable is captured by the model. It ranges from `0` to `1`, and the *p* value tells us if the model is significant.

From the preceding output, we can see that the `R-square` value is `0.265`, which isn't great. We can see that the model shows `x3` as the most significant variable, which is the `success_field_goals` variable. As a rule of thumb, any *p* value of a variable less than 0.05 can be considered significant.

Let's recreate the model with only the successful field goals variable and see how the model performs:

```
>>> result_alternate = sm.OLS( y_train,
                  add_constant(X_train[:,2]) ).fit()
>>> result_alternate.summary()
```

OLS Regression Results

Dep. Variable:	y	**R-squared:**	0.078
Model:	OLS	**Adj. R-squared:**	0.056
Method:	Least Squares	**F-statistic:**	3.492
Date:	Sun, 22 Mar 2015	**Prob (F-statistic):**	0.0688
Time:	05:11:44	**Log-Likelihood:**	-135.11
No. Observations:	43	**AIC:**	274.2
Df Residuals:	41	**BIC:**	277.7
Df Model:	1		
Covariance Type:	nonrobust		

	coef	std err	t	P>|t|	[95.0% Conf. Int.]
const	-2.5735	7.546	-0.341	0.735	-17.814 12.667
x1	31.4348	16.823	1.869	0.069	-2.539 65.409

Omnibus:	5.440	**Durbin-Watson:**	1.810
Prob(Omnibus):	0.066	**Jarque-Bera (JB):**	4.382
Skew:	0.760	**Prob(JB):**	0.112
Kurtosis:	3.370	**Cond. No.**	23.1

We can see that the variable has become less significant, and the r square value has become really low. The preceding model can be iterated multiple times with the different combination of variables till the best model is arrived at.

Let's apply both the models on the test data and see how the mean squared error between the actual and the predicted value is. The model that gives the least mean squared error is a good model:

```
>>> ypred = result.predict(add_constant(X_valid))
>>> print mse(ypred,y_valid)

35.208
```

In the following code, we use the predict function of the regression model object to predict the given test dataset:

```
>>> ypred_alternate = result_alternate.predict(add_constant(X_valid[:,
2]))
>>> print mse(ypred_alternate,y_valid)

26.3
```

We can see that the second model has a lower mean squared error as compared to the first one.

Let's also plot the predicted versus actual plot for both the models:

```
>>> fig, ax = plt.subplots(1, 1)
>>> ax.scatter(y_valid, ypred)
>>> ax.set_xlabel('Actual')
>>> ax.set_ylabel('Predicted')
>>> plt.show()
```

Here is the output for the preceding code:

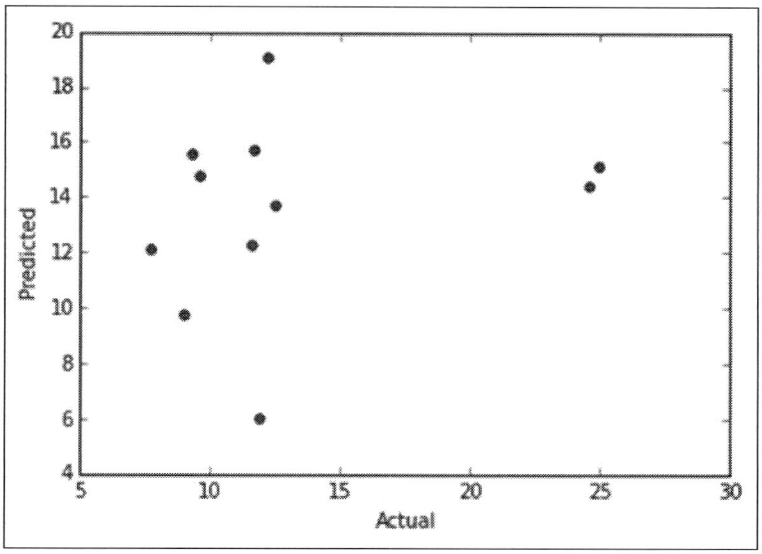

Now, let's plot the scatter for the alternate model:

```
>>> fig, ax = plt.subplots(1, 1)
>>> ax.scatter(y_valid, ypred_alternate)
>>> ax.set_xlabel('Actual')
>>> ax.set_ylabel('Predicted')
>>> plt.show()
```

Here is the output for the preceding code:

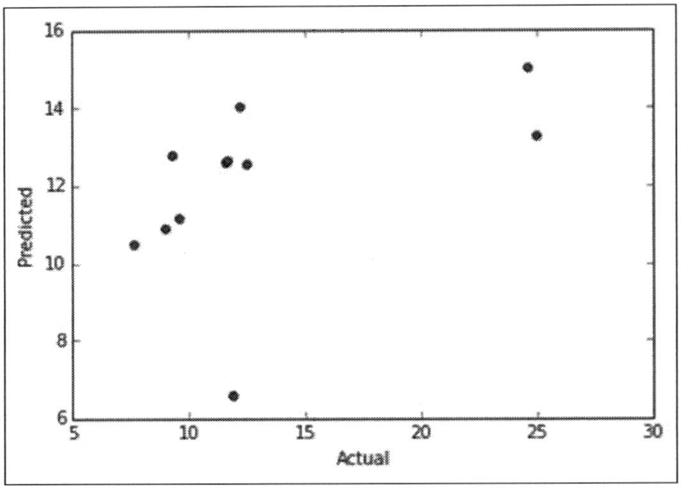

This clearly shows that our models are not good enough since the predictions are quite random.

To make a highly accurate model, we need some more variables, which have an influence on the average points that are scored.

The preceding model was constructed using the statsmodels package. We'll now build a model using SciKit.

The following code creates a Linear Regression object and then fits it with dependent and independent variables:

```
# Create linear regression object
>>> lm = linear_model.LinearRegression()


# Train the model using the training sets
```

```
>>> lm.fit(X_train, y_train)
```

```
>>> print 'Intercept is %f' % lm.intercept_)
Intercept is 15.5129271596
```

```
>>> pd.DataFrame(zip(b_data.columns,lm.coef_), columns = ['features',
        'estimatedCoefficients'])
```

Here is the output of the preceding code:

	features	estimatedCoefficients
0	height	-5.927749
1	weight	0.016150
2	success_field_goals	55.164717
3	success_free_throws	9.725042

The coefficient and intercepts are similar to the model that was built using the statsmodels package.

To calculate the r square in SciKit, the cross-validation module of the SciKit package is utilized:

```
>>> cross_validation.cross_val_score(lm, X_train,
          y_train, scoring='r2')
array([-0.3043391 , -0.42402161,  0.26890649])
```

Multiple runs of the cross-validation takes place and, by default, it is `3` due to which you can see three values in the preceding output. The highest value is of relevance and you can see that it is similar to the one we built with the statsmodels.

Let's see how the mean squared error is calculated:

```
>>> ypred = lm.predict(X_valid)
>>> mean_squared_error(ypred,y_valid)
35.208
```

We used the `mean_squared_error` function of the SciKit package here.

Finally, the actual versus the predicted plot will be same as the first model plot of statsmodels:

```
>>> fig, ax = plt.subplots(1, 1)
>>> ax.scatter(y_valid, ypred)
>>> ax.set_xlabel('Actual')
>>> ax.set_ylabel('Predicted')
>>> plt.show()
```

Here is the output for the preceding code:

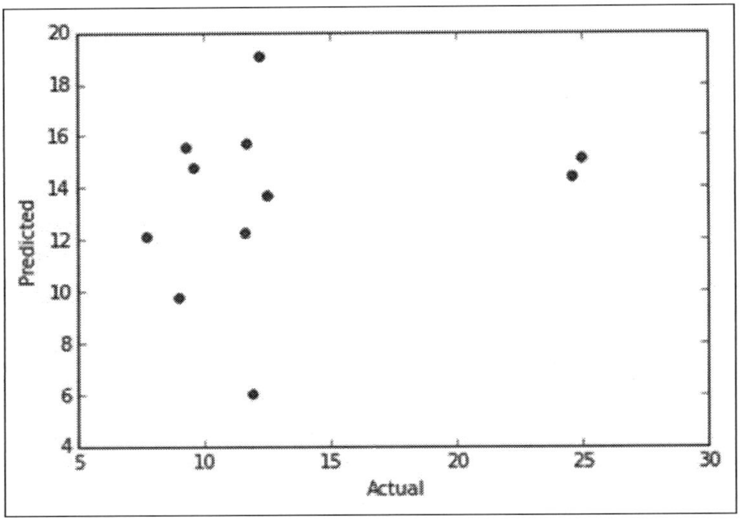

Summary

In this chapter, we learned how to create a simple linear regression model followed by multiple regressions, where there was an initial inspection analysis done on the data in order to understand it. We then created regression models using the statsmodels and SciKit package.

In the next chapter, we'll learn how to perform the probability scoring of an event that takes place using logistic regression.

7
Estimating the Likelihood of Events

Logistic regression is a type of regression analysis that helps in estimating the likelihood of an event to occur based on some given parameters. It is used as a classification technique with a binary outcome. The probabilities describing the possible outcomes of a single trial are modeled, as a function of the explanatory (predictor) variables, using a logistic function.

You have been already introduced to *Logisitc regression* in *Chapter 5, Uncovering Machine Learning*. In this chapter, you'll learn to:

- Build a logistic regression model with statsmodels
- Build a logistic regression model with SciKit
- Evaluate and test the model

Logistic regression

We'll use the Titanic dataset, which was utilized in *Chapter 3, Finding a Needle in a Haystack*, to help us build the logistic regression model. Since we have already explored the data, we won't be performing any exploratory data analysis as we already have a context for this data.

This is a recap of the field descriptions of the Titanic dataset:

- **Survival**: This refers to the survival of the passengers (`0` = No and `1` = Yes)
- **Pclass**: This refers to the passenger class (`1` = 1st, `2` = 2nd, and `3` = 3rd)
- **Name**: This refers to the names of the passengers
- **Sex**: This refers to the gender of the passengers

- **Age**: This refers to the age of the passengers
- **Sibsp**: This refers to the number of siblings/spouses aboard
- **Parch**: This refers to the number of parents/children aboard
- **Ticket**: This refers to the ticket number
- **Fare**: This refers to the passenger fares
- **Cabin**: This refers to the cabin
- **Embarked**: This refers to the port of embarkation (C = Cherbourg, Q = Queenstown, and S = Southampton)

Data preparation

Let's start off by reading the data:

```
>>> df = pd.read_csv('Data/titanic data.csv')
```

Let's clean the data a bit by taking care of columns that have lots of missing values:

```
>>> df.count(0)
```

```
PassengerId    891
Survived       891
Pclass         891
Name           891
Sex            891
Age            714
SibSp          891
Parch          891
Ticket         891
Fare           891
Cabin          204
Embarked       889
dtype: int64
```

We can see that the `Ticket` and `Cabin` columns won't add much value to the model building process as the `Ticket` column is basically a unique identifier for each passenger and the `Cabin` column is mostly empty. Also, we'll remove the rows with the missing values.

We'll remove these two columns from our DataFrame:

```
>>> # Applying axis as 1 to remove the  columns with the following labels
>>> df = df.drop(['Ticket','Cabin','Name'], axis=1)
>>> # Remove missing values
>>> df = df.dropna()
```

Creating training and testing sets

In the preceding code, we removed the `Ticket`, `Cabin`, and `Name` columns, followed by the missing values.

We'll use a Python package called Patsy, which helps in describing statistical models. It helps in defining a dependent and independent variable formula that is similar to R. The variable that is defined left of '~' is the dependent variable, and the variable that is defined to right of it are the independent variables. The variables enclosed within `C()` are treated as categorical variables.

Now, we'll create the training and test sets from the data:

```
>>> formula = 'Survived ~ C(Pclass) + C(Sex) + Age + SibSp  + C(Embarked)
         +  Parch'


>>> # create a results dictionary to hold our regression results for easy
>>> # analysis later
>>> df_train = df.iloc[ 0: 600, : ]
>>> df_test = df.iloc[ 600: , : ]


>>> #Splitting the data into dependent and independent variables
>>> y_train,x_train = dmatrices(formula, data=df_train,
                                     return_type='dataframe')
>>> y_test,x_test = dmatrices(formula, data=df_test,
                                     return_type='dataframe')
```

In the preceding code, we define the equation in the formula variables where `survived` is the dependent variable and the ones to the right of it are the independent variables. After this, we take the first `600` rows as the training set and the remaining rows in the `df` DataFrame as the test set.

Finally, we use the `dmatrices` of the Patsy package, which takes in the formula and input a DataFrame to create a DataFrame. This is ready to be inputted to the modeling functions of statsmodels and SciKit.

Building a model

We'll use the statsmodels package to build a model:

```
>>> # instantiate our model
>>> model = sm.Logit(y_train,x_train)
>>> res = model.fit()
>>> res.summary()
```

Here is the output of the preceding code:

Logit Regression Results

Dep. Variable:	Survived	**No. Observations:**	600
Model:	Logit	**Df Residuals:**	591
Method:	MLE	**Df Model:**	8
Date:	Mon, 06 Apr 2015	**Pseudo R-squ.:**	0.3333
Time:	16:14:07	**Log-Likelihood:**	-270.02
converged:	True	**LL-Null:**	-404.99
		LLR p-value:	1.009e-53

	coef	std err	z	P>|z|	[95.0% Conf. Int.]
Intercept	4.3332	0.510	8.490	0.000	3.333 5.334
C(Pclass)[T.2]	-1.2030	0.325	-3.703	0.000	-1.840 -0.566
C(Pclass)[T.3]	-2.4673	0.320	-7.705	0.000	-3.095 -1.840
C(Sex)[T.male]	-2.6312	0.244	-10.797	0.000	-3.109 -2.154
C(Embarked)[T.Q]	-0.4359	0.647	-0.674	0.501	-1.704 0.832
C(Embarked)[T.S]	-0.2910	0.297	-0.980	0.327	-0.873 0.291
Age	-0.0397	0.009	-4.464	0.000	-0.057 -0.022
SibSp	-0.3202	0.136	-2.354	0.019	-0.587 -0.054
Parch	-0.1420	0.136	-1.041	0.298	-0.409 0.125

We can see that the Maximum Likelihood Estimation has been used to predict the coefficients. The pseudo r square is similar to the r square of linear regression, which is used to measure the goodness of it. A pseudo r square value between `0.2` and `0.4` is considered good that we have got a value of `0.33`.

From the preceding table, we can see that the port of embarkation and number of parents/children are significant predictors as their p-values are higher than `0.05`.

We'll rebuild the model by using predictors, such as class, age, sex and number of siblings:

```
>>> formula = 'Survived ~ C(Pclass) + C(Sex) + Age + SibSp '


>>> y_train,x_train = dmatrices(formula, data=df_train, return_
type='dataframe')

>>> y_test,x_test = dmatrices(formula, data=df_test, return_
type='dataframe')


>>> # instantiate our model

>>> model = sm.Logit(y_train,x_train)

>>> res = model.fit()

>>> res.summary()
```

Logit Regression Results

Dep. Variable:	Survived	**No. Observations:**	600
Model:	Logit	**Df Residuals:**	594
Method:	MLE	**Df Model:**	5
Date:	Tue, 07 Apr 2015	**Pseudo R-squ.:**	0.3307
Time:	12:36:09	**Log-Likelihood:**	-271.08
converged:	True	**LL-Null:**	-404.99
		LLR p-value:	8.172e-56

	coef	**std err**	**z**	**P>|z|**	**[95.0% Conf. Int.]**
Intercept	4.1050	0.479	8.575	0.000	3.167 5.043
C(Pclass)[T.2]	-1.2971	0.306	-4.242	0.000	-1.896 -0.698
C(Pclass)[T.3]	-2.5739	0.305	-8.433	0.000	-3.172 -1.976
C(Sex)[T.male]	-2.5808	0.235	-10.996	0.000	-3.041 -2.121
Age	-0.0401	0.009	-4.549	0.000	-0.057 -0.023
SibSp	-0.3691	0.130	-2.840	0.005	-0.624 -0.114

We can see that all the predictors are significant in the preceding model.

Model evaluation

Now, let's see the distribution of the predictions on the training data with the following code:

```
>>> kde_res = KDEUnivariate(res.predict())
>>> kde_res.fit()
>>> plt.plot(kde_res.support,kde_res.density)
>>> plt.fill_between(kde_res.support,kde_res.density, alpha=0.2)
>>> plt.title("Distribution of our Predictions")
```

In the preceding code, we use the kernel density estimation to find the probability density of the predicted values. This helps us to understand which areas of the predicted probability are denser.

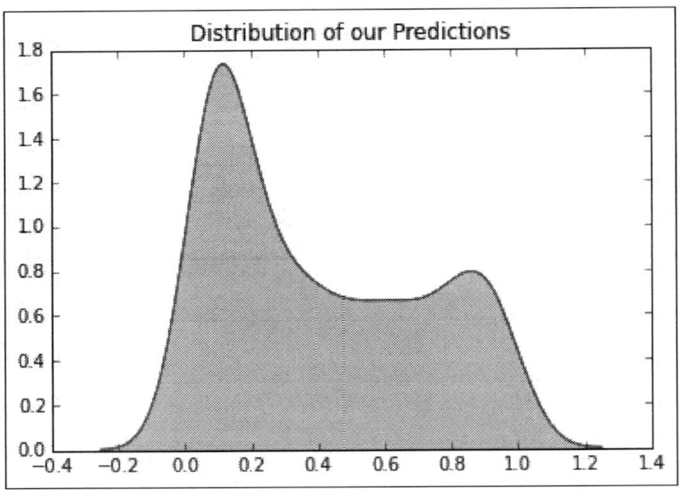

From the preceding plot, we can see that the density is higher near the probabilities of `0` and `1`, which is a good sign and shows that the model is able to predict some patterns from the data given. It also shows that the density is the highest near 0, which means that a lot of people did not survive. This proves the analysis we performed in *Chapter 3, Finding a Needle in a Haystack*.

Let's see the prediction distribution based on the male gender:

```
>>> plt.scatter(res.predict(),x_train['C(Sex)[T.male]'] , alpha=0.2)
>>> plt.grid(b=True, which='major', axis='x')
>>> plt.xlabel("Predicted chance of survival")
>>> plt.ylabel("Male Gender")
>>> plt.title("The Change of Survival Probability by Gender being Male")
```

In the preceding code, we created a scatter plot between the predicted probability of survival and a flag indicating that the passengers are male.

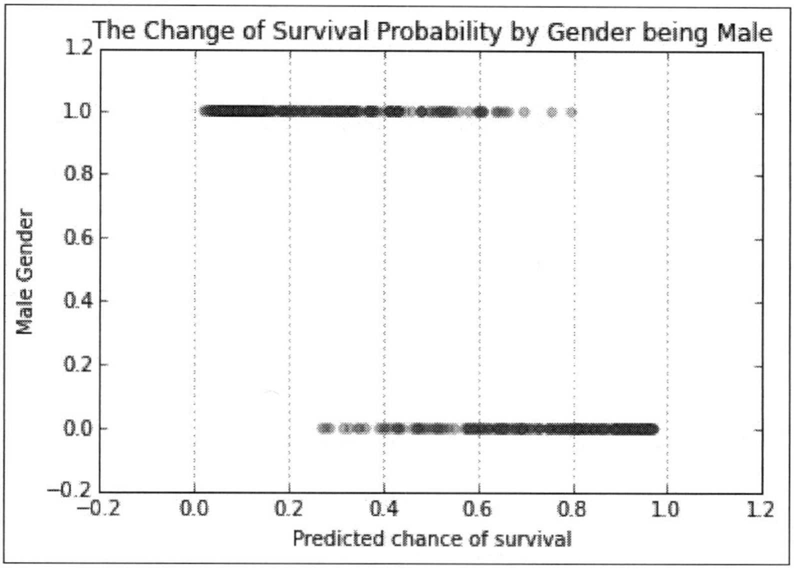

We can see that the model prediction shows that if the passenger is male, then the chances of survival are lower compared to females. This was also shown in our analysis in *Chapter 3, Finding a Needle in a Haystack*, where it was seen that females had a higher survival rate.

Now, let's see the distribution of the prediction based on the lower class of the passengers:

```
>>> plt.scatter(res.predict(),x_train['C(Pclass)[T.3]'] , alpha=0.2)
>>> plt.xlabel("Predicted chance of survival")
>>> plt.ylabel("Class Bool") # Boolean class to show if its 3rd class
>>> plt.grid(b=True, which='major', axis='x')
>>> plt.title("The Change of Survival Probability by Lower
                        Class which is 3rd class")
```

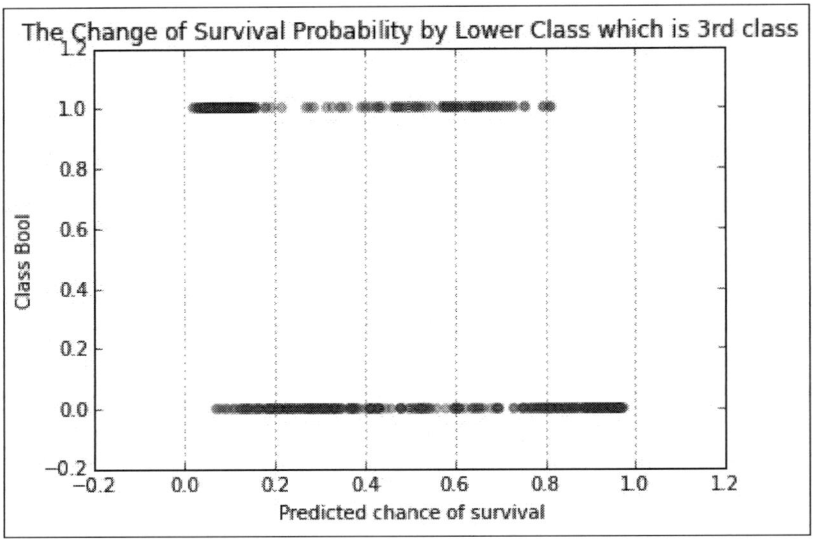

We can see that the lower class passengers have a lower probability of survival as the probability is more concentrated toward 0 when compared to the other classes.

Let's see the distribution of the probability with respect to the age of the passengers:

```
>>> plt.scatter(res.predict(),x_train.Age , alpha=0.2)
>>> plt.grid(True, linewidth=0.15)
>>> plt.title("The Change of Survival Probability by Age")
>>> plt.xlabel("Predicted chance of survival")
>>> plt.ylabel("Age")
```

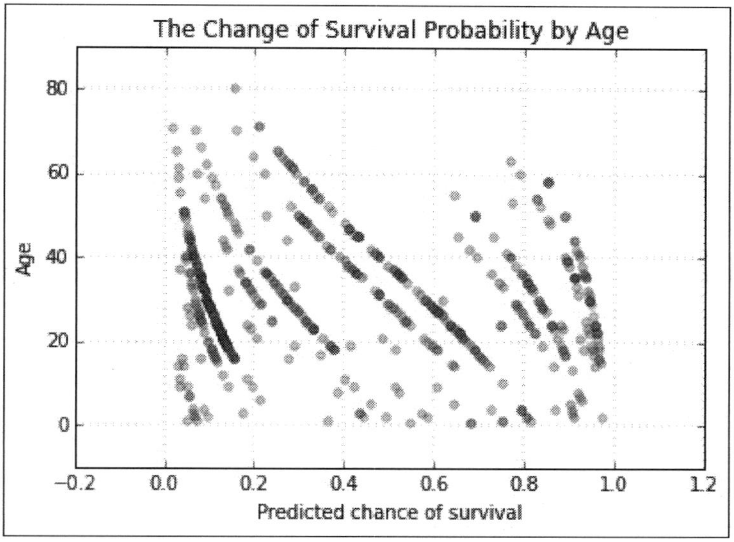

If you observe the preceding plot, it can be seen that as the age of the passenger increases, the probability leans toward the left-hand side of the graph, which shows that elderly people have a lower probability of survival.

Let's see the distribution of the probability with respect to the number of siblings/spouses:

```
>>> plt.scatter(res.predict(),x_train.SibSp , alpha=0.2)
>>> plt.grid(True, linewidth=0.15)
>>> plt.title("The Change of Survival Probability by Number of
                     siblings/spouses")
>>> plt.xlabel("Predicted chance of survival")
>>> ylabel("No. of Siblings/Spouses")
```

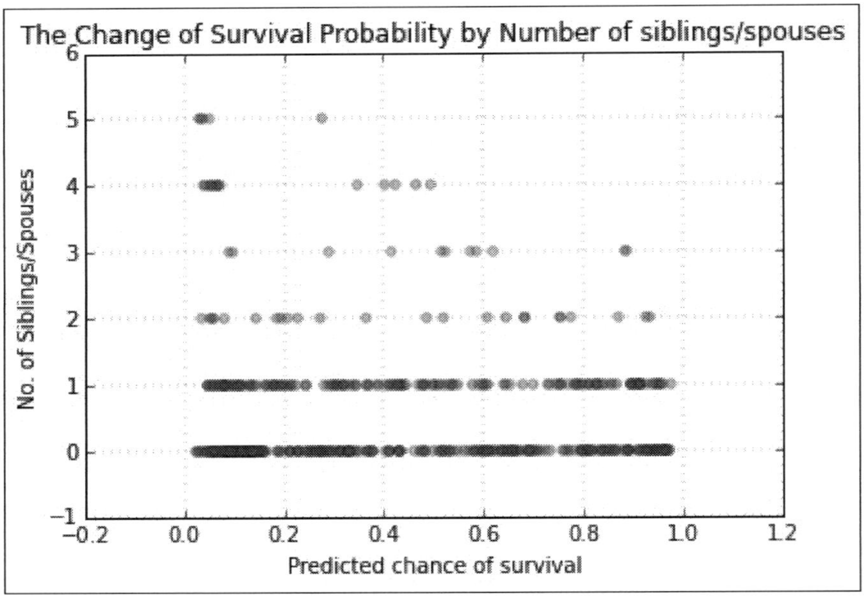

From the preceding graph, the only pattern we can see is that passengers with four to five siblings/spouses had a lower probability of survival. For the remaining passengers, there is a more or less random distribution.

Evaluating a model based on test data

Let's predict by using the model on the test data and also show the performance of the model through precision and recall by maintaining a threshold of `0.7`:

```
>>> y_pred = res.predict(x_test)
>>> y_pred_flag = y_pred > 0.7
>>> print pd.crosstab(y_test.Survived
                      ,y_pred_flag
```

```
                  ,rownames = ['Actual']
                  ,colnames = ['Predicted'])

>>> print '\n \n'

>>> print classification_report(y_test,y_pred_flag)
```

In the preceding code, we get the predicted probability on the test data followed by assigning `True` or `False` for an event based on the threshold of `0.7`. We use the crosstab function of pandas, which helps in displaying the frequency distribution between two variables. We'll use this to get the crosstab between the actual and predicted values, and then we will use the `classification_report` function of SciKit to get the precision and recall values:

Predicted	False	True
Actual		
0	67	0
1	21	24

The following image shows the precision and recall on the test data:

	precision	recall	f1-score	support
0.0	0.76	1.00	0.86	67
1.0	1.00	0.53	0.70	45
avg / total	0.86	0.81	0.80	112

We can see that all the nonsurvivors have been predicted correctly, but the model is able to predict only half of the survivors correctly based on the 0.7 threshold. Note that the precision and recall values will vary with the threshold that is used.

Let's understand what precision and recall mean.

- **Precision**: Precision tells you that among all the predictions of class 0 or class 1, how many of them have been correctly predicted. So, in the preceding case, 76% of the prediction of nonsurvivors is correct and 100% of the prediction of those who have survived is correct.
- **Recall**: Recall tells you that out of the actual instances, how many of them have been predicted correctly. So, in the preceding case, all the people who did not survive have been predicted correctly with an accuracy of 100%, but of all the people who survived, only 53% of them have been predicted correctly.

Let's plot the **Receiver Operating Characteristic** (**ROC**) curve, which will be explained as follows:

```
>>> # Compute ROC curve and area the curve
>>> fpr, tpr, thresholds = roc_curve(y_test, y_pred)
>>> roc_auc = auc(fpr, tpr)
>>> print "Area under the ROC curve : %f" % roc_auc

Area under the ROC curve : 0.879934
```

The area under the curve is `0.87`, which is a good value. In the preceding code, we use the `roc_curve` function to get the False and True Positive rates, respectively, which are defined as follows:

The False Positive rate is $\frac{FP}{FP+TN}$ which is also called fallout, and the True Positive rate is $TPR = TP/P = TP/(TP+FN)$ which is also called sensitivity.

Here are some of our observations:

- `False Positive` (`FP`): This is a positive prediction, which is actually wrong. So, in the preceding crosstab, `0` is False Positive
- `True Positive` (`TP`): This is a positive prediction, which is actually right. So, in the preceding crosstab, `24` is True Positive
- `True Negative` (`TN`): This is a negative prediction, which is actually right. So, in the above crosstab, `67` is True Negative
- `False Negative` (`FN`): This is a negative prediction, which is actually wrong. So, in the preceding cross tab, `21` is False Negative

So, a False Positive rate tells us that among all the people who did not survive, what percentage have been predicted as survived. The True Positive rate tells us that among all the people who survived, what percentage of them have been predicted as survived. Ideally, False Positive rates should be low and True Positive rates should be high.

The `roc_curve` function is created by taking the TPR and FPR at different threshold values and then plotting them against each other.

The `roc_curve` function gives the False and True Positive rates at different thresholds, and this will be utilized to plot the ROC curve:

```
>>> # Plot ROC curve
>>> plt.clf()
```

```
>>> plt.plot(fpr, tpr, label='ROC curve (area = %0.2f)' % roc_auc)
>>> plt.plot([0, 1], [0, 1], 'k--')
>>> plt.xlim([0.0, 1.0])
>>> plt.ylim([0.0, 1.0])
>>> plt.xlabel('False Positive Rate')
>>> plt.ylabel('True Positive Rate')
>>> plt.title('Receiver operating characteristic example')
>>> plt.legend(loc="lower right")
>>> plt.show()
```

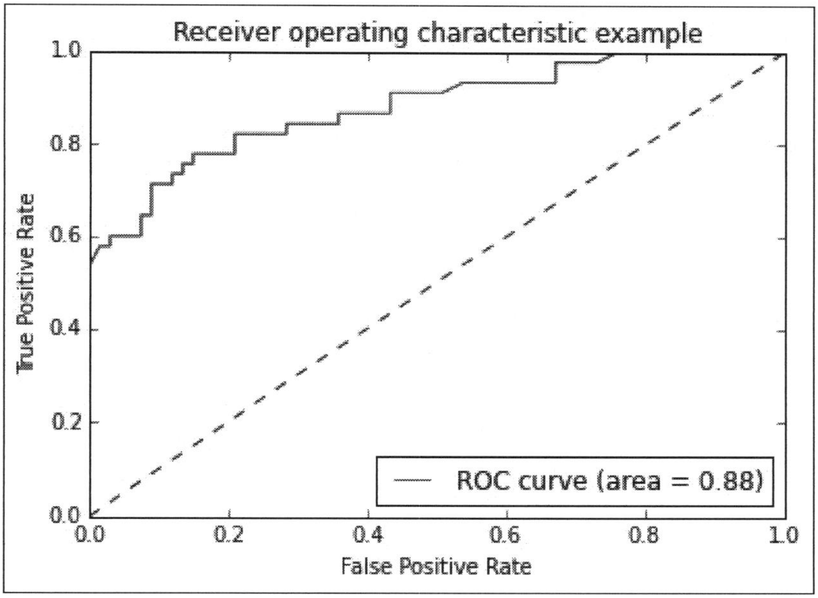

Accuracy is measured by the area under the ROC curve. An area of 1 represents a perfect test; an area of `0.5` represents that the model is as good as a random guess. A rough guide to classify the accuracy of a diagnostic test is the traditional academic point system as follows:

Range	Category
0.90-1	This refers to excellent (A)
0.80-0.90	This refers to good (B)
0.70-0.80	This refers to fair (C)
0.60-0.70	This refers to poor (D)
0.50-0.60	This refers to fail (F)

The dotted line in the preceding graph has an AUC of `0.50`, which is not good. Our model gives us an AUC of `0.88`, which is really good and is the blue line on the graph.

Model building and evaluation with SciKit

Let's build the same model shown earlier by using SciKit:

```
>>> # instantiate a logistic regression model, and fit with X and y
>>> model = LogisticRegression()
>>> model = model.fit(x_train, y_train.Survived)
```

In the preceding code, we create an object of the `LogisticRegression` method and then fit the model using our training data:

```
>>> # examine the coefficients
>>> pd.DataFrame(zip(x_train.columns, np.transpose(model.coef_)))
```

	0	1
0	Intercept	[1.67901054914]
1	C(Pclass)[T.2]	[-0.941153862481]
2	C(Pclass)[T.3]	[-2.13935207654]
3	C(Sex)[T.male]	[-2.34378496065]
4	Age	[-0.0314323464392]
5	SibSp	[-0.297688747773]

The first column contains our dependent variable name and the second column contains the coefficient values. We can see that the coefficients of our predictor are similar but not same as the model built using the statsmodels package.

Let's see how our precision and recall are performing:

```
>>> y_pred = model.predict_proba(x_test)
>>> y_pred_flag = y_pred[:,1] > 0.7


>>> print pd.crosstab(y_test.Survived
                      ,y_pred_flag
```

```
                    ,rownames = ['Actual']
                    ,colnames = ['Predicted'])

>>> print '\n \n'

>>> print classification_report(y_test,y_pred_flag)
```

```
Predicted  False  True
Actual
0             67     0
1             23    22
```

The following shows the precision and recall on the test data:

```
             precision    recall  f1-score   support

        0.0       0.74      1.00      0.85        67
        1.0       1.00      0.49      0.66        45

avg / total       0.85      0.79      0.77       112
```

We can see that there is a slight difference in performance compared to the previous model that we created. There are two instances of positive predictions that have shifted to negative predictions.

Let's compute the ROC and area under the curve:

```
>>> # Compute ROC curve and area the curve
>>> fpr, tpr, thresholds = roc_curve(y_test, y_pred[:,1])
>>> roc_auc = auc(fpr, tpr)
>>> print "Area under the ROC curve : %f" % roc_auc
Area under the ROC curve :0.878275
```

It's nearly the same but slightly less than the AUC of the previous model.

Let's plot the ROC curve, which will be almost identical to the previous model:

```
>>> # Plot ROC curve
>>> plt.clf()
>>> plt.plot(fpr, tpr, label='ROC curve (area = %0.2f)' % roc_auc)
>>> plt.plot([0, 1], [0, 1], 'k--')
```

```
>>> plt.xlim([0.0, 1.0])
>>> plt.ylim([0.0, 1.0])
>>> plt.xlabel('False Positive Rate')
>>> plt.ylabel('True Positive Rate')
>>> plt.title('Receiver operating characteristic example')
>>> plt.legend(loc="lower right")
>>> plt.show()
```

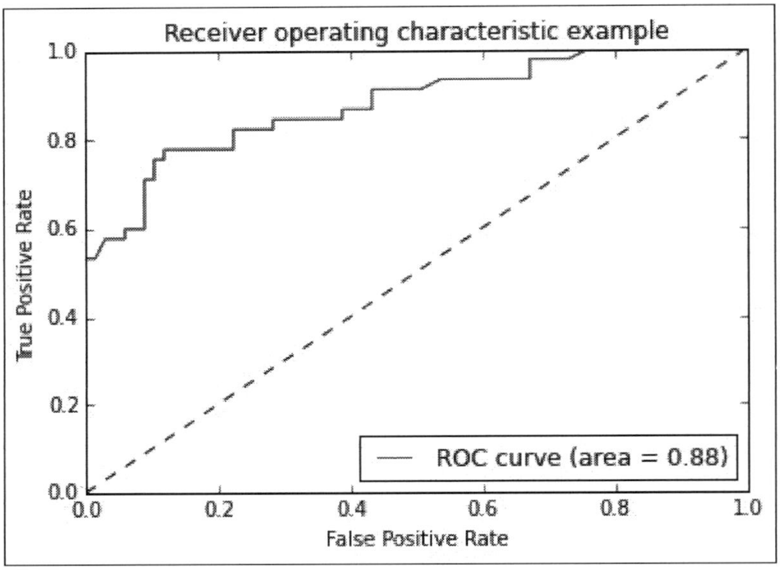

Summary

In this chapter, you learned the purpose of logistic regression. You learned how to build a logistic regression model using statsmodels and SciKit, and then how to evaluate the model and see whether it's a good model or not.

In the next chapter, you'll learn how to generate recommendations, such as the ones you see on `http://www.amazon.com/`, where you'll be recommended new items based on your purchase history. Similar items can also be shown to you based on the product that you are currently browsing.

8
Generating Recommendations with Collaborative Filtering

Collaborative filtering is the process of filtering for information or patterns using techniques including collaboration among multiple agents, viewpoints, data sources, and so on. Collaborative filtering methods have been applied to many different kinds of data, including sensing and monitoring data, such as mineral exploration, environmental sensing over large areas or multiple sensors; financial data, such as financial service institutions that integrate many financial sources; or in electronic commerce and web applications where the focus is on user data and so on.

The basic principle behind the collaborative filtering approach is that it tries to find people who are similar to each other by looking at their tastes. Let's say if a person primarily likes action movies, then it will try to find a person who has seen similar kinds of movies and it will try to recommend the one that hasn't been seen by the first person, but seen by the second person.

We'll be focusing on the following types of collaborative filtering in this chapter:

- User-based collaborative filtering
- Item-based collaborative filtering

Recommendation data

We will use a set of users who have given ratings to the movies of their choice. The following is a dictionary object containing the different users in the form of keys and their values in the form of a dictionary of movies, with each movie's value being the rating given by a user:

```
movie_user_preferences={'Jill': {'Avenger: Age of Ultron': 7.0,
 'Django Unchained': 6.5,
 'Gone Girl': 9.0,
 'Kill the Messenger': 8.0},
'Julia': {'Avenger: Age of Ultron': 10.0,
 'Django Unchained': 6.0,
 'Gone Girl': 6.5,
 'Kill the Messenger': 6.0,
 'Zoolander': 6.5},
'Max': {'Avenger: Age of Ultron': 7.0,
 'Django Unchained': 7.0,
 'Gone Girl': 10.0,
 'Horrible Bosses 2': 6.0,
 'Kill the Messenger': 5.0,
 'Zoolander': 10.0},
'Robert': {'Avenger: Age of Ultron': 8.0,
 'Django Unchained': 7.0,
 'Horrible Bosses 2': 5.0,
 'Kill the Messenger': 9.0,
 'Zoolander': 9.0},
'Sam': {'Avenger: Age of Ultron': 10.0,
 'Django Unchained': 7.5,
 'Gone Girl': 6.0,
 'Horrible Bosses 2': 3.0,
 'Kill the Messenger': 5.5,
 'Zoolander': 7.0},
'Toby': {'Avenger: Age of Ultron': 8.5,
 'Django Unchained': 9.0,
 'Zoolander': 2.0},
'William': {'Avenger: Age of Ultron': 6.0,
```

```
 'Django Unchained': 8.0,
 'Gone Girl': 7.0,
 'Horrible Bosses 2': 4.0,
 'Kill the Messenger': 6.5,
 'Zoolander': 4.0}}
```

```
movie_user_preferences['William']['Gone Girl']
7.0
```

User-based collaborative filtering

Let's start to build a user-based collaborative filter by finding users who are similar to each other.

Finding similar users

When you have data about what people like, you need a way to determine the similarity between different users. The similarity between different users is determined by comparing each user with every other user and computing a similarity score. This similarity score can be computed using the Pearson correlation, the Euclidean distance, the Manhattan distance, and so on.

The Euclidean distance score

The Euclidean distance is the minimum distance between two points in space. Let's try to understand this by plotting the users who have watched Django Unchained and Avengers.

We'll create a DataFrame that contains the `user`, `django`, and `avenger` columns, where `django` and `avenger` contain the ratings given by the user:

```
>>> data = []
>>> for i in movie_user_preferences.keys():
        try:
            data.append( (i
            ,movie_user_preferences[i]['Django Unchained']
            ,movie_user_preferences[i]['Avenger: Age of Ultron']) )
        except:
```

```
            pass


>>> df = pd.DataFrame(data = data, columns = ['user', 'django',
                      'avenger'])

>>> df
```

	user	django	avenger
0	Sam	7.5	10.0
1	Max	7.0	7.0
2	Robert	7.0	8.0
3	Toby	9.0	8.5
4	Julia	6.0	10.0
5	William	8.0	6.0
6	Jill	6.5	7.0

Using the preceding DataFrame, we'll plot the different users by keeping `Django` as the y axis and `Avengers` as the x axis:

```
>>> plt.scatter(df.django, df.avenger)
>>> plt.xlabel('Django')
>>> plt.ylabel('Avengers')
>>> for i,txt in enumerate(df.user):
        plt.annotate(txt, (df.django[i],df.avenger[i]))
>>> plt.show()
```

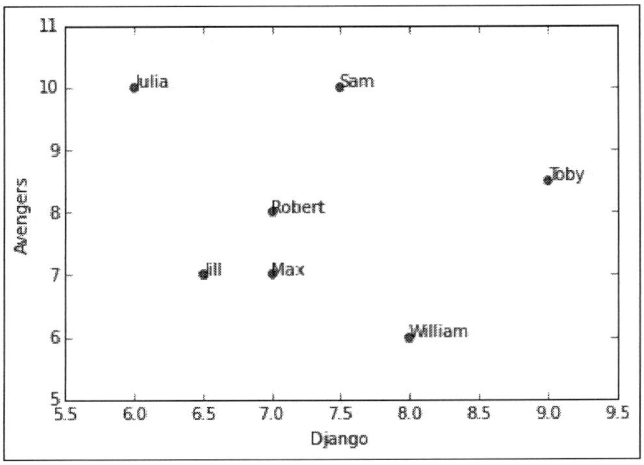

We can see that `Jill` and `Toby` are quite far away from each other, whereas `Robert` and `Max` are quite close to each other. Let's compute the Euclidean distance between the two:

```
>>> #Euclidean distance between Jill and Toby rating
>>> sqrt(pow(8.5-7,2)+pow(9-6.5,2))

2.9154759474226504


>>> #Euclidean distance between Robert and Max rating
>>> sqrt(pow(8-7,2)+pow(7-7,2))

1.0
```

We can see that the further the users are away from each other, the higher the Euclidean distance. As seen in the preceding code, the smaller the Euclidean distance, the greater is the similarity. We'll divide the Euclidean distance by `1` so that we get a metric that represents a greater similarity for a higher number. We'll also add `1` in the denominator to avoid getting `ZeroDivisionError`.

```
>>> #Similarity Score based on Euclidean distance between Jill and Toby
>>> 1/(1 + sqrt(pow(8.5-7,2)+pow(9-6.5,2)) )
0.2553967929896867


>>> #Similarity Score based on Euclidean distance between Robert and Max
>>> 1/(1 + sqrt(pow(8-7,2)+pow(7-7,2)) )

0.5
```

Let's create a function that calculates the similarity score based on the Euclidean distance between two users where all the movies that they watched are taken into consideration, apart from the two movies that we mentioned earlier:

```
>>> # Returns a distance-based similarity score for person1 and person2
>>> def sim_distance(prefs,person1,person2):
      # Get the list of shared_items
      si={}
      for item in prefs[person1]:
          if item in prefs[person2]:
```

```
            si[item]=1

    # if they have no ratings in common, return 0
    if len(si)==0: return 0

    # Add up the squares of all the differences
    sum_of_squares=sum([pow(prefs[person1][item] -
                        prefs[person2][item],2)
    for item in prefs[person1] if item in prefs[person2]])

    return 1/(1+sum_of_squares)
```

Let's apply the preceding function to calculate the similarity score between `Sam` and `Toby`:

```
>>> sim_distance(movie_user_preferences,'Sam','Toby')

0.03278688524590164
```

The Pearson correlation score

We have already studied what the Pearson correlation is in *Chapter 2, Inferential Statistics*. The Euclidean distance is how far apart the users are from each other, whereas the Pearson correlation takes into account the association between two people. We'll use the Pearson correlation to compute the similarity score between two users.

Let's see how `Sam` and `Toby` are correlated to each other:

```
>>> def create_movie_user_df(input_data, user1, user2):
      data = []
      for movie in input_data[user1].keys():
          if movie in input_data[user2].keys():
              try:
                  data.append( (movie
                  ,input_data[user1][movie]
                  ,input_data[user2][movie]) )
              except:
                  pass


      return pd.DataFrame(data = data, columns = ['movie', user1,
                            user2])

>>> df = create_movie_user_df(movie_user_preferences, 'Sam', 'William')
>>> df
```

	movie	Sam	William
0	Gone Girl	6.0	7.0
1	Horrible Bosses 2	3.0	4.0
2	Django Unchained	7.5	8.0
3	Zoolander	7.0	4.0
4	Avenger: Age of Ultron	10.0	6.0
5	Kill the Messenger	5.5	6.5

Once we have created the preceding DataFrame, we will plot the scatter plot as we did earlier:

```
>>> plt.scatter(df.Sam, df.William)
>>> plt.xlabel('Sam')
>>> plt.ylabel('William')
>>> for i,txt in enumerate(df.movie):
      plt.annotate(txt, (df.Sam[i],df.William[i]))
>>> plt.show()
```

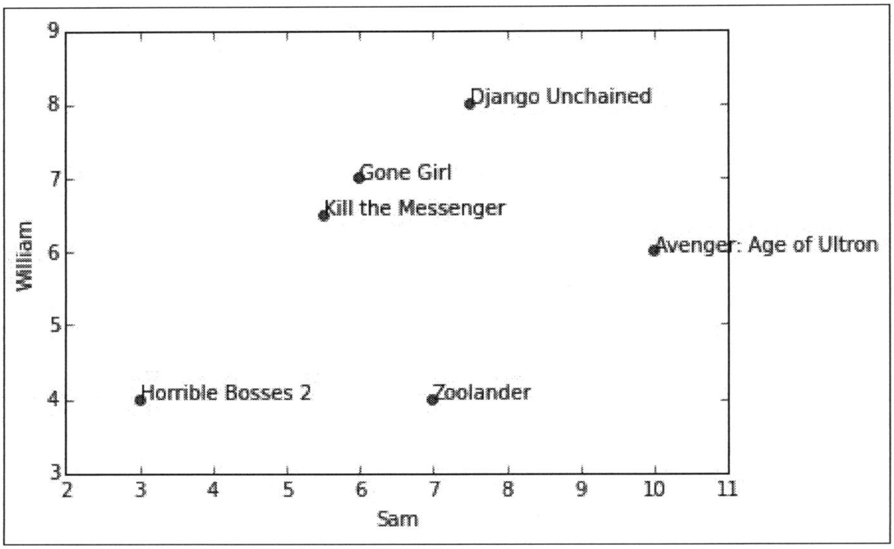

Let's compute the Pearson correlation between `Sam` and `William`:

```
>>> pearsonr(df.Sam,df.William)

(0.37067401970178415, 0.46945413268410929)
```

Let's see the scatter plot of correlation between `Sam` and `Julia`:

```
>>> df = create_movie_user_df(movie_user_preferences, 'Sam', 'Julia')
>>> df

>>> plt.scatter(df.Sam, df.Julia)
>>> plt.xlabel('Sam')
>>> plt.ylabel('Julia')
```

```
>>> for i,txt in enumerate(df.movie):
      plt.annotate(txt, (df.Sam[i],df.Julia[i]))
>>> plt.show()
```

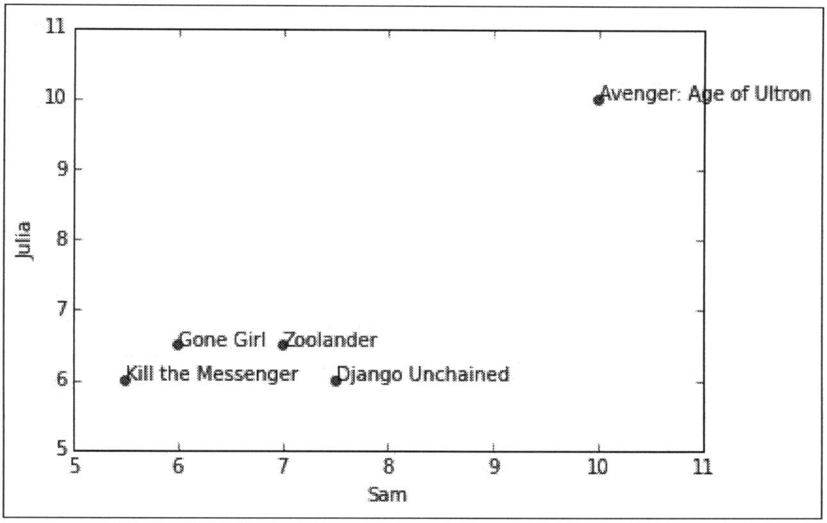

Let's compute the Pearson correlation between `Sam` and `Julia`:

```
>>> pearsonr(df.Sam,df.Julia)

(0.88285183326025096, 0.047277507003439537)
```

We can see that `Sam` and `Julia` are very similar to each other as the correlation value of `0.88` is close to 1.

We'll now create a function that takes in the data and calculates the Pearson correlation between the two users:

```
>>> # Returns the Pearson correlation coefficient for p1 and p2
>>> def sim_pearson(prefs,p1,p2):
      # Get the list of mutually rated items
      si={}
      for item in prefs[p1]:
          if item in prefs[p2]: si[item]=1

      # Find the number of elements
```

```
    n=len(si)

    # if they are no ratings in common, return 0
    if n==0: return 0

    # Add up all the preferences
    sum1=sum([prefs[p1][it] for it in si])
    sum2=sum([prefs[p2][it] for it in si])

    # Sum up the squares
    sum1Sq=sum([pow(prefs[p1][it],2) for it in si])
    sum2Sq=sum([pow(prefs[p2][it],2) for it in si])

    # Sum up the products
    pSum=sum([prefs[p1][it]*prefs[p2][it] for it in si])

    # Calculate Pearson score
    num=pSum-(sum1*sum2/n)
    den=sqrt((sum1Sq-pow(sum1,2)/n)*(sum2Sq-pow(sum2,2)/n))
    if den==0: return 0

    r=num/den

    return r
```

Let's compute the Pearson correlation between `Sam` and `Julia` by using the preceding function and verify if it's computing correctly:

```
>>> sim_pearson(movie_user_preferences,'Sam','Julia')

0.8828518332602507
```

Ranking the users

Once we have the methods of computing the similarity between users, we then proceed to rank them based on the similarity between particular users. I would like to know the people who are most similar to me. We can achieve this with the following code:

```
>>> def top_matches(prefs,person,n=5,similarity=sim_pearson):
        scores=[(similarity(prefs,person,other),other)
            for other in prefs if other!=person]

        # Sort the list so the highest scores appear at the top
        scores.sort( )
        scores.reverse( )
        return scores[0:n]
```

Let's see the top three people who are similar to `Sam`:

```
>>> top_matches(movie_user_preferences,'Toby',
                              n = 3, similarity = sim_distance)

[(0.10526315789473684, 'Jill'),
(0.08163265306122448, 'William'),
(0.03278688524590164, 'Sam')]
```

Recommending items

Once you know who is similar to you, you would now like to know the movies that are recommended for you. The following image shows how to compute a score for the movies so that we can find out what the most recommended movie is:

User	Similiarity	GoneGirl	R.Gone	HorribleBosses2	R.HorribleBosses2	KillTheMessenger	R.Kill the Messenger
Jill	0.105	9	0.945			8	0.84
William	0.081	7	0.567	4	0.324	6.5	0.5265
Sam	0.032	6	0.192	3	0.096	5.5	0.176
Total			1.704		0.42		1.5425
Sim Sum			0.218		0.113		0.218
Total/ Sim Sum			7.8165137615		3.7168141593		7.0756880734

We multiply the similarity score by the movie ratings of each user. We then sum up this new score and then divide it by the applicable similarity score. In summary, we are taking the weighted average based on the similarity score.

From the preceding output, we can see that Gone Girl has a very good score in terms of being recommended, and this is then followed by Kill the Messenger.

We'll now create a function that will generate recommendations for a user by encompassing the preceding logic:

```
>>> # Gets recommendations for a person by using a weighted average
>>> # of every other user's rankings
>>> def get_recommendations(prefs,person,similarity=sim_pearson):
    totals={}
    simSums={}
    for other in prefs:
        # don't compare me to myself
        if other==person: continue
        sim=similarity(prefs,person,other)

        # ignore scores of zero or lower
        if sim<=0: continue
        for item in prefs[other]:

            # only score movies I haven't seen yet
            if item not in prefs[person] or prefs[person][item]==0:
                # Similarity * Score
                totals.setdefault(item,0)
                totals[item]+=prefs[other][item]*sim
                # Sum of similarities
                simSums.setdefault(item,0)
                simSums[item]+=sim

    # Create the normalized list
    rankings=[(total/simSums[item],item) for item,total in
               totals.items( )]

    # Return the sorted list
```

```
        rankings.sort( )
        rankings.reverse( )
        return rankings
```

Let's get the recommendation by using the preceding function:

```
>>> get_recommendations(movie_user_preferences,'Toby')

[(6.587965809121004, 'Gone Girl'),
(6.087965809121004, 'Kill the Messenger'),
(3.608127720528246, 'Horrible Bosses 2')]

>>> getRecommendations(movie_user_preferences,'Toby',
                       similarity = sim_distance)

[(7.773043918833565, 'Gone Girl'),
(6.976295282563891, 'Kill the Messenger'),
(4.093380589669568, 'Horrible Bosses 2')]
```

We have now created a user-based collaborative filter.

Item-based collaborative filtering

User-based collaborative filtering finds the similarities between users, and then using these similarities between users, a recommendation is made.

Item-based collaborative filtering finds the similarities between items. This is then used to find new recommendations for a user.

To begin with item-based collaborative filtering, we'll first have to invert our dataset by putting the movies in the first layer, followed by the users in the second layer:

```
>>> def transform_prefs(prefs):
        result={}
        for person in prefs:
            for item in prefs[person]:
                result.setdefault(item,{})

                # Flip item and person
```

```
                result[item][person]=prefs[person][item]
        return result
```

```
{'Avenger: Age of Ultron': {'Jill': 7.0,
 'Julia': 10.0,
 'Max': 7.0,
 'Robert': 8.0,
 'Sam': 10.0,
 'Toby': 8.5,
 'William': 6.0},
'Django Unchained': {'Jill': 6.5,
 'Julia': 6.0,
 'Max': 7.0,
 'Robert': 7.0,
 'Sam': 7.5,
 'Toby': 9.0,
 'William': 8.0},
'Gone Girl': {'Jill': 9.0,
 'Julia': 6.5,
 'Max': 10.0,
 'Sam': 6.0,
 'William': 7.0},
'Horrible Bosses 2': {'Max': 6.0, 'Robert': 5.0, 'Sam': 3.0,
   'William': 4.0},
'Kill the Messenger': {'Jill': 8.0,
 'Julia': 6.0,
 'Max': 5.0,
 'Robert': 9.0,
 'Sam': 5.5,
 'William': 6.5},
'Zoolander': {'Julia': 6.5,
 'Max': 10.0,
 'Robert': 9.0,
 'Sam': 7.0,
 'Toby': 2.0,
 'William': 4.0}}
```

Now, we would like to find similar movies for each of the movies:

```
>>> def calculate_similar_items(prefs,n=10):
        # Create a dictionary of items showing which other items they
        # are most similar to.
        result={}

        # Invert the preference matrix to be item-centric
        itemPrefs=transform_prefs(prefs)
        c=0
        for item in itemPrefs:
            # Status updates for large datasets
            c+=1
            if c%100==0: print "%d / %d" % (c,len(itemPrefs))
            # Find the most similar items to this one
            scores=top_matches(itemPrefs, item, n=n,
                    similarity=sim_distance)
            result[item]=scores
        return result

>>> itemsim=calculate_similar_items(movie_user_preferences)
>>> itemsim

{'Avenger: Age of Ultron': [(0.034782608695652174, 'Django
  Unchained'),
 (0.023121387283236993, 'Gone Girl'),
 (0.022988505747126436, 'Kill the Messenger'),
 (0.015625, 'Horrible Bosses 2'),
 (0.012738853503184714, 'Zoolander')],
'Django Unchained': [(0.05714285714285714, 'Kill the Messenger'),
 (0.05063291139240506, 'Gone Girl'),
 (0.034782608695652174, 'Avenger: Age of Ultron'),
 (0.023668639053254437, 'Horrible Bosses 2'),
 (0.012578616352201259, 'Zoolander')],
'Gone Girl': [(0.09090909090909091, 'Zoolander'),
 (0.05063291139240506, 'Django Unchained'),
 (0.036036036036036036, 'Kill the Messenger'),
```

```
 (0.02857142857142857, 'Horrible Bosses 2'),
 (0.023121387283236993, 'Avenger: Age of Ultron')],
'Horrible Bosses 2': [(0.03278688524590164, 'Kill the Messenger'),
 (0.02857142857142857, 'Gone Girl'),
 (0.023668639053254437, 'Django Unchained'),
 (0.02040816326530612, 'Zoolander'),
 (0.015625, 'Avenger: Age of Ultron')],
'Kill the Messenger': [(0.05714285714285714, 'Django Unchained'),
 (0.036036036036036036, 'Gone Girl'),
 (0.03278688524590164, 'Horrible Bosses 2'),
 (0.02877697841726619, 'Zoolander'),
 (0.022988505747126436, 'Avenger: Age of Ultron')],
'Zoolander': [(0.09090909090909091, 'Gone Girl'),
 (0.02877697841726619, 'Kill the Messenger'),
 (0.02040816326530612, 'Horrible Bosses 2'),
 (0.012738853503184714, 'Avenger: Age of Ultron'),
 (0.012578616352201259, 'Django Unchained')]}
```

Once we have similarities between all the movies, we would like to generate the recommendations for a user.

The following table shows the movies seen by `Toby` under the `Movie` column and the rating given by `Toby`. The `Movie` column contains movies similar to the ones seen by `Toby`. The columns with R as a prefix are the products of the rating and similarity score.

Finally, we normalize the values by summing the `R` prefixed column, then dividing it by the sum of the similarity score of the `Movie` column.

The following table shows Kill The Messenger as the most recommended movie:

Movie	Rating	GoneGirl	R.GoneGirl	KillTheMessenger	R.KillTheMessenger	HorribleBosses2	R.HorribleBosses2
Avengers	8.5	0.023	0.1955	0.022	0.187	0.015	0.1275
Django	9	0.051	0.459	0.057	0.513	0.023	0.207
Zoolander	2	0.091	0.182	0.028	0.056	0.02	0.04
Total		0.165	0.8365	0.107	0.756	0.058	0.3745
Normalized			5.0696969697		7.0654205607		6.4568965517

We would now like to generate the recommendations by encompassing the preceding logic:

```
>>> def get_recommendedItems(prefs,itemMatch,user):
      userRatings=prefs[user]
      scores={}
      totalSim={}

      # Loop over items rated by this user
      for (item,rating) in userRatings.items( ):

          # Loop over items similar to this one
          for (similarity,item2) in itemMatch[item]:

              # Ignore if this user has already rated this item
              if item2 in userRatings: continue

              # Weighted sum of rating times similarity
              scores.setdefault(item2,0)
              scores[item2]+=similarity*rating

              # Sum of all the similarities
              totalSim.setdefault(item2,0)
              totalSim[item2]+=similarity

      # Divide each total score by total weighting to get an average
      rankings=[(score/totalSim[item],item) for
                   item,score in scores.items( )]

      # Return the rankings from highest to lowest
      rankings.sort( )
      rankings.reverse( )
      return rankings
    # Divide each total score by total weighting to get an average
```

```
    rankings=[(score/totalSim[item],item) for
              item,score in scores.items( )]


    # Return the rankings from highest to lowest
    rankings.sort( )
    rankings.reverse( )
    return rankings
```

Let's generate recommendations for `Toby`, using the item-based recommender:

```
>>> get_recommendedItems(movie_user_preferences, itemsim,'Toby')

[(7.044841200971884, 'Kill the Messenger'),
(6.476296577225752, 'Horrible Bosses 2'),
(5.0651585538275095, 'Gone Girl')]
```

Summary

In this chapter, you learned how to perform user-based and item-based collaborative filtering. You also learned some of the metrics that can be used to compute the similarity between users as well as items, and how to apply this similarity to generate recommendations for end users.

The next chapter will cover different ensemble models that basically combine multiple models to increase the performance of predictions.

9
Pushing Boundaries with Ensemble Models

Ensemble modeling is a process where two or more models are generated and then their results are combined. In this chapter, we'll cover a random forest, which is a nonparametric modeling technique where multiple decision trees are created during training time, and then the result of these decision trees are averaged to give the required output. It's called a **random forest** because many decision trees are created during training time on randomly selected features.

An analogy of this would be to try to guess the number of pebbles in a glass jar. There are groups of people who try to guess the number of pebbles in the jar. Individually, each person would be very wrong in guessing the number of pebbles in the glass jar, but when you average each of their guesses, the resulting averaged guess would be pretty close to the actual number of pebbles in the jar.

In this chapter, you'll learn how to:

- Work with census data on US earnings and explore this data
- Make decision trees to predict if a person is earning more than $50K
- Make random forest models and get improved data performance

The census income dataset

The following table is a census dataset on income created by the University of California, Irvine:

Columns	Description
`age`	This refers to the age of a person
`work class`	This refers to the type of employment a person is involved in
`education`	This refers to the education level of a person
`marital_status`	This refers to whether a person is married or not
`occupation`	This refers to the type of jobs a person is involved in
`relationship`	This refers to the type of relationship of the person
`race`	This refers to the ethnicity of a person
`gender`	This refers to the gender of a person
`hours_per_week`	This refers to the average hours worked per week
`native_country`	This refers to the country of origin
`greater_than_50k`	This refers to the flag that indicates whether a person is earning more than $50K in a year

Let's load this data:

```
>>> data = pd.read_csv('./Data/census.csv')
```

Let's check the fill rate of the data:

```
>>> data.count(0)/data.shape[0] * 100
age                  100.000000
workclass             94.361179
education            100.000000
education_num        100.000000
marital_status       100.000000
occupation            94.339681
relationship         100.000000
race                 100.000000
gender               100.000000
capital_gain         100.000000
capital_loss         100.000000
```

```
hours_per_week       100.000000
native_country        98.209459
greater_than_50k     100.000000
dtype: float64
```

We can see that the columns have a good fill rate. We'll remove the rows that have empty values and also remove the `education_num` column as it contains the same information, such as education and its unique codes:

```
>>> data = data.dropna(how='any')
>>> del data['education_num']
```

Exploring the census data

Let's explore the census data and understand the patterns with the data before building the model.

Hypothesis 1: People who are older earn more

We'll create a histogram of people who earn more than $50K:

```
>>> hist_above_50 = plt.hist(data[data.greater_than_50k ==
                    1].age.values, 10, facecolor='green', alpha=0.5)
>>> plt.title('Age distribution of Above 50K earners')
>>> plt.xlabel('Age')
>>> plt.ylabel('Frequency')
```

Here is the histogram for the preceding code:

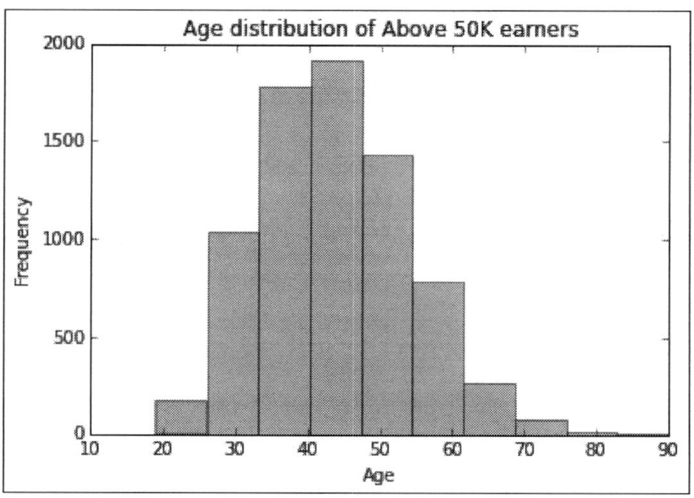

Now, we'll plot a histogram of the age of the people who earn less than $50K a year, using this code:

```
>>> hist_below_50 = plt.hist(data[data.greater_than_50k ==
                    0].age.values, 10, facecolor='green', alpha=0.5)
>>> plt.title('Age distribution of below 50K earners')
>>> plt.xlabel('Age')
>>> plt.ylabel('Frequency)
```

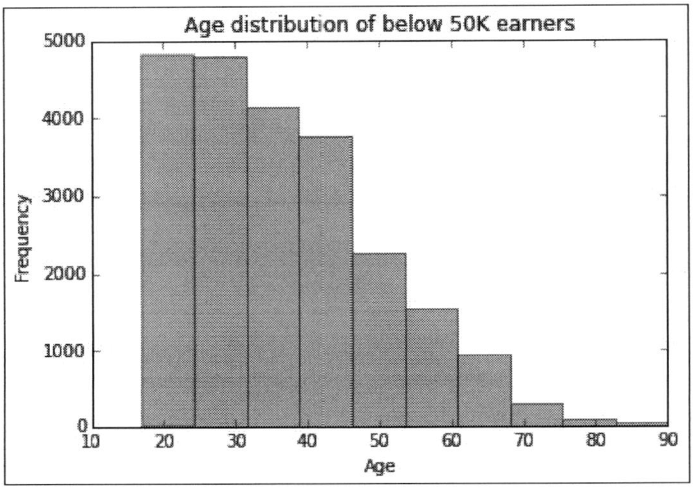

We can see that people who earn above $50K are mostly aged between their late 30s and mid 50s, whereas people who earn less than $50K are primarily aged between 20 and 30.

Hypothesis 2: Income bias based on working class

Let's see what the distribution of people earning more than $50K between different working class groups is. We'll see the percentage of earners who earn more than $50K in each of the groups, using the following code:

```
>>> dist_data = pd.concat([data[data.greater_than_50k == 1]
              .groupby('workclass').workclass.count()
               , data[data.greater_than_50k == 0]
                 .groupby('workclass').workclass.count()], axis=1)
>>> dist_data.columns = ['wk_class_gt50','wk_class_lt50']
>>> dist_data_final = dist_data.wk_class_gt50 /
                     (dist_data.wk_class_lt50 +
                     dist_data.wk_class_gt50 )
>>> dist_data_final.sort(ascending=False)
```

```
>>> ax = dist_data_final.plot(kind = 'bar', color = 'r',
                              y='Percentage')
>>> ax.set_xticklabels(dist_data_final.index, rotation=30,
                       fontsize=8, ha='right')
>>> ax.set_xlabel('Working Class')
>>> ax.set_ylabel('Percentage of People')
```

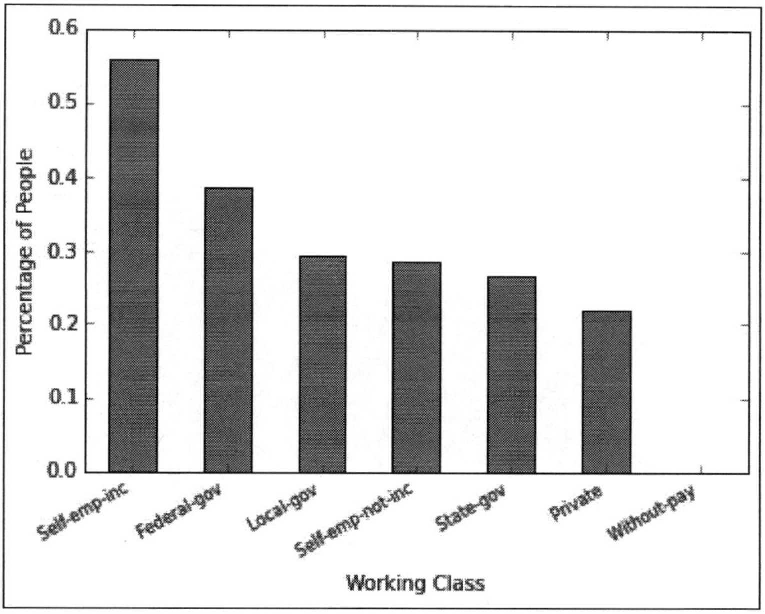

We see that people who are self-employed and have a company have got the maximum share of people who earn more than $50K. The second most well-off group in terms of earning are federal government employees.

Hypothesis 3: People with more education earn more

Education is an important field. It should be related to the level of earning power of an individual:

```
>>> dist_data = pd.concat([data[data.greater_than_50k == 1]
              .groupby('education').education.count()
              , data[data.greater_than_50k ==
                0].groupby('education').education.count()],
                axis=1)
```

```
>>> dist_data.columns = ['education_gt50','education_lt50']

>>> dist_data_final = dist_data.education_gt50 /
                (dist_data.education_gt50 +
                dist_data.education_lt50)

>>> dist_data_final.sort(ascending = False)
>>> ax = dist_data_final.plot(kind = 'bar', color = 'r')
>>> ax.set_xticklabels(dist_data_final.index,
                rotation=30, fontsize=8, ha='right')
>>> ax.set_xlabel('Education Level')
>>> ax.set_ylabel('Percentage of People')
```

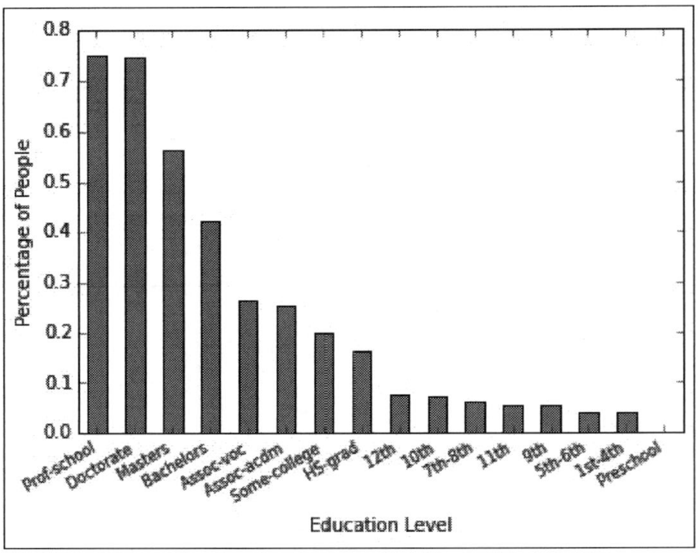

We can see that the more the person is educated, the greater the number of people in their group who earn more than $50K.

Hypothesis 4: Married people tend to earn more

Let's see how distribution is based on marital status:

```
>>> dist_data = pd.concat([data[data.greater_than_50k == 1]
              .groupby('marital_status').marital_status.count()
              , data[data.greater_than_50k == 0]
                  .groupby('marital_status')
                  .marital_status.count()],
                  axis=1)
```

```
>>> dist_data.columns = ['marital_status_gt50','marital_status_lt50']

>>> dist_data_final = dist_data.marital_status_gt50 /
        (dist_data.marital_status_gt50+dist_data.marital_status_lt50)

>>> dist_data_final.sort(ascending = False)

>>> ax = dist_data_final.plot(kind = 'bar', color = 'r')
>>> ax.set_xticklabels(dist_data_final.index, rotation=30,
              fontsize=8, ha='right')
>>> ax.set_xlabel('Marital Status')
>>> ax.set_ylabel('Percentage of People')
```

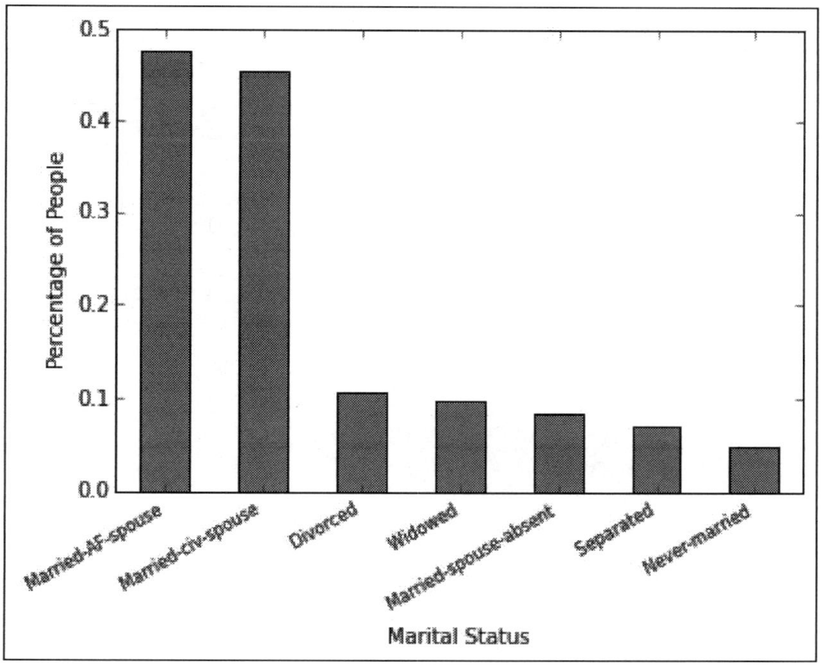

We can see that people who are married earn better as compared to people who are single.

Hypothesis 5: There is a bias in income based on race

Let's see how earning power is based on the race of the person:

```
>>> dist_data = pd.concat([data[data.greater_than_50k == 1]
                .groupby('race').race.count()
                  , data[data.greater_than_50k ==
                    0].groupby('race').race.count()], axis=1)

>>> dist_data.columns = ['race_gt50','race_lt50']

>>> dist_data_final = dist_data.race_gt50 / (dist_data.race_gt50 +
                        dist_data.race_lt50 )

>>> dist_data_final.sort(ascending = False)

>>> ax = dist_data_final.plot(kind = 'bar', color = 'r')

>>> ax.set_xticklabels(dist_data_final.index, rotation=30,
                         fontsize=8, ha='right')
>>> ax.set_xlabel('Race')
>>> ax.set_ylabel('Percentage of People')
```

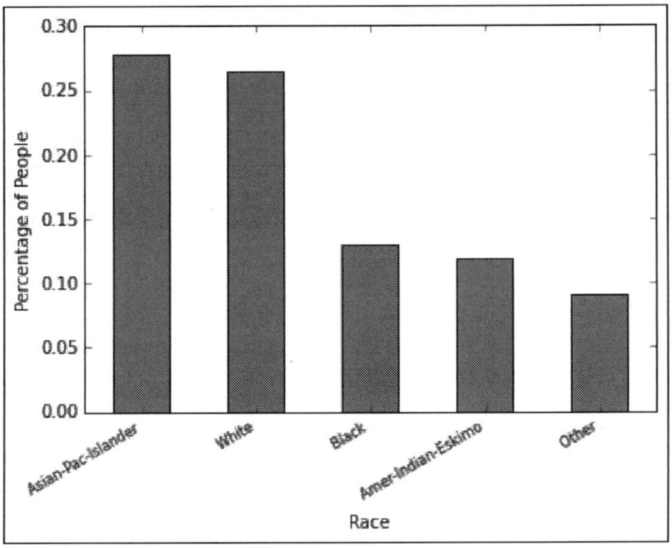

Asian Pacific people and Whites have the highest earning power.

Hypothesis 6: There is a bias in the income based on occupation

Let's see how earning power is based on the occupation of a person:

```
>>> dist_data = pd.concat([data[data.greater_than_50k == 1]
                  .groupby('occupation').occupation.count()
                  , data[data.greater_than_50k == 0]
                      .groupby('occupation').occupation.count()],
                       axis=1)

>>> dist_data.columns = ['occupation_gt50','occupation_lt50']

>>> dist_data_final = dist_data.occupation_gt50 /
                          (dist_data.occupation_gt50 +
                           dist_data.occupation_lt50 )

>>> dist_data_final.sort(ascending = False)

>>> ax = dist_data_final.plot(kind = 'bar', color = 'r')

>>> ax.set_xticklabels(dist_data_final.index, rotation=30,
                           fontsize=8, ha='right')
>>> ax.set_xlabel('Occupation')
>>> ax.set_ylabel('Percentage of People')
```

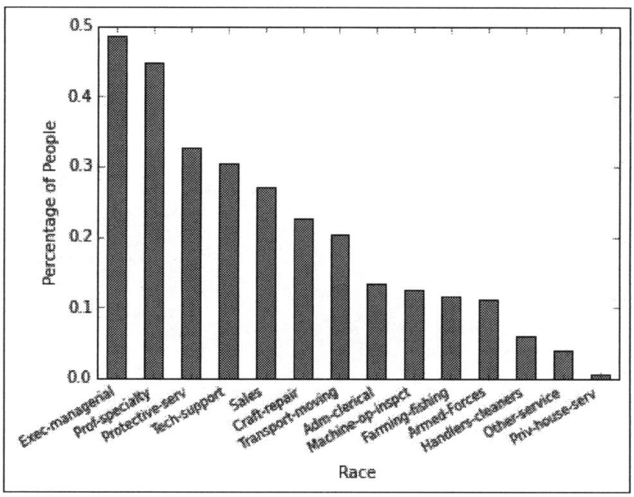

We can see that people who are in specialized or managerial positions earn more.

Hypothesis 7: Men earn more

Let's see how earning power is based on gender:

```
>>> dist_data = pd.concat([data[data.greater_than_50k == 1]
                  .groupby('gender').gender.count()
                   , data[data.greater_than_50k == 0]
                      .groupby('gender').gender.count()], axis=1)
>>> dist_data.columns = ['gender_gt50','gender_lt50']


>>> dist_data_final = dist_data.gender_gt50 /
                      (dist_data.gender_gt50 + dist_data.gender_lt50)


>>> dist_data_final.sort(ascending = False)


>>> ax = dist_data_final.plot(kind = 'bar', color = 'r')


>>> ax.set_xticklabels(dist_data_final.index, rotation=30,
                       fontsize=8, ha='right')
>>> ax.set_xlabel('Gender')
>>> ax.set_ylabel('Percentage of People')
```

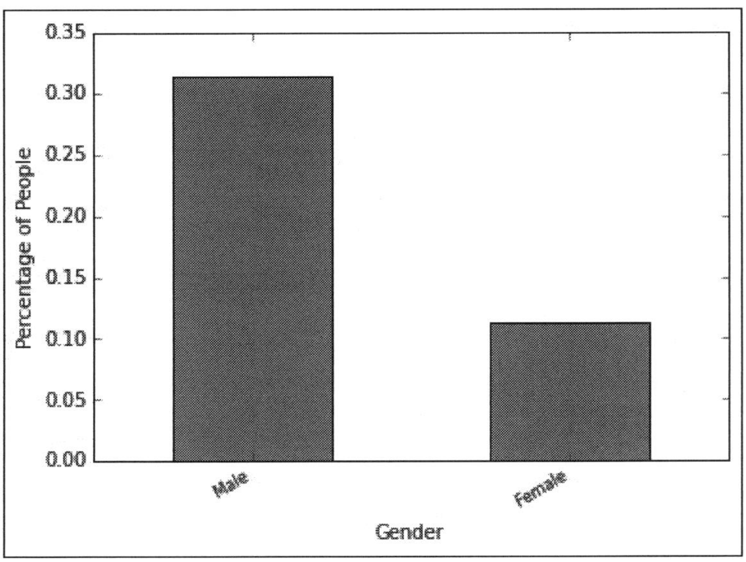

It's no surprise to see that males have a higher earning power as compared to females. It will be good to see the two bars at an equal level sometime in the future.

Hypothesis 8: People who clock in more hours earn more

Let's see the distribution of people who earn above $50K based on their working hours per week:

```
>>> hist_above_50 = plt.hist(data[data.greater_than_50k == 1]
                    .hours_per_week.values, 10, facecolor='green',
                    alpha=0.5)
>>> plt.title('Hours per week distribution of Above 50K earners')
```

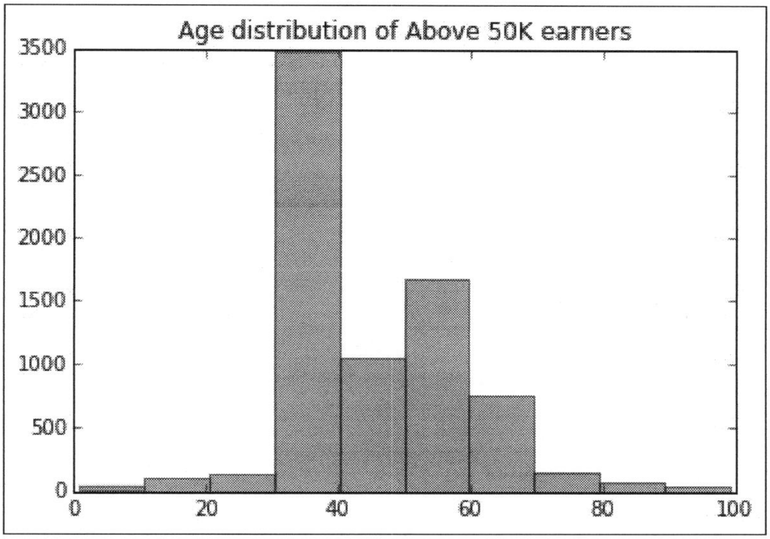

Now, let's see the distribution of the earners below $50K based on their working hours per week:

```
>>> hist_below_50 = plt.hist(data[data.greater_than_50k ==
        0].hours_per_week.values, 10, facecolor='green', alpha=0.5)
>>> plt.title('Hours per week distribution of Below 50K earners')
```

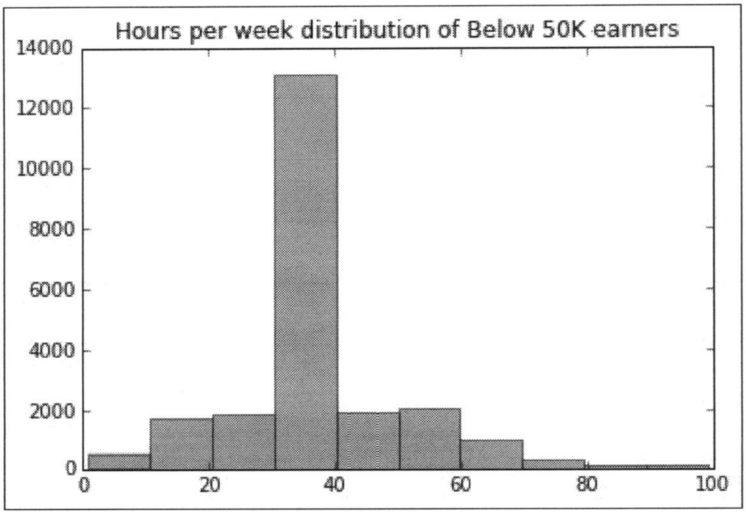

We can see that people who earn more than $50K and less than this have an average of 40 working hours per week, but it can be seen that people who earn above $50K have a higher number of people who work more than 40 hours.

Hypothesis 9: There is a bias in income based on the country of origin

Let's see how earning power is based on a person's country of origin:

```
>>> plt.figure(figsize=(10,5))
>>> dist_data = pd.concat([data[data.greater_than_50k == 1]
                .groupby('native_country').native_country.count()
                , data[data.greater_than_50k == 0]
                  .groupby('native_country').native_country
                  .count()], axis=1)

>>> dist_data.columns = ['native_country_gt50','native_country_lt50']
```

```
>>> dist_data_final = dist_data.native_country_gt50 /
                       (dist_data.native_country_gt50 +
                          dist_data.native_country_lt50 )


>>> dist_data_final.sort(ascending = False)


>>> ax = dist_data_final.plot(kind = 'bar', color = 'r')


>>> ax.set_xticklabels(dist_data_final.index, rotation=40,
                        fontsize=8, ha='right')
>>> ax.set_xlabel(Country)
>>> ax.set_ylabel('Percentage of People')
```

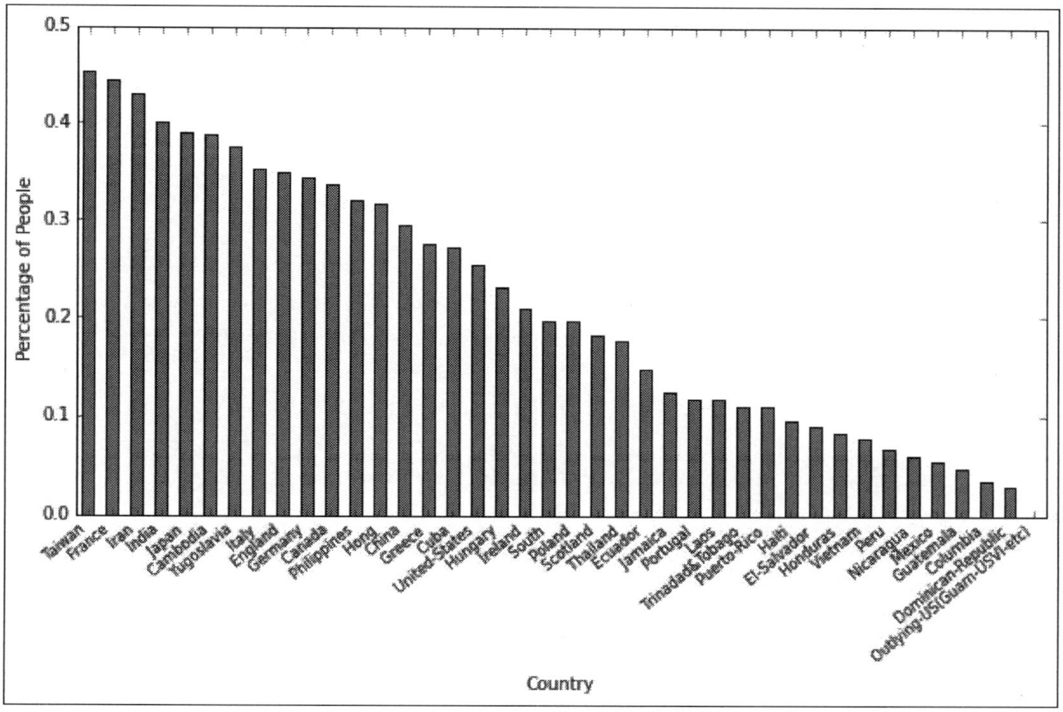

We can see that Taiwanese, French, Iranians, and Indians are the most well-earning people among different counties.

Decision trees

To understand decision tree-based models, let's try to imagine that Google wants to recruit people for a software development job. Based on the employees that they already have and the ones they have rejected previously, we can determine whether an applicant was from an Ivy League college or not and what the **Grade Point Average (GPA)** of the applicant was.

The decision tree will split the applicants into Ivy League and non-Ivy League groups. The Ivy League group will then be split into high GPA and low GPA so that people with a high GPA are likely to be tagged highly and the ones with a low GPA are likely to get recruited.

Applicants who have a high GPA and belong to non-Ivy League colleges have a slightly better chance of getting recruited as compared to those who have a low GPA and belong to non-Ivy League colleges.

The preceding explanation is what a decision tree does in simple terms.

Let's create a decision tree on the basis of our data to predict what the likelihood of a person earning more than $50K is going to be:

```
>>> data_test = pd.read_csv('./Data/census_test.csv')
>>> data_test = data_test.dropna(how='any')
>>> formula = 'greater_than_50k ~  age + workclass + education +
                marital_status + occupation + race + gender +
                hours_per_week + native_country '
>>> y_train,x_train = dmatrices(formula, data=data,
                                 return_type='dataframe')
>>> y_test,x_test = dmatrices(formula, data=data_test,
                               return_type='dataframe')
>>> clf = tree.DecisionTreeClassifier()
>>> clf = clf.fit(x_train, y_train)
```

Let's see how the model performs:

```
>>> from sklearn.metrics import classification_report
>>> y_pred = clf.predict(x_test)
>>> print pd.crosstab(y_test.greater_than_50k
                      ,y_pred
                      ,rownames = ['Actual']
                       ,colnames = ['Predicted'])
```

```
>>> print '\n \n'

>>> print classification_report(y_test.greater_than_50k,y_pred)
```

```
Predicted      0     1
Actual
0           9832  1528
1           1781  1919


              precision    recall  f1-score   support

        0.0        0.85      0.87      0.86     11360
        1.0        0.56      0.52      0.54      3700

avg / total        0.78      0.78      0.78     15060
```

We can see that the people who don't earn more than $50K can be predicted well as there is a precision of 85% and a recall of 87%. People who earn more than $50K can only be predicted with a precision of 56% and a recall of 52%

Note that the order of the dependent variables given in the formula will change these values slightly. You can experiment to see whether changing the order of the variables will improve their precision/recall.

Random forests

We have learned how to create a decision tree but, at times, decision tree models don't hold up well when there are many variables and a large dataset. This is where ensemble models, such as random forest, come to rescue.

A random forest basically creates many decision trees on the dataset and then averages out the results. If you see a singing competition, such as American Idol, or a sporting competition, such as the Olympics, there are multiple judges. The reason for having multiple judges is to eliminate bias and give fair results, and this is what a random forest tries to achieve.

A decision tree can change drastically if the data changes slightly and it can easily overfit the data.

Let's try to create a random forest model and see how its precision/recall is compared to the decision tree that we just created:

```
>>> import sklearn.ensemble as sk
>>> clf = sk.RandomForestClassifier(n_estimators=100)
>>> clf = clf.fit(x_train, y_train.greater_than_50k)
```

After building the model, let's cross-validate the model on the test data:

```
>>> y_pred = clf.predict(x_test)
>>> print pd.crosstab(y_test.greater_than_50k
                      ,y_pred
                      ,rownames = ['Actual']
                      ,colnames = ['Predicted'])
>>> print '\n \n'
>>> print classification_report(y_test.greater_than_50k,y_pred)
```

```
Predicted      0     1
Actual
0          10148  1212
1           1685  2015


             precision    recall  f1-score   support

        0.0       0.86      0.89      0.88     11360
        1.0       0.62      0.54      0.58      3700

avg / total       0.80      0.81      0.80     15060
```

We can see that we have improved the precision and recall for the people who don't earn more than $50K, as well as for the people who do.

Let's try to do some fine-tuning to achieve better performance for the model by using the `min_samples_split` parameter and setting it to `5`. This parameter tells us that the minimum number of samples required to create a split is `5`:

```
>>> clf = sk.RandomForestClassifier(n_estimators=100,
        oob_score=True,min_samples_split=5)
>>> clf = clf.fit(x_train, y_train.greater_than_50k)
>>> y_pred = clf.predict(x_test)
>>> print pd.crosstab(y_test.greater_than_50k
                      ,y_pred
                      ,rownames = ['Actual']
                      ,colnames = ['Predicted'])
>>> print '\n \n'
>>> print classification_report(y_test.greater_than_50k,y_pred)
```

```
Predicted       0     1
Actual
0           10269  1091
1            1636  2064



             precision    recall  f1-score   support

        0.0       0.86      0.90      0.88     11360
        1.0       0.65      0.56      0.60      3700

avg / total       0.81      0.82      0.81     15060
```

We increased the recall of 0% to 90%, 1% to 56%, and the precision of 1% to 65%.

We'll fine-tune the model further by increasing the minimum number of leaves to 2 by using the `min_leaf` parameter. The meaning of this parameter indicates that the minimum number of nodes to be created are 2:

```
>>> clf = sk.RandomForestClassifier(n_estimators=100,
        oob_score=True,min_samples_split=5, min_samples_leaf= 2)
>>> clf = clf.fit(x_train, y_train.greater_than_50k)


>>> y_pred = clf.predict(x_test)


>>> print pd.crosstab(y_test.greater_than_50k
                      ,y_pred
                      ,rownames = ['Actual']
                      ,colnames = ['Predicted'])


>>> print '\n \n'


>>> print classification_report(y_test.greater_than_50k,y_pred)
```

```
Predicted      0     1
Actual
0          10453   907
1           1621  2079



             precision    recall  f1-score   support

        0.0       0.87      0.92      0.89     11360
        1.0       0.70      0.56      0.62      3700

avg / total       0.82      0.83      0.83     15060
```

We have further significantly increased the recall of 0% to 92% and the precision of 1% to 70%. This model performs decently.

Let's see the importance of the variables that are contributing to the prediction. We'll use the feature importance attribute of the `clf` object, and using this, we'll plot important features, such as dependent variables that are sorted by their importance:

```
>>> model_ranks = pd.Series(clf.feature_importances_,
                   index=x_train.columns, name='Importance')
                   .sort(ascending=False, inplace=False)

>>> model_ranks.index.name = 'Features'

>>> top_features = model_ranks.iloc[:31].sort(ascending=True,
                   inplace=False)

>>> plt.figure(figsize=(15,7))

>>> ax = top_features.plot(kind='barh')

>>> _ = ax.set_title("Variable Ranking")

>>> _ = ax.set_xlabel('Performance')

>>> _ = ax.set_yticklabels(top_features.index, fontsize=8)
```

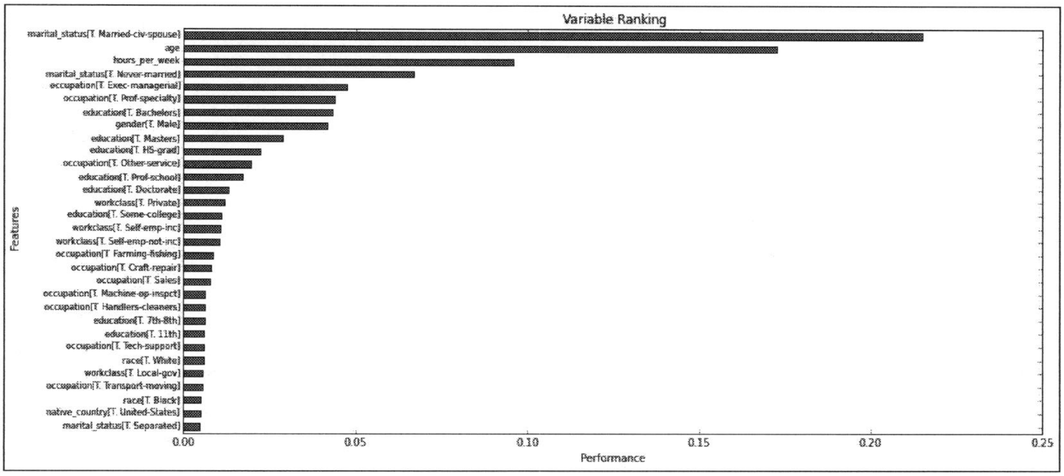

We can see that those people who are married to a civilian spouse are very good indicators of whether a particular group of people earn more than $50K or not. This is followed by the age of a person, and finally, the number of hours a week a person works. Also, people who aren't married are good indicators of predicting the group of people who earn less than $50K.

Summary

In this chapter, we explored the patterns in the census data and then understood how a decision tree was constructed and also built a decision tree model on the data given. You then learned the concept of ensemble models with the help of a random forest and improved the performance of prediction by using the random forest model.

In the next chapter, you'll learn clustering, which is basically grouping elements together that are similar to each other. We will use the k-means cluster for this.

10
Applying Segmentation with k-means Clustering

Clustering comes under unsupervised learning and helps in segmenting an instance into groups in such a way that instances in the group have similar characteristics. Amazon might want to understand who their high-value, medium-value and low-value users are. In the simplest form, we can determine this by bucketing the total transaction amount of each user into three buckets. The high value customers will come under the top 20 percentile bucket, the medium value will come under the 20th to 80th percentile bucket, and the bottom 20 percentile will contain the low-value customers. Amazon will know who their high value customers are through this and ensure that they are taken care of in case of scenarios, such as payment failures for transactions. Here, we've used a single variable, such as the transaction amount, and we've manually bucketed the data.

We require an algorithm that can take multiple variables and helps us in bucketing instances. The k-means is one of the most popular algorithms to perform clustering as it is the easiest machine learning algorithm to understand under clustering. Also, segmentation is the process of dividing customers into groups, and clustering is the technique that helps in finding the similarities in a group and help assign customers to a particular group.

In this chapter, you'll learn the following topics:

- Determining the ideal number of clusters through the k-means technique
- Clustering with the k-means algorithm

The k-means algorithm and its working

The k-means clustering algorithm operates by computing the average of features, such as the variables that we use for clustering. For example, segmenting customers based on the average transaction amount and the average number of products purchased in a quarter of a year. This mean then becomes the center of a cluster. The *K* number is the number of clusters, that is, the technique consists of computing a *K* number of means that lead to the clustering of data around these k-means.

How do we choose this *K*? If we have some idea of what we are looking for or how many clusters we expect or want, then we can set *K* to be this number before we start the engines and let the algorithm compute along.

If we don't know how many clusters there are, then our exploration will take a little longer and involve some trial and error, say, as we try *K=3,4*, and *5*.

The k-means algorithm is iterative. It starts by choosing *K* points at random from the data and uses these as cluster centers just to get started. Then, at each iterative step, this algorithm decides which row values are closest to the cluster center and assigns *K* points to them.

Once this is done, we have a new arrangement of points. Thus, the center or mean of the clusters is computed again as it may have changed. When does it not shift? When we have stable clusters, and we have iterated till we get no benefit from iterating further, then this is our result.

There are conditions under which k-means do not converge, that is, there are no stable clusters, but we won't get into that here. You can read further about the convergence of k-means at `http://webdocs.cs.ualberta.ca/~nray1/CMPUT466_551/kmeans_convergence.pdf`.

A simple example

Let's look at a simple example before getting into k-means clustering. We'll use a dataset of t-shirt sizes with the following columns:

- `Size`: This refers to the size of a t-shirt
- `Height`: This refers to the height of a person
- `Weight`: This refers to the weight of a person

Let's look at the data:

```
>>> import numpy as np
>>> import pandas as pd
>>> import matplotlib.pyplot as plt
>>> #Reading the data from the file
>>> df = pd.read_csv('./Data/tshirt_sizes.csv')
>>> print df[:10]

   Height  Weight Size
0     150      54    S
1     150      55    S
2     151      55    S
3     151      47    S
4     152      58    S
5     155      53    S
6     155      59    S
7     157      60    S
8     157      56    S
9     157      55    S
```

We'll plot a scatter plot of the height and weight of people and group it on the basis of t-shirt sizes using the following code:

```
>>> d_color = {
        "S": "b",
        "M": "r",
        "L": "g",
    }
>>> fig, ax = plt.subplots()
>>> for size in ["S", "M", "L"]:
        color = d_color[size]
        df[df.Size == size].plot(kind='scatter', x='Height', y='Weight',
                                 label=size, ax=ax, color=color)
>>> handles, labels = ax.get_legend_handles_labels()
>>> _ = ax.legend(handles, labels, loc="upper left")
```

After the preceding code is executed we'll get the following output:

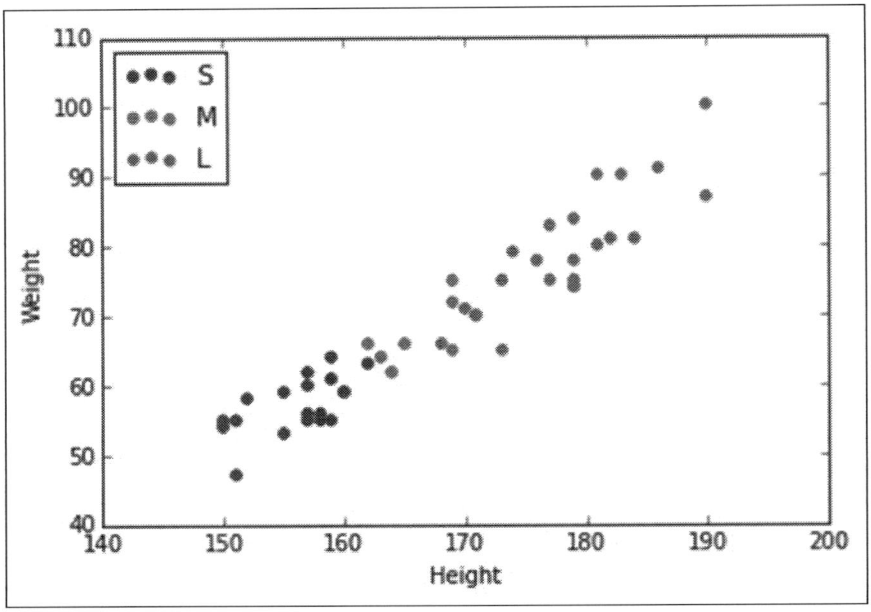

You can see that people who have sizes, such as small, are short in height and they weigh less and are blue in color. Similarly, for the other t-shirt sizes, the height and weight of people are grouped together around each other.

In the preceding case, we had labels for the t-shirt sizes. However, if we don't have t-shirt sizes with us but have the height and weight of the individual instead and we want to estimate the sizes based on height and weight, then this is where a k-means algorithm helps us:

```
>>> from math import sqrt
>>> from scipy.stats.stats import pearsonr
>>> from sklearn.cluster import KMeans
>>> from scipy.cluster.vq import kmeans,vq
>>> from scipy.spatial.distance import cdist


>>> km = KMeans(3,init='k-means++', random_state=3425) # initialize
>>> km.fit(df[['Height','Weight']])
>>> df['SizePredict'] = km.predict(df[['Height','Weight']])
>>> df.groupby(['Size','SizePredict']).Size.count()
>>> print pd.crosstab(df.Size
```

```
                    ,df.SizePredict
                    ,rownames = ['Size']
                    ,colnames = ['SizePredict'])

SizePredict    0   1   2
Size
L             13   0   1
M              0   6  14
S              0  15   0
```

We have assumed three clusters in the k-means algorithm based on the t-shirt sizes that we know (later on we'll discuss how to determine the number of clusters), and then we input the height and weight in the k-means algorithm. Post this, we predict buckets and assign these buckets to the `SizePredict` variable. We then look at the confusion matrix between the actual and the predicted values to see where the predicted bucket belongs. We can see that `0` bucket belongs to the `L` shirt size, `1` to `S` and `2` to `M`. We'll now map the buckets back to the t-shirt sizes and plot the scatter plot:

```
>>> c_map = {
        2: "M",
        1: "S",
        0: "L",
    }

>>> df['SizePredict'] = df['SizePredict'].map(c_map)
>>> df['SizePredict'][:10]
0    S
1    S
2    S
3    S
4    S
5    S
6    S
7    S
8    S
9    S
Name: SizePredict, dtype: object
```

We'll now plot the scatter plot:

```
>>> fig, ax = plt.subplots()
>>> for size in ["S", "M", "L"]:
        color = d_color[size]
        df[df.SizePredict == size].plot(kind='scatter', x='Height',
                                        y='Weight', label=size, ax=ax,
                                        color=color)
>>> handles, labels = ax.get_legend_handles_labels()
>>> _ = ax.legend(handles, labels, loc="upper left")
```

After the preceding code is executed we'll get the following output:

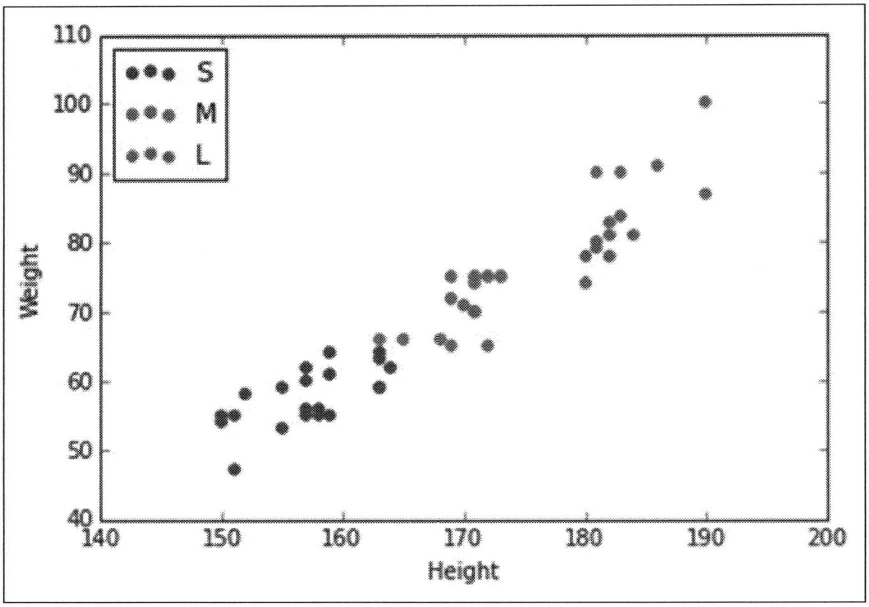

We can see from the plot that the k-means algorithm was able to bucket people into appropriate buckets where the shirt sizes can be used to identify a bucket as unique.

The k-means clustering with countries

We have UN data on different countries of the world with regard to education of people to Gross Domestic Product. We'll use this data to bucket the countries based on their development. Here are the descriptions of the columns:

country	Name of the country
region	Continent the country belongs to
tfr	Total Fertility Rate
contraception	Percentage of people taking contraceptions
educationMale	Percentage of male population who are educated
educationFemale	Percentage of male population who are educated
lifeMale	Life Expectancy of Male
lifeFemale	Life Expectancy of Female
infantMortality	Infant Mortality Rate
GDPperCapita	GDP per capita
economicActivityMale	Males who generate income
economicActivityFemale	Females who generate income
illiteracyMale	Illiteracy rate in Male
illiteracyFemale	Illiteracy rate in Female

Here is a screenshot of the data:

country	region	tfr	contraception	educationMale	educationFemale	lifeMale	lifeFemale	infantMortality	GDPperCapita	economicActivityMale	economicActivityFem	illiteracyMal	illiteracyF
Afghanist	Asia	6.9				45	46	154	2848	87.5	7.2	52.8	85
Albania	Europe	2.6				68	74	32	863				
Algeria	Africa	3.81	52	11.1	9.9	67.5	70.3	44	1531	76.4	7.8	26.1	51
American	Asia					68	73	11		58.8	42.4	0.264	0.36
Andorra	Europe												
Angola	Africa	6.69				44.9	48.1	124	355				
Antigua	America		53					24	6966	74.4	56.2		
Argentina	America	2.62				69.6	76.8	22	8055	76.2	41.3	3.8	3.8
Armenia	Europe	1.7	22			67.2	74	25	354	65	52	0.3	0.5
Australia	Oceania	1.89	76	16.3	16.1	75.4	81.2	6	20046	74	53.8		
Austria	Europe	1.42	71	14.4	14.2	73.7	80.1	6	29006	69.5	47.7		
Azerbaija	Asia	2.3	17			66.5	74.5	33	321			0.3	0.5
Bahamas	America	1.95	62	12.1	13.2	70.5	77.1	14	12545	81.2	67	1.5	2

Lets see the data type of each column:

```
>>> df = pd.read_csv('./Data/UN.csv')
>>> # print the raw column information plus summary header
>>> print('----')
>>> # look at the types of each column explicitly
>>> [(col, type(df[col][0])) for col in df.columns] [(x, type(df[x][0]))
   for x in df.columns]
        [('country', str),
        ('region', str),
        ('tfr', numpy.float64),
        ('contraception', numpy.float64),
        ('educationMale', numpy.float64),
        ('educationFemale', numpy.float64),
        ('lifeMale', numpy.float64),
        ('lifeFemale', numpy.float64),
        ('infantMortality', numpy.float64),
        ('GDPperCapita', numpy.float64),
        ('economicActivityMale', numpy.float64),
        ('economicActivityFemale', numpy.float64),
        ('illiteracyMale', numpy.float64),
        ('illiteracyFemale', numpy.float64)]
```

Let's check the **fill rate** of the columns, which is basically the percentage of rows and columns that have values:

```
>>> print('Percentage of the values complete in the columns')
>>> s_col_fill = df.count(0)/df.shape[0] * 100
>>> s_col_fill
country                    100.000000
region                     100.000000
tfr                         95.169082
contraception               69.565217
educationMale               36.714976
educationFemale             36.714976
lifeMale                    94.685990
lifeFemale                  94.685990
infantMortality             97.101449
```

```
GDPperCapita                 95.169082
economicActivityMale         79.710145
economicActivityFemale       79.710145
illiteracyMale               77.294686
illiteracyFemale             77.294686
dtype: float64
```

We can see that the education column does not have a good fill rate followed by the contraception column.

The columns with a good fill rate are life expectancy of `lifeMale` and `lifeFemale`, `infantMortality` and `GDPperCapita`. With these columns, we'll remove only a few countries, whereas if we include other columns, we'll remove a lot of countries.

There should be a clustering influence based on the life expectancy of males and females and the infant mortality rate based on the GDP of a country. This is because a higher GDP is better for the economy of the country, and a country with a good economy is presumed to have a good life expectancy and low infant mortality rate:

```
>>> df = df[['lifeMale', 'lifeFemale', 'infantMortality',
             'GDPperCapita']]


>>> df = df.dropna(how='any')
```

Determining the number of clusters

Before applying the k-means algorithm, we would like to estimate the ideal number of clusters to the group called countries:

```
>>> K = range(1,10)


>>> # scipy.cluster.vq.kmeans
>>> KM = [kmeans(df.values,k) for k in K] # apply kmeans 1 to 10
>>> KM[:3]
[(array([[   63.52606383,    68.30904255,    44.30851064,
          5890.59574468]]),    6534.9809626620172),
(array([[  6.12227273e+01,   6.57779221e+01,   5.23831169e+01,
          2.19273377e+03],     [  7.39588235e+01,   7.97735294e+01,
  7.73529412e+00,     2.26397353e+04]]),     2707.2294867471232),
(array([[  7.43050000e+01,   8.02350000e+01,   6.60000000e+00,
          2.76644500e+04],     [  6.02309353e+01,   6.46640288e+01,
  5.61007194e+01,     1.47384173e+03],      [  7.18862069e+01,
  7.75551724e+01,    1.37931034e+01,     1.20441034e+04]]),
  1874.0284870915732)]
```

In the preceding code, we define a number of clusters from 1 to 10. Using the SciPy library's **k-mean function**, we compute centroids and the distortion between these centroids and observed values associated to the distortion that is computed between the centroid and the observed values of the cluster:

```
>>> euclidean_centroid = [cdist(df.values, centroid, 'euclidean') for
      (centroid,var) in k_clusters]
>>> print '-----with 1 cluster------'
>>> print euclidean_centroid[0][:5]


-----with 1 cluster------
[[ 3044.71049474]
 [ 5027.61602297]
 [ 4359.59802141]
 [ 5536.23755972]
 [ 2164.54439528]]
>>> print '-----with 2 cluster------'
>>> print euclidean_centroid[1][:5]


-----with 2 cluster------
[[ 19792.32574968    663.5918709 ]
 [ 21776.75039319   1329.9326654 ]
 [ 21108.76955936    661.83208396]
 [ 22285.08003662   1839.28608809]
 [ 14584.74322443   5862.36131557]]
```

We take the centroids in each of the group of clusters and compute the **euclidean distance** from all the points in space to the centroids of the cluster using the `dist` function in SciPy.

You can see that the first cluster has only one column since it has only one cluster in it, and the second cluster has two columns as it has two clusters in it:

```
>>> dist = [np.min(D,axis=1) for D in D_k]
>>> print '-----with 1st cluster------'
>>> print dist[0][:5]
>>> print '-----with 2nd cluster------'
>>> print dist[1][:5]


-----with 1st cluster------
```

```
[ 3044.71049474
5027.61602297
4359.59802141
5536.23755972
2164.54439528]
-----with 2nd cluster------
[  663.5918709
1329.9326654
661.83208396
1839.28608809
5862.36131557]
```

As we have the distance of each of the observed points from the different centroids, we can find the minimum distance of each observed point from the closest centroid.

You can see in the preceding code that the first and second clusters contain a single value, which is the distance from the centroid.

We'll now compute the average of the sum of the square of the distance:

```
>>> avgWithinSS = [sum(d)/df.values.shape[0] for d in dist]
>>> avgWithinSS

[6534.9809626620136,
 2790.2101193300132,
 1890.9166153060164,
 1438.7793254224125,
 1120.3902815703975,
 903.15438285732,
 740.45942949866003,
 645.91915410445336,
 604.37878538964185]
```

Each of the values in the array is the average sum of the square that has one cluster to a group of ten clusters.

We'll now plot the **elbow curve** (this is the point at which a curve starts flattening out) for the k-means clustering using this data:

```
>>> #Choosing the cluster number
>>> kIdx = 2

>>> # plot elbow curve
>>> fig = plt.figure()

>>> ax = fig.add_subplot(111)

>>> ax.plot(K, avgWithinSS, 'b*-')

>>> ax.plot(K[kIdx], avgWithinSS[kIdx], marker='o', markersize=12,
      markeredgewidth=2, markeredgecolor='r', markerfacecolor='None')

>>> plt.grid(True)

>>> plt.xlabel('Number of clusters')

>>> plt.ylabel('Average within-cluster sum of squares')

>>> tt = plt.title('Elbow for K-Means clustering')
```

After the preceding code is executed we'll get the following output:

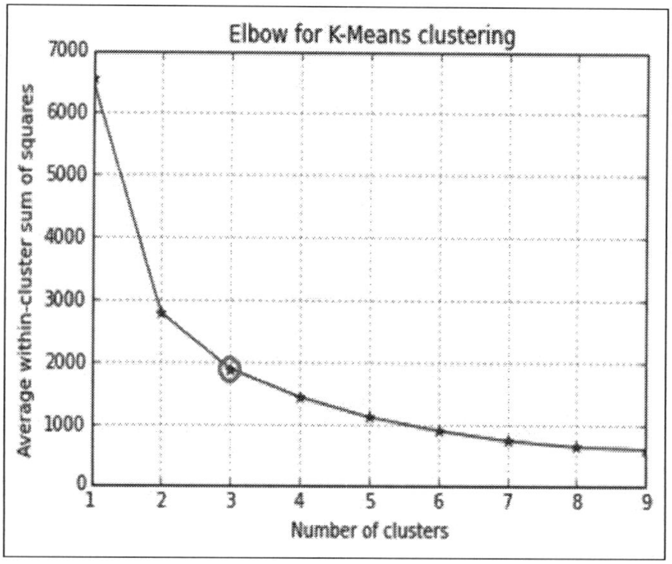

By looking at the curve, we can see that there is big jump from one cluster to the other, and then a significant jump from cluster `2` to cluster `3`. There is a slight jump from cluster `3` to cluster `4`, and then the jump to the subsequent number of clusters is very small. Let's fix the elbow point at cluster `3` and create three clusters to segment the countries.

Clustering the countries

We'll now apply the k-means algorithm to cluster the countries together:

```
>>> km = KMeans(3, init='k-means++', random_state = 3425) # initialize
>>> km.fit(df.values)
>>> df['countrySegment'] = km.predict(df.values)
>>> df[:5]
```

After the preceding code is executed we'll get the following output:

	lifeMale	lifeFemale	infantMortality	GDPperCapita	countrySegment
0	45.0	46.0	154	2848	1
1	68.0	74.0	32	863	1
2	67.5	70.3	44	1531	1
5	44.9	48.1	124	355	1
7	69.6	76.8	22	8055	0

Let's find the average GDP per capita for each country segment:

```
>>> df.groupby('countrySegment').GDPperCapita.mean()
>>> countrySegment
0     13800.586207
1      1624.538462
2     29681.625000
Name: GDPperCapita, dtype: float64
```

We can see that cluster `2` has the highest average GDP per capita and we can assume that this includes developed countries. Cluster `0` has the second highest GDP, we can assume this includes developing countries, and finally, cluster `1` has a very low average GDP per capita. We can assume this includes developed nations:

```
>>> clust_map = {
        0:'Developing',
        1:'Under Developed',
        2:'Developed'
   }

>>> df.countrySegment = df.countrySegment.map(clust_map)
>>> df[:10]
```

After the preceding code is executed we'll get the following output:

	lifeMale	lifeFemale	infantMortality	GDPperCapita	countrySegment
0	45.0	46.0	154	2848	Under Developed
1	68.0	74.0	32	863	Under Developed
2	67.5	70.3	44	1531	Under Developed
5	44.9	48.1	124	355	Under Developed
7	69.6	76.8	22	8055	Developing
8	67.2	74.0	25	354	Under Developed
9	75.4	81.2	6	20046	Developing
10	73.7	80.1	6	29006	Developed
11	66.5	74.5	33	321	Under Developed
12	70.5	77.1	14	12545	Developing

Let's see the GDP versus infant mortality rate of the countries for each of the clusters:

```
>>> d_color = {
        'Developing':'y',
        'Under Developed':'r',
        'Developed':'g'
   }


>>> fig, ax = plt.subplots()
>>> for clust in clust_map.values():
        color = d_color[clust]
        df[df.countrySegment == clust].plot(kind='scatter',
             x='GDPperCapita', y='infantMortality', label=clust,
             ax=ax, color=color)
>>> handles, labels = ax.get_legend_handles_labels()
>>> _ = ax.legend(handles, labels, loc="upper right")
```

After the preceding code is executed we'll get the following output:

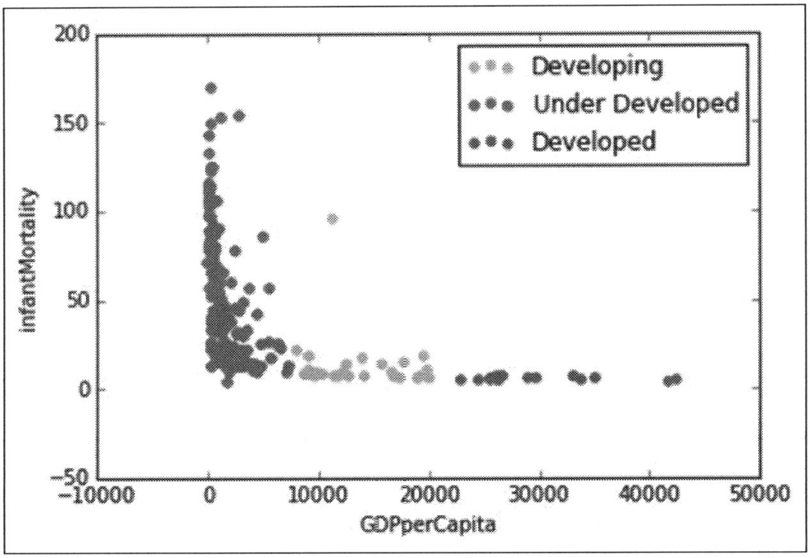

We can see from the preceding graph that when the GDP is low, the `infantMortality` rate is really high, and as the GDP increases, the `InfantMortality` rate decreases.

We can also clearly see that the countries in green are the underdeveloped nations, the one in dark blue are the developing nations, and the ones in red are the developed nations.

Let's see the life expectancy of males with respect to the GDP:

```
>>> fig, ax = plt.subplots()
>>> for clust in clust_map.values():
       color = d_color[clust]
       df[df.countrySegment == clust].plot(kind='scatter',
                   x='GDPperCapita', y='lifeMale', label=clust,
                   ax=ax, color=color)
>>> handles, labels = ax.get_legend_handles_labels()
>>> _ = ax.legend(handles, labels, loc="lower right")
```

After the preceding code is executed we'll get the following output:

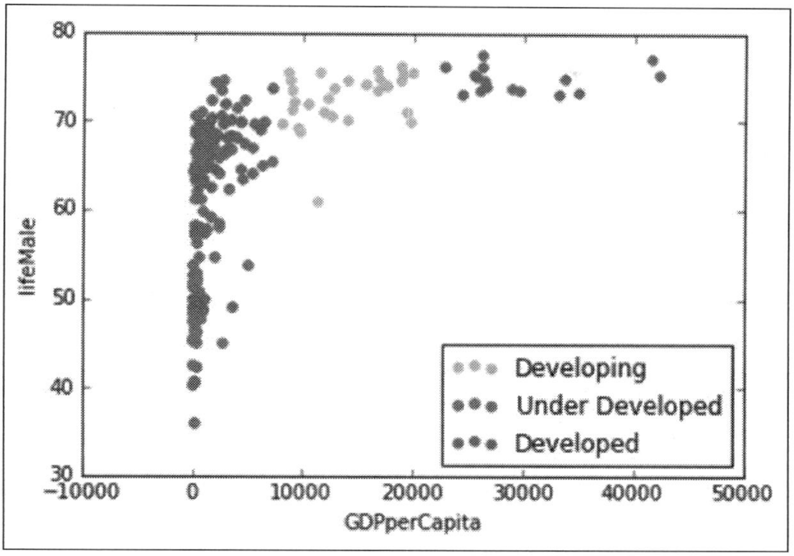

We can see that the life expectancy of males also increases with the GDP for the different kinds of nations.

Now, for the life expectancy of females with regard to the GDP, we'll use this code:

```
>>> fig, ax = plt.subplots()
>>> for clust in clust_map.values():
       color = d_color[clust]
       df[df.countrySegment == clust].plot(kind='scatter',
                                  x='GDPperCapita', y='lifeFemale',
                                  label=clust, ax=ax, color=color)
>>> handles, labels = ax.get_legend_handles_labels()
>>> _ = ax.legend(handles, labels, loc="lower right")
```

After the preceding code is executed we'll get the following output:

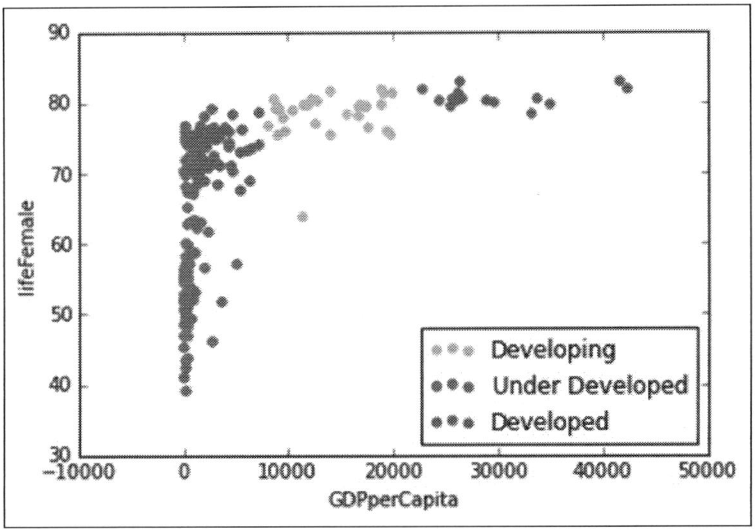

There is a similar trend for females too.

Summary

In this chapter, you were made to understand the concept of clustering and learned an unsupervised learning technique called the k-means technique. You also learned how to determine the number of clusters before segmenting data using k-means, and finally, you saw the results of this using the k-means clustering.

In the next chapter, you'll learn how to explore unstructured data and use text mining techniques on unstructured data.

11
Analyzing Unstructured Data with Text Mining

There is a lot of unstructured data out there, such as news articles, customer feedbacks, Twitter tweets and so on, that contains information and needs to be analyzed. Text mining is a data mining technique that helps us to perform an analysis of this unstructured data.

In this chapter, we'll learn the following:

- Preprocessing data
- Plotting a wordcloud from data
- Word and sentence tokenization
- Tagging parts of speech
- Stemming and lemmatization
- Applying Stanford Named Entity Recognizer

Preprocessing data

We'll use the reviews of Mad Max: Fury Road from the online portals of BBC, Forbes, Guardian, and Movie Pilot.

We'll extensively use the **Natural Language Toolkit** (**NLTK**) package of Python in this chapter for text mining. You can install it with the help of instructions at `http://www.nltk.org/install.html`

We'll be performing the following actions on data:

- Removing punctuation
- Removing numbers
- Converting text to lowercase
- Removing the most common words in the English language, called stop words, such as `be`, `the`, `on`, and so on.

Let's start by loading the data first:

```
>>> data = {}


>>> #data['bbc'] =


>>> data['bbc'] = open('./Data/madmax_review/bbc.txt','r').read()


>>> data['forbes'] =
               open('./Data/madmax_review/forbes.txt','r').read()


>>> data['guardian'] =
               open('./Data/madmax_review/guardian.txt','r').read()


>>> data['moviepilot'] =
               open('./Data/madmax_review/moviepilot.txt','r').read()


>>> # We'll convert the text to lower case


>>> #Conversion to lower case
>>> for k in data.keys():
>>>     data[k] = data[k].lower()


>>> print data['bbc'][:800]
```

```
when the creator of a 1970s/1980s blockbuster franchise decides to dust it off again
decades later, the results can be ... well, the results can be the phantom menace,
prometheus, or indiana jones and the kingdom of the crystal skull: legacy-tarnishing
messes that fans try to forget. and then there's mad max: fury road. the first mad max
film to be made by george miller in 30 years, this belated reboot is missing its original
star, mel gibson, and its director has spent the intervening years on such children's fare
as happy feet and babe: pig in the city. you might assume, then, that fury road would join
the phantom menace on the scrapheap reserved for unloved revivals. and yet, somehow, this
explosive new barrage of action and eccentricity isn't only a faithful continuation of the
series,
```

Now, we'll remove the punctuation from the text as we'll be analyzing the frequency of each word:

```
>>> #Removing punctuation
>>> for k in data.keys():
        data[k] = re.sub(r'[-./?!,":;()\']',' ',data[k])


>>> print data['bbc'][:800]
```

```
when the creator of a 1970s 1980s blockbuster franchise decides to dust it off again
decades later  the results can be     well  the results can be the phantom menace
prometheus  or indiana jones and the kingdom of the crystal skull  legacy tarnishing
messes that fans try to forget  and then there s mad max  fury road  the first mad max
film to be made by george miller in 30 years  this belated reboot is missing its original
star  mel gibson  and its director has spent the intervening years on such children s fare
as happy feet and babe  pig in the city  you might assume  then  that fury road would join
the phantom menace on the scrapheap reserved for unloved revivals  and yet  somehow  this
explosive new barrage of action and eccentricity isn t only a faithful continuation of the
series
```

We'll remove the numbers from the text:

```
>>> #Removing number
>>> for k in data.keys():
        data[k] = re.sub('[-|0-9]',' ',data[k])


>>> print data['bbc'][:800]
```

```
when the creator of a     s     s blockbuster franchise decides to dust it off again
decades later  the results can be     well  the results can be the phantom menace
prometheus  or indiana jones and the kingdom of the crystal skull  legacy tarnishing
messes that fans try to forget  and then there s mad max  fury road  the first mad max
film to be made by george miller in    years  this belated reboot is missing its original
star  mel gibson  and its director has spent the intervening years on such children s fare
as happy feet and babe  pig in the city  you might assume  then  that fury road would join
the phantom menace on the scrapheap reserved for unloved revivals  and yet  somehow  this
explosive new barrage of action and eccentricity isn t only a faithful continuation of the
series
```

We'll need to download and install the `stopwords` package for `nltk`, which can be done using the following command:

```
>>> import nltk
>>> nltk.download_gui()
```

You'll get the following GUI from which you can install the stopwords:

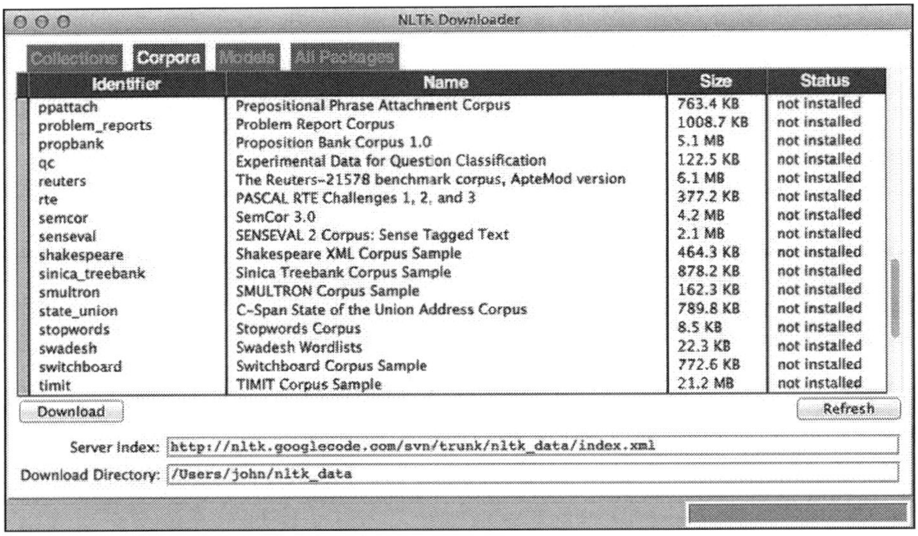

Post this, we'll remove commonly occurring stop words, such as `ours`, `yours`, `that`, `this`, and so on:

```
>>> #Removing stopwords
>>> for k in data.keys():
        data[k] = data[k].split()


>>> stopwords_list = stopwords.words('english')
>>> stopwords_list = stopwords_list +
                        ['mad','max','film','fury','miller','road']


>>> for k in data.keys():
```

```
        data[k] = [ w for w in data[k] if not w in stopwords_list ]

>>> print data['bbc'][:80]

['creator', 'blockbuster', 'franchise', 'decides', 'dust',
'decades', 'later', 'results', 'well', 'results', 'phantom',
'menace', 'prometheus', 'indiana', 'jones', 'kingdom', 'crystal',
'skull', 'legacy', 'tarnishing', 'messes', 'fans', 'try',
'forget', 'first', 'made', 'george', 'years', 'belated', 'reboot',
'missing', 'original', 'star', 'mel', 'gibson', 'director',
'spent', 'intervening', 'years', 'children', 'fare', 'happy',
'feet', 'babe', 'pig', 'city', 'might', 'assume', 'would', 'join',
'phantom', 'menace', 'scrapheap', 'reserved', 'unloved',
'revivals', 'yet', 'somehow', 'explosive', 'new', 'barrage',
'action', 'eccentricity', 'isn', 'faithful', 'continuation',
'series', 'also', 'exhilarating', 'high', 'point', 'made',
'trilogy', 'three', 'decades', 'ago', 'seems', 'revving',
'benefit', 'uninitiated']
```

Creating a wordcloud

A worldcloud is a collage of words and those words that are bigger in size have a high frequency.

You can download wordcloud with the following command if you use Ubuntu:

```
$ pip install git+git://github.com/amueller/word_cloud.git
```

You can follow the instructions to do this by referring to `https://github.com/amueller/word_cloud`.

Let's plot the wordcloud for the BBC by using the following code:

```
>>> wordcloud = WordCloud(width = 1000, height = 500)
                            .generate(' '.join(data['bbc']))


>>> plt.figure(figsize=(15,8))


>>> plt.imshow(wordcloud)


>>> plt.axis("off")


>>> plt.show()
```

From the preceding wordcloud, we can make out that there are mentions about the long duration between the 80s Mad Max and the current Mad Max. The article talks about Mel Gibson, the cars, and the villain Immortan Joe as these are the most frequently occurring keywords. There is also an emphasis on different aspects of the movie given by the *one* keyword

Now, let's see how the wordcloud looks like for Forbes by using this code:

```
>>> wordcloud = WordCloud(width = 1000, height = 500)
                          .generate(' '.join(data['forbes']))
>>> plt.figure(figsize=(15,8))
>>> plt.imshow(wordcloud)
>>> plt.axis("off")
>>> plt.show()
```

Forbes talks more about the female characters.

This is what the wordcloud for The Guardian looks like:

```
>>> wordcloud = WordCloud(width = 1000, height = 500)
                              .generate(' '.join(data['guardian']))


>>> plt.figure(figsize=(15,8))


>>> plt.imshow(wordcloud)


>>> plt.axis("off")


>>> plt.show()
```

The Guardian lays an emphasis on women and water. If you have seen the movie, then you'll understand that The Guardian emphasizes the female characters and the lack of water in their wasteland.

Finally, this is what the word cloud looks like for moviepilot:

```
>>> wordcloud = WordCloud(width = 1000, height = 500)
                          .generate(' '.join(data['moviepilot']))


>>> plt.figure(figsize=(15,8))


>>> plt.imshow(wordcloud)


>>> plt.axis("off")


>>> plt.show()
```

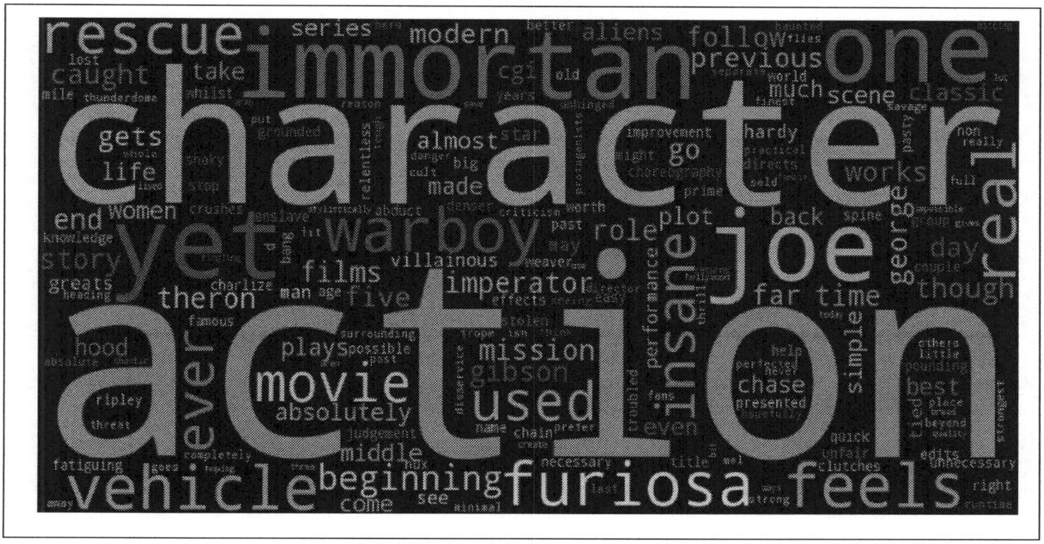

The http://moviepilot.com/ emphasizes the character of Immortan Joe, the characters in general, and the war boys shown in the film.

Word and sentence tokenization

We have dealt with word tokenization previously, but we can perform this using NLTK as well as sentence tokenization, which is quite tricky, as the English language has period symbols for abbreviations and other purposes. Thankfully, the sentence tokenizer is a instance of **PunktSentenceTokenizer** from the `tokenize.punkt` module of `nltk`, which helps in tokenizing sentences.

Let's look at word tokenization using this code:

```
>>> #Loading the forbes data
>>> data = open('./Data/madmax_review/forbes.txt','r').read()


>>> word_data = nltk.word_tokenize(data)
>>> word_data[:15]
['Pundits',
 'and',
 'critics',
 'like',
 'to',
 'blame',
 'the',
 'twin',
 'successes',
 'of',
 'Jaws',
 'and',
 'Star',
 'Wars',
 'for']
```

Now, let's perform the sentence tokenization of the Forbes article:

```
>>> sent_tokenize(data)[:5]


['Pundits and critics like to blame the twin successes of Jaws and
Star Wars for turning Hollywood into something of a blockbuster
factory.', "We can debate the merits of said accusation, but for
me it comes down to one simple factor: If every would-be
blockbuster, or even most would-be blockbusters were as good as
Jaws and/or Star Wars, I imagine most of us wouldn't be
complaining nearly as much.", "That brings us to George Miller's
Mad Max: Fury Road.", "It is a revamp/reboot/sequel for a 30-year
old franchise, directed by the original helmer who hasn't been
culturally relevant in decades, featuring a new and somewhat
flavor-of-the-month actor, and seemingly only existing because of
the fact that the property is vaguely known and thus has a token
amount of built-in awareness.", "If  you think that sounds like
the kind of thing I complain about rather regularly, you'd be
correct."]
```

You can see that each of the sentences is an element of the list after sentence tokenization has been performed.

Parts of speech tagging

Parts of speech tagging is one of the important tasks of text analysis. It helps tag each word based on the context of a sentence or the role that a word plays in a sentence.

Let's see how to perform part of speech tagging using `nltk`:

```
>>> pos_word_data = nltk.pos_tag(word_data)

>>> pos_word_data[ : 10]

[('Pundits', 'NNS'),
 ('and', 'CC'),
 ('critics', 'NNS'),
 ('like', 'IN'),
 ('to', 'TO'),
 ('blame', 'VB'),
 ('the', 'DT'),
 ('twin', 'NN'),
 ('successes', 'NNS'),
 ('of', 'IN')]
```

You can see tags, such as `NNS`, `CC`, `IN` , `TO`, `DT`, and `NN`. Let's see what they mean using this code:

```
>>> nltk.help.upenn_tagset('NNS')


NNS: noun, common, plural
    undergraduates scotches bric-a-brac products bodyguards facets
    coasts divestitures storehouses designs clubs fragrances
    averages subjectivists apprehensions muses factory-jobs


>>> nltk.help.upenn_tagset('NN')


NN: noun, common, singular or mass
    common-carrier cabbage knuckle-duster Casino afghan shed
    thermostat investment slide humour falloff slick wind hyena
    override subhumanity machinist


>>> nltk.help.upenn_tagset('IN')


IN: preposition or conjunction, subordinating
    astride among uppon whether out inside pro despite on by
    throughout below within for towards near behind atop around if
    like until below next into if beside


>>> nltk.help.upenn_tagset('TO')


TO: "to" as preposition or infinitive marker
    to


>>> nltk.help.upenn_tagset('DT')


DT: determiner
    all an another any both del each either every half la many
    much nary neither no some such that the them these this those


>>> nltk.help.upenn_tagset('CC')


CC: conjunction, coordinating
    & 'n and both but either et for less minus neither nor or plus
    so therefore times v. versus vs. whether yet
```

You can get more information about the tags used in the preceding code at `https://www.ling.upenn.edu/courses/Fall_2003/ling001/penn_treebank_pos.html`.

You can see words used in the preceding code are tagged well. This tagging can help us create heuristics over data and then extract information out of it. For example, we can take out all the nouns in our article and analyze the theme of the article.

Stemming and lemmatization

Text documents can contain words in different forms, such as play, playing, and played. They are similar and they have a common root.

Stemming and lemmatization are techniques that are used to find these common roots. Finding the roots will help us count, play, playing, and played as a single entity as all the words talk about play.

Stemming is more of a crude form of arriving at the root of a word; so, in the case of the preceding example, playing would be reduced to play. Lemmatization brings into context words, such as worse and bad, that can have a common bad root.

Stemming

Stemming is a process of reducing a word to its root form. The root form is not a word by itself, but words can be formed by adding the right suffix to it.

If you take fish, fishes, and fishing, they all can be stemmed to fishing. Also, study, studying, and studies can be stemmed to study, which is not a part of the English language.

There are various types of stemming algorithms, such as Porter, Lancaster, Snowball, and so on.

Porter is the most commonly used stemmer. It is also one of the gentlest stemmers and is computationally intensive with regard to algorithms.

The Snowball algorithm is regarded as an improvement over Porter. Porter himself, in fact, admits that the Snowball algorithm is better than his algorithm.

Lancaster is a more aggressive stemming algorithm. Porter and Snowball stemming is understandable by readers, but Lancaster isn't, as it makes words more obscure. Lancaster is considered to be the fastest algorithm among the three and it will work very well with a large set of words, but if you are looking for something more distinctive, then Lancaster is not for you.

Let's try out the Porter Stemming Algorithm using this code:

```
>>> from nltk.stem.porter import PorterStemmer

>>> porter_stemmer = PorterStemmer()

>>> for w in word_data[:20]:
        print "Actual: %s  Stem: %s"  % (w,porter_stemmer.stem(w))

Actual: Pundits  Stem: Pundit
Actual: and  Stem: and
Actual: critics  Stem: critic
Actual: like  Stem: like
Actual: to  Stem: to
Actual: blame  Stem: blame
Actual: the  Stem: the
Actual: twin  Stem: twin
Actual: successes  Stem: success
Actual: of  Stem: of
Actual: Jaws  Stem: Jaw
Actual: and  Stem: and
Actual: Star  Stem: Star
Actual: Wars  Stem: War
Actual: for  Stem: for
Actual: turning  Stem: turn
Actual: Hollywood  Stem: Hollywood
Actual: into  Stem: into
Actual: something  Stem: someth
Actual: of  Stem: of
```

Let's try out the Lancaster Algorithm using this code:

```
>>> from nltk.stem.lancaster import LancasterStemmer

>>> lancaster_stemmer = LancasterStemmer()

>>> for w in word_data[:20]:
```

```
        print "Actual: %s  Stem: %s"  % (w,lancaster_stemmer.stem(w))

Actual: Pundits  Stem: pundit
Actual: and  Stem: and
Actual: critics  Stem: crit
Actual: like  Stem: lik
Actual: to  Stem: to
Actual: blame  Stem: blam
Actual: the  Stem: the
Actual: twin  Stem: twin
Actual: successes  Stem: success
Actual: of  Stem: of
Actual: Jaws  Stem: jaw
Actual: and  Stem: and
Actual: Star  Stem: star
Actual: Wars  Stem: war
Actual: for  Stem: for
Actual: turning  Stem: turn
Actual: Hollywood  Stem: hollywood
Actual: into  Stem: into
Actual: something  Stem: someth
Actual: of  Stem: of
```

Now, let's try out the Snowball Algorithm using this code:

```
>>> from nltk.stem.snowball import SnowballStemmer

>>> snowball_stemmer = SnowballStemmer("english")

>>> for w in word_data[:20]:
        print "Actual: %s  Stem: %s"  % (w,snowball_stemmer.stem(w))

Actual: Pundits  Stem: pundit
Actual: and  Stem: and
Actual: critics  Stem: critic
Actual: like  Stem: like
Actual: to  Stem: to
```

```
Actual: blame  Stem: blame
Actual: the  Stem: the
Actual: twin  Stem: twin
Actual: successes  Stem: success
Actual: of  Stem: of
Actual: Jaws  Stem: jaw
Actual: and  Stem: and
Actual: Star  Stem: star
Actual: Wars  Stem: war
Actual: for  Stem: for
Actual: turning  Stem: turn
Actual: Hollywood  Stem: hollywood
Actual: into  Stem: into
Actual: something  Stem: someth
Actual: of  Stem: of
```

Lemmatization

Lemmatization is similar to stemming but unlike stemming, it brings in a context of the word.

A lemmatization-based algorithm will match a train to the word locomotive, but a stemming algorithm won't be able to do this. A lemmatization algorithm makes use of a dictionary to link up words.

The `WordNet` is a lexical database for English by Princeton, and we'll use their lemmatization techniques:

```
Actual: Pundits  Lemma: Pundits
Actual: and  Lemma: and
Actual: critics  Lemma: critic
Actual: like  Lemma: like
Actual: to  Lemma: to
Actual: blame  Lemma: blame
Actual: the  Lemma: the
Actual: twin  Lemma: twin
```

```
Actual: successes  Lemma: success
Actual: of  Lemma: of
Actual: Jaws  Lemma: Jaws
Actual: and  Lemma: and
Actual: Star  Lemma: Star
Actual: Wars  Lemma: Wars
Actual: for  Lemma: for
Actual: turning  Lemma: turning
Actual: Hollywood  Lemma: Hollywood
Actual: into  Lemma: into
Actual: something  Lemma: something
Actual: of  Lemma: of
Actual: a  Lemma: a
Actual: blockbuster  Lemma: blockbuster
Actual: factory  Lemma: factory
Actual: .  Lemma: .
Actual: We  Lemma: We
Actual: can  Lemma: can
Actual: debate  Lemma: debate
Actual: the  Lemma: the
Actual: merits  Lemma: merit
Actual: of  Lemma: of
```

The Stanford Named Entity Recognizer

The Named Entity Recognizer is a task that classifies the elements of a sentence into categories, such as person, organization, location, and so on. Stanford Named Entity Recognizer is one of the most popular out there and can be found at `http://nlp.stanford.edu/`.

The Stanford Named Entity Recognizer can be downloaded at `http://nlp.stanford.edu/software/stanford-ner-2014-06-16.zip`.

The following code shows the Stanford Named Entity Recognizer in action:

```
>>> from nltk.tag.stanford import NERTagger.

>>> st = NERTagger('./lib/stanford-ner
         /classifiers/english.all.3class.distsim.crf.ser.gz',
         './lib/stanford-ner/stanford-ner.jar')

>>> st.tag('''Barrack Obama is the president of the United States of
           America . His father is from Kenya and Mother from United
           States of America.
           He has two daughters with his wife. He has strong
           opposition in Congress due to Republicans'''.split())


[[(u'Barrack', u'PERSON'),
  (u'Obama', u'PERSON'),
  (u'is', u'O'),
  (u'the', u'O'),
  (u'president', u'O'),
  (u'of', u'O'),
  (u'the', u'O'),
  (u'United', u'LOCATION'),
  (u'States', u'LOCATION'),
  (u'of', u'LOCATION'),
  (u'America', u'LOCATION'),
  (u'.', u'O')],
 [(u'His', u'O'),
  (u'father', u'O'),
  (u'is', u'O'),
  (u'from', u'O'),
  (u'Kenya', u'LOCATION'),
  (u'and', u'O'),
  (u'Mother', u'O'),
  (u'from', u'O'),
  (u'United', u'LOCATION'),
  (u'States', u'LOCATION'),
  (u'of', u'O'),
```

```
(u'America.', u'O'),
(u'He', u'O'),
(u'has', u'O'),
(u'two', u'O'),
(u'daughters', u'O'),
(u'with', u'O'),
(u'his', u'O'),
(u'wife.', u'O'),
(u'He', u'O'),
(u'has', u'O'),
(u'strong', u'O'),
(u'opposition', u'O'),
(u'in', u'O'),
(u'Congress', u'ORGANIZATION'),
(u'due', u'O'),
(u'to', u'O'),
(u'Republicans', u'O')]]
```

You can see that the Stanford Named Entity Tagger does a pretty good job of tagging a `PERSON`, `LOCATION`, and `ORGANIZATION`.

Performing sentiment analysis on world leaders using Twitter

Before we start analyzing tweets, we'll need to install the `Twython` package of Python, which helps interact with the Twitter API to get tweets from Twitter. This can be downloaded from `https://github.com/ryanmcgrath/twython`.

Also, you need to get the consumer key and consumer secret key from `https://apps.twitter.com/app/new`.

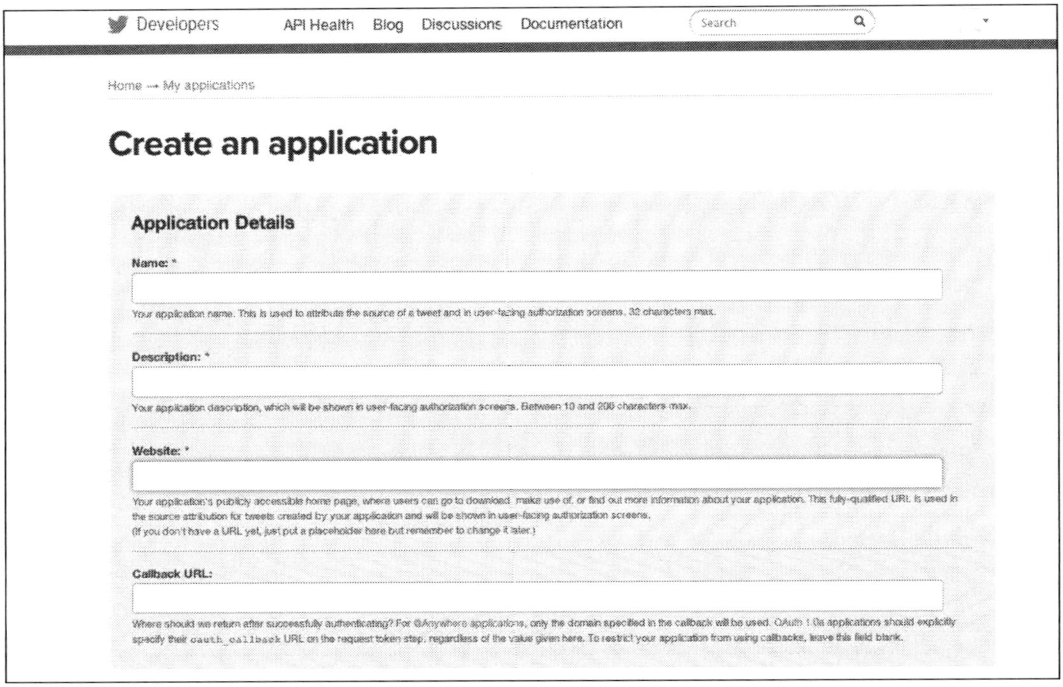

Once you have details about your app, you'll get the consumer key and consumer secret key:

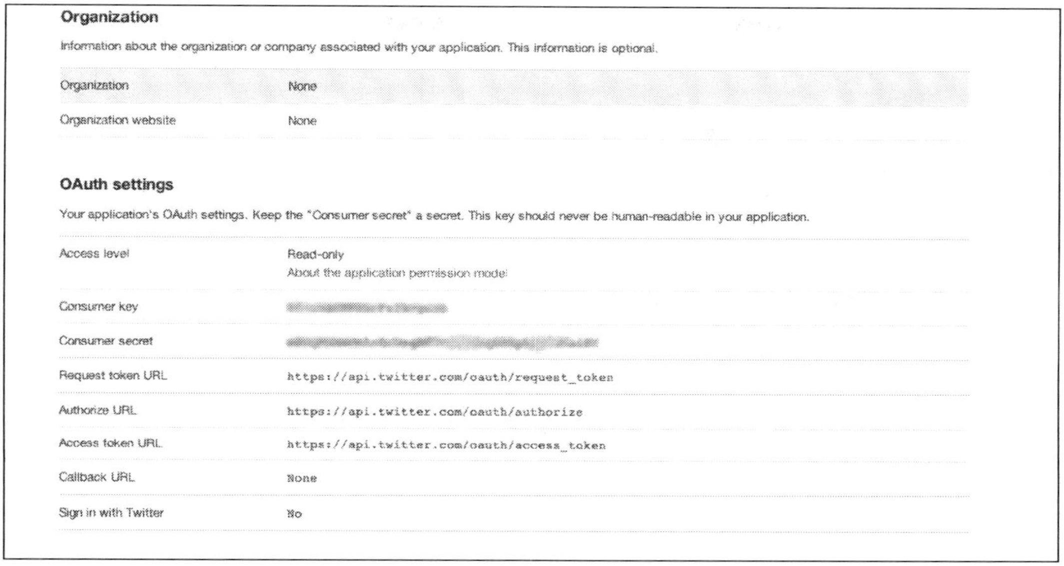

After this, go to the Key and Access Tokens tab to generate your access token:

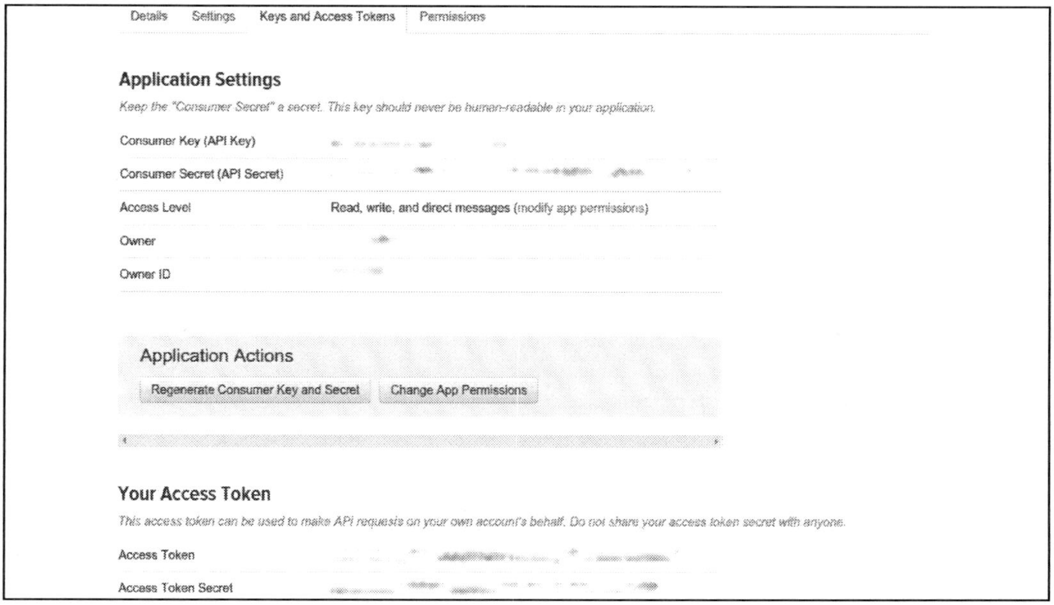

Once you have the required keys, we'll add the details to the following code:

```
#Please provide your keys here


TWITTER_APP_KEY = 'XXXXXXXXXXXXXXXXXXXXXX'
TWITTER_APP_KEY_SECRET = 'XXXXXXXXXXXXXXXXXXXXXX'
TWITTER_ACCESS_TOKEN = 'XXXXXXXXXXXXXXXXXXXXXX' TWITTER_ACCESS_TOKEN_
SECRET = 'XXXXXXXXXXXXXXXXXXXXXX'


t = Twython(app_key=TWITTER_APP_KEY,
            app_secret=TWITTER_APP_KEY_SECRET,
            oauth_token=TWITTER_ACCESS_TOKEN,
            oauth_token_secret=TWITTER_ACCESS_TOKEN_SECRET)


def get_tweets(twython_object, query, n):
    count = 0
    result_generator = twython_object.cursor(twython_object.search,
                                             q = query)
    result_set = []
    for r in result_generator:
        result_set.append(r['text'])
        count += 1
        if count == n: break

    return result_set
```

Now, we have access to the tweets and can fetch them.

We'll analyze the sentiment of tweets from Obama, Putin, Modi, Xi Jin Ping, and David Cameron. Here are a few assumptions that we'll be making for our analysis:

1. The tweets are in English.
2. We set a limit of a maximum of 500 tweets.

You can load the tweets from the following JSON file:

```
>>> with open('./Data/politician_tweets.json', 'w') as fp:
>>> tweets=json.load(fp)
```

You can fetch fresh tweets of these politicians:

```
>>> tweets = {}
>>> max_tweets = 500
>>> tweets['obama'] = [re.sub(r'[-.#/?!,":;()\']',' ',tweet.lower())
                    for tweet in get_tweets(t,'#obama', max_tweets )]


>>> tweets['putin'] = [re.sub(r'[-.#/?!,":;()\']',' ',tweet.lower())
                    for tweet in get_tweets(t,'#putin', max_tweets )]


>>> tweets['modi'] = [re.sub(r'[-.#/?!,":;()\']',' ',tweet.lower())
                    for tweet in get_tweets(t,'#modi', max_tweets )]


>>> tweets['xijinping'] = [re.sub(r'[-.#/?!,":;()\']','
                    ',tweet.lower()) for tweet in
                    get_tweets(t,'#xijinping', max_tweets )]
>>> tweets['davidcameron'] = [re.sub(r'[-.#/?!,":;()\']','
                    ',tweet.lower()) for tweet in
                    get_tweets(t,'#davidcameron', max_tweets )]
```

Now, let's define a function to score the sentiments of the tweets. We have a positive and negative word list from Hu and Liu's lexicon at `http://www.cs.uic.edu/~liub/FBS/sentiment-analysis.html`.

This will be used to compare the tweets and give them a score. Every positive word that matches will be given a `+1` point and every negative score that is matched will be given a `-1` point:

```
>>> positive_words = open('./Data/positive-words.txt')
                     .read().split('\n')
>>> negative_words = open('./Data/negative-words.txt')
                     .read().split('\n')


>>> def sentiment_score(text, pos_list, neg_list):
    positive_score = 0
    negative_score = 0

    for w in text.split(' '):
        if w in pos_list: positive_score+=1
        if w in neg_list: negative_score+=1

    return positive_score - negative_score
```

Let's now score the sentiments of each tweet in the list:

```
>>> tweets_sentiment = {}


>>> tweets_sentiment['obama'] = [
                sentiment_score(tweet,positive_words,negative_words)
                for tweet in  tweets['obama'] ]


>>> tweets_sentiment['putin'] = [
                sentiment_score(tweet,positive_words,negative_words)
                for tweet in tweets['putin'] ]


>>> tweets_sentiment['modi'] = [
                sentiment_score(tweet,positive_words,negative_words)
                for tweet in tweets['modi'] ]


>>> tweets_sentiment['xijinping'] = [
                sentiment_score(tweet,positive_words,negative_words)
                for tweet in tweets['xijinping'] ]


>>> tweets_sentiment['davidcameron'] = [
                sentiment_score(tweet,positive_words,negative_words)
                for tweet in tweets['davidcameron'] ]
```

We have defined `dict` and called `tweets_sentiment` where we have scored the sentiments of each of the tweets for the politicians.

Now, as we have the sentiment score for each of the politicians, we'll now analyze the sentiments for each politician.

Let's see how people feel about Obama:

```
>>> obama = plt.hist(tweets_sentiment['obama'], 5,
                  facecolor='green', alpha=0.5)
>>> plt.xlabel('Sentiment Score')
>>> _=plt.xlim([-4,4])
```

After the preceding code is executed we'll get the following output:

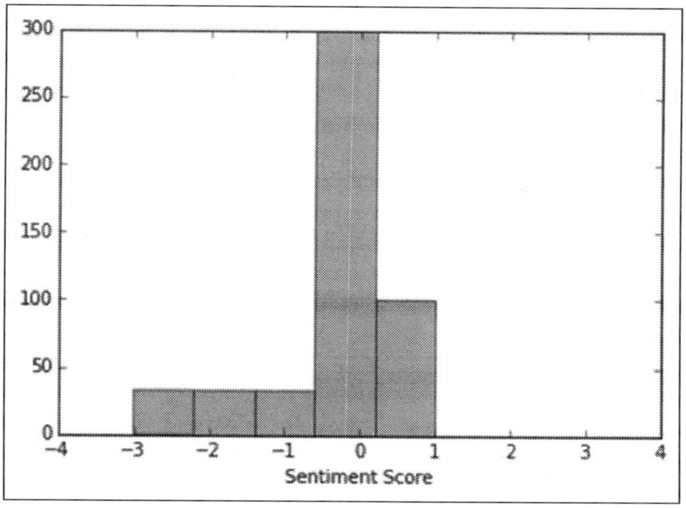

We mostly see neutral tweets about Obama.

Let's see the tweets for Putin:

```
>>> putin = plt.hist(tweets_sentiment['putin'], 5,
                    facecolor='green', alpha=0.5)
>>> plt.xlabel('Sentiment Score')
>>> _=plt.xlim([-4,4])
```

After the preceding code is executed we'll get the following output:

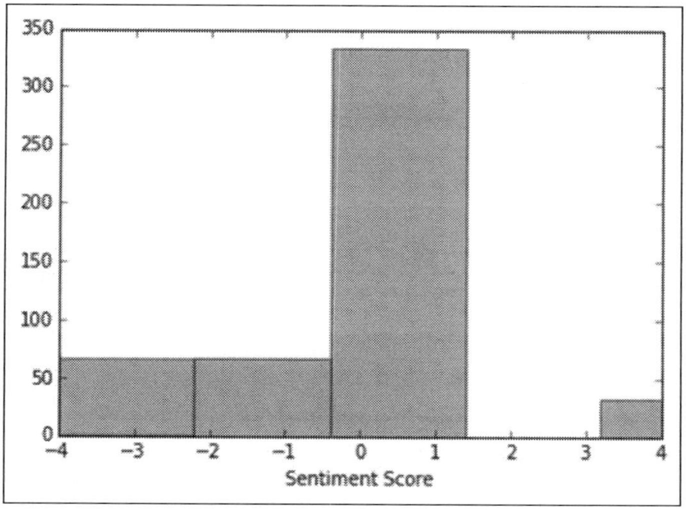

Most tweets are neutral with a slight negativity.

Let's see the tweets for Modi:

```
>>> modi = plt.hist(tweets_sentiment['modi'], 5,
                    facecolor='green', alpha=0.5)
>>> plt.xlabel('Sentiment Score')
>>> _=plt.xlim([-4,4])
```

After the preceding code is executed we'll get the following output:

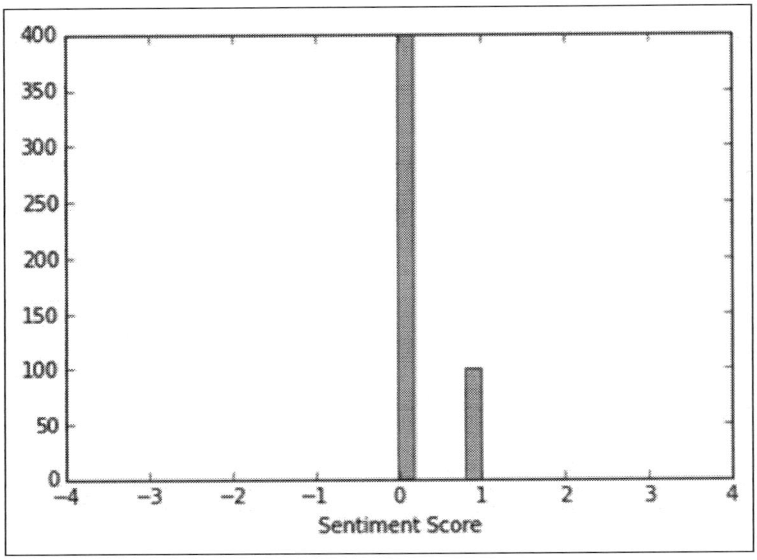

Most tweets are neutral for Modi with a slight positivity.

Let's see the tweets for Xi Jin Ping:

```
>>> xijinping = plt.hist(tweets_sentiment['xijinping'], 5,
                         facecolor='green', alpha=0.5)
>>> plt.xlabel('Sentiment Score')
>>> _=plt.xlim([-4,4])
```

After the preceding code is executed we'll get the following output:

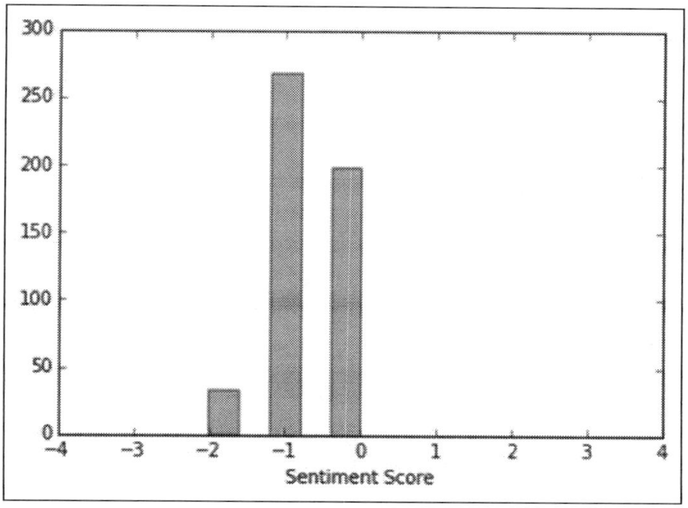

So, the tweets for Xi Jin Ping are mostly negative:

```
>>> davidcameron = plt.hist(tweets_sentiment['davidcameron'], 5,
                            facecolor='green', alpha=0.5)

>>> plt.xlabel('Sentiment Score')

>>> _=plt.xlim([-4,4])
```

After the preceding code is executed we'll get the following output:

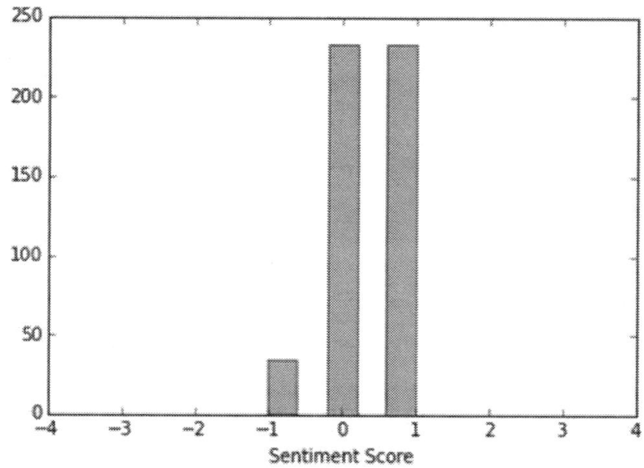

The tweets for David Cameron are more toward positive in nature.

Summary

In this chapter, you learned how to clean unstructured text data and then plotted a wordcloud out of this data. You learned how to tokenize words and sentences using NLTK. You learned how to perform parts of speech tagging and also the concepts of stemming and lemmatization. You were introduced to Named Entity Recognition and learned how to apply it using Stanford NER. Finally, you learned how to fetch tweets using the Twitter API and then perform sentiment analysis on it.

In the next chapter, you'll learn how to use Python in the world of big data.

12
Leveraging Python in the World of Big Data

We are generating more and more data day by day. We have generated more data this century than in the previous century and we are currently only 15 years into this century. big data is the new buzz word and everyone is talking about it. It brings new possibilities. Google Translate is able to translate any language, thanks to big data. We are able to decode our human genome due to it. We can predict the failure of a turbine and do the required maintenance on it because of big data.

There are three Vs of big data and they are defined as follows:

- **Volume**: This defines the size of the data. Facebook has petabytes of data on its users.
- **Velocity**: This is the rate at which data is generated.
- **Variety**: Data is not only in a tabular form. We can get data from text, images, and sound. Data comes in the form of JSON, XML, and other types as well.

Let's take a look at the following screenshot:

In this chapter, we'll learn how to use Python in the world of big data by doing the following:

- Understanding Hadoop
- Writing a MapReduce program in Python
- Using a Hadoop library

What is Hadoop?

According to the Apache Hadoop's website, Hadoop stores data in a distributed manner and helps in computing it. It has been designed to scale easily to any number of machines with the help of computing power and storage. Hadoop was created by Doug Cutting and Mike Cafarella in the year 2005. It was named after Doug Cutting's son's toy elephant.

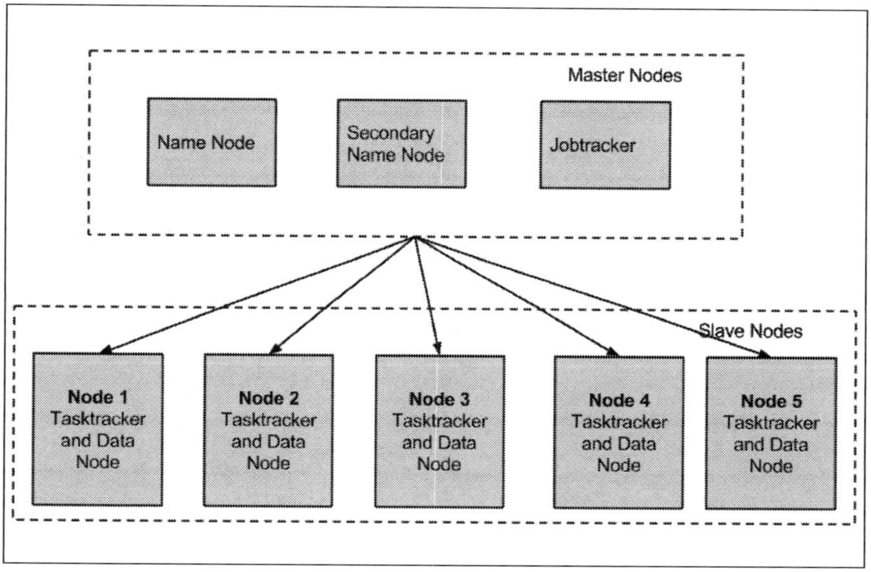

The programming model

Hadoop is a programming paradigm that takes a large distributed computation as a sequence of distributed operations on large datasets of key-value pairs. The MapReduce framework makes use of a cluster of machines and executes MapReduce jobs across these machines. There are two phases in MapReduce—a mapping phase and a reduce phase. The input data to MapReduce is key value pairs of data.

During the mapping phase, Hadoop splits the data into smaller pieces, which is then fed to the mappers. These mappers are distributed across machines within the cluster. Each mapper takes the input key-value pairs and generates intermediate key-value pairs by invoking a user-defined function within them.

After the mapper phase, Hadoop sorts the intermediate dataset by key and generates a set of key-value tuples so that all the values belonging to a particular key are together.

During the reduce phase, the reducer takes in the intermediate key-value pair and invokes a user-defined function, which then generates a output key-value pair. Hadoop distributes the reducers across the machines and assigns a set of key-value pairs to each of the reducers.

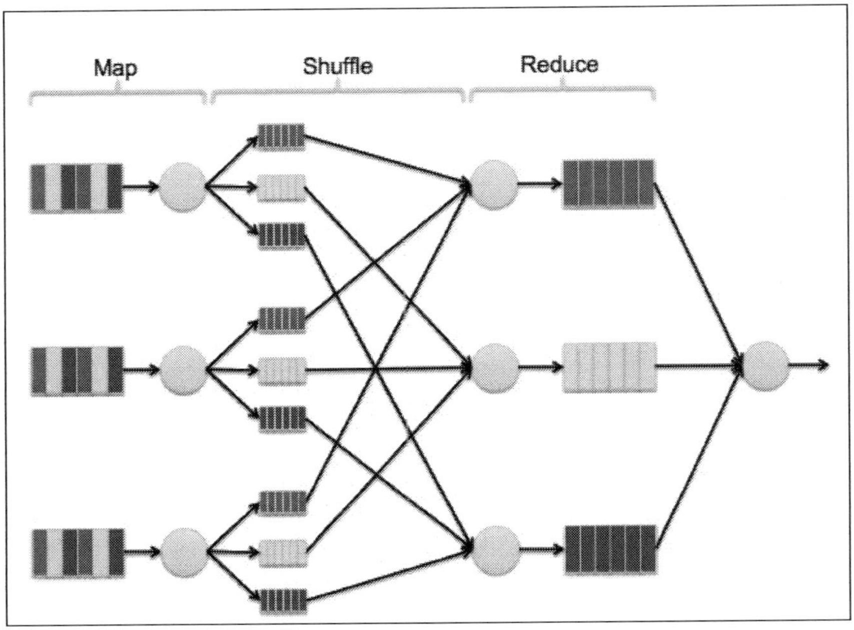

Data processing through MapReduce

The MapReduce architecture

MapReduce has a master-slave architecture, where the master is the JobTracker and TaskTracker is the slave. When a MapReduce program is submitted to Hadoop, the JobTracker assigns the mapping/reducing task to the TaskTracker and it takes of the task over executing the program.

The Hadoop DFS

Hadoop's distributed filesystem has been designed to store very large datasets in a distributed manner. It has been inspired by the Google File system, which is a proprietary distributed filesystem designed by Google. The data in HDFS is stored in a sequence of blocks, and all blocks are of the same size except for the last block. The block sizes are configurable in Hadoop.

Hadoop's DFS architecture

It also has a master/slave architecture where NameNode is the master machine and DataNode is the slave machine. The actual data is stored in the data node. The NameNode keeps a tab on where certain kinds of data is stored and whether it has the required replication. It also helps in managing a filesystem by creating, deleting, and moving directories and files in the filesystem.

Python MapReduce

Hadoop can be downloaded and installed from `https://hadoop.apache.org/`. We'll be using the Hadoop streaming API to execute our Python MapReduce program in Hadoop. The Hadoop Streaming API helps in using any program that has a standard input and output as a MapReduce program.

We'll be writing three MapReduce programs using Python, they are as follows:

- A basic word count
- Getting the sentiment Score of each review
- Getting the overall sentiment score from all the reviews

The basic word count

We'll start with the word count MapReduce. Save the following code in a `word_mapper.py` file:

```
import sys
for l in sys.stdin:
    # Trailing and Leading white space is removed
    l = l.strip()

    # words in the line is split
    word_tokens = l.split()

  # Key Value pair is outputted
  for w in word_tokens:
    print '%s\t%s' % (w, 1)
```

In the preceding mapper code, each line of the file is stripped of the leading and trailing white spaces. The line is then divided into tokens of words and then these tokens of words are outputted as a key value pair of `1`.

Save the following code in a `word_reducer.py` file:

```
from operator import itemgetter
import sys

current_word_token = None
counter = 0
word = None

# STDIN Input
for l in sys.stdin:
  # Trailing and Leading white space is removed
  l = l.strip()

  # input from the mapper is parsed
  word_token, counter = l.split('\t', 1)

  # count is converted to int
  try:
    counter = int(counter)
    except ValueError:
      # if count is not a number then ignore the line
      continue

  #Since Hadoop sorts the mapper output by key, the following
  # if else statement works
  if current_word_token == word_token:
    current_counter += counter
  else:
    if current_word_token:
      print '%s\t%s' % (current_word_token, current_counter)

      current_counter = counter
      current_word_token = word_token

# The last word is outputed
```

```
if current_word_token == word_token:
  print '%s\t%s' % (current_word_token, current_counter)
```

In the preceding code, we use the `current_word_token` parameter to keep track of the current word that is being counted. In the `for` loop, we use the `word_token` parameter and a counter to get the value out of the key-value pair. We then convert the counter to an `int` type.

In the `if/else` statement, if the `word_token` value is same as the previous instance, which is `current_word_token`, then we keep counting `else` statement's value. If it's a new word that has come as the output, then we output the word and its count. The last `if` statement is to output the last word.

We can check out if the mapper is working fine by using the following command:

```
$ echo 'dolly dolly max max jack tim max' | ./BigData/word_mapper.py
```

The output of the preceding command is shown as follows:

```
dolly1
dolly1
max1
max1
jack1
tim1
max1
```

Now, we can check if the reducer is also working fine by piping the reducer to the sorted list of the mapper output:

```
$ echo "dolly dolly max max jack tim max" | ./BigData/word_mapper.py
| sort -k1,1 | ./BigData/word_reducer.py
```

The output of the preceding command is shown as follows:

```
dolly2
jack1
max3
tim1
```

Now, let's try to apply the same code on a local file containing the summary of `mobydick`:

```
$ cat ./Data/mobydick_summary.txt | ./BigData/word_mapper.py | sort
  -k1,1  | ./BigData/word_reducer.py
```

The output of the preceding command is shown as follows:

```
a28
A2
abilities1
aboard3
about2
```

A sentiment score for each review

We had written a program in the preceding chapter to calculate the sentiment score. We'll extend this to write a MapReduce program to determine the sentiment score for each review. Write the following code in the `senti_mapper.py` file:

```
import sys
import re

positive_words = open('positive-words.txt').read().split('\n')
negative_words = open('negative-words.txt').read().split('\n')

def sentiment_score(text, pos_list, neg_list):
  positive_score = 0
  negative_score = 0

  for w in text.split(''):
    if w in pos_list: positive_score+=1
    if w in neg_list: negative_score+=1

  return positive_score - negative_score

for l in sys.stdin:
  # Trailing and Leading white space is removed
  l = l.strip()

  #Convert to lower case
  l = l.lower()

  #Getting the sentiment score
```

```
score = sentiment_score(l, positive_words, negative_words)


# Key Value pair is outputted
print '%s\t%s' % (l, score)
```

In the preceding code, we used the `sentiment_score` function from the preceding chapter. For each line, we strip the leading and trailing white spaces and then get the sentiment score for a review. Finally, we output a sentence and the score.

For this program, we don't require a reducer as we can calculate the sentiment in the mapper itself and we just have to output the sentiment score.

Let's test whether the mapper is working fine locally with a file containing the reviews for Jurassic World:

```
$ cat ./Data/jurassic_world_review.txt | ./BigData/senti_mapper.py


there is plenty here to divert, but little to leave you enraptored.
such is the fate of the sequel: bigger. louder. fewer teeth.0
if you limit your expectations for jurassic world to "more teeth," it
will deliver on that promise. if you dare to hope for anything more-
relatable characters, narrative coherence-you'll only set yourself up
for disappointment.-1
there's a problem when the most complex character in a film is the
dinosaur-2
not so much another bloated sequel as it is the fruition of dreams
deferred in the previous films. too bad the genre dictates that those
dreams are once again destined for disaster.-2
```

We can see that our program is able to calculate the sentiment score well.

The overall sentiment score

To calculate the overall sentiment score, we would require the reducer and we'll use the same mapper but with slight modifications.

Here is the mapper code that we'll use stored in the `overall_senti_mapper.py` file:

```
import sys
import hashlib


positive_words = open('./Data/positive-words.txt').
read().split('\n')
```

```
negative_words = open('./Data/negative-words.txt').
read().split('\n')


def sentiment_score(text, pos_list, neg_list):
  positive_score = 0
  negative_score = 0

  for w in text.split(''):
    if w in pos_list: positive_score+=1
    if w in neg_list: negative_score+=1
  return positive_score - negative_score


for l in sys.stdin:
  # Trailing and Leading white space is removed
  l = l.strip()
  #Convert to lower case
  l = l.lower()
  #Getting the sentiment score
  score = sentiment_score(l, positive_words, negative_words)
  #Hashing the review to use it as a string
  hash_object = hashlib.md5(l)
  # Key Value pair is outputted
  print '%s\t%s' % (hash_object.hexdigest(), score)
```

This mapper code is similar to the previous mapper code, but here we use the `MD5` hash library to review and then to get the output as the key.

Here is the reducer code that is utilized to determine the overall sentiments score of the movie. Store the following code in the `overall_senti_reducer.py` file:

```
from operator import itemgetter
import sys


total_score = 0


# STDIN Input
for l in sys.stdin:
  # input from the mapper is parsed
```

```
    key, score = l.split('\t', 1)
    # count is converted to int
    try:
      score = int(score)
    except ValueError:
      # if score is not a number then ignore the line
      continue

    #Updating the total score
    total_score += score

print '%s' % (total_score,)
```

In the preceding code, we strip the value containing the score and we then keep adding to the `total_score` variable. Finally, we output the `total_score` variable, which shows the sentiment of the movie.

Let's locally test the overall sentiment on Jurassic World, which is a good movie, and then test the sentiment for the movie, Unfinished Business, which was critically deemed poor:

```
$ cat ./Data/jurassic_world_review.txt |
    ./BigData/overall_senti_mapper.py | sort -k1,1 |
    ./BigData/overall_senti_reducer.py
19

$ cat ./Data/unfinished_business_review.txt |
    ./BigData/overall_senti_mapper.py | sort -k1,1 |
    ./BigData/overall_senti_reducer.py
-8
```

We can see that our code is working well and we also see that Jurassic World has a more positive score, which means that people have liked it a lot. On the contrary, Unfinished Business has a negative value, which shows that people haven't liked it much.

Deploying the MapReduce code on Hadoop

We'll create a directory for data on Moby Dick, Jurassic World, and Unfinished Business in the HDFS `tmp` folder:

```
$ Hadoop fs -mkdir /tmp/moby_dick
$ Hadoop fs -mkdir /tmp/jurassic_world
$ Hadoop fs -mkdir /tmp/unfinished_business
```

Let's check if the folders are created:

```
$ Hadoop fs -ls /tmp/


Found 6 items
drwxrwxrwx   - mapred Hadoop          0 2014-11-14 15:42 /tmp/
Hadoop-mapred
drwxr-xr-x   - samzer Hadoop          0 2015-06-18 18:31
/tmp/jurassic_world
drwxrwxrwx   - hdfs   Hadoop          0 2014-11-14 15:41 /tmp/mapred
drwxr-xr-x   - samzer Hadoop          0 2015-06-18 18:31
/tmp/moby_dick
drwxr-xr-x   - samzer Hadoop          0 2015-06-16 18:17
/tmp/temp635459726
drwxr-xr-x   - samzer Hadoop          0 2015-06-18 18:31
/tmp/unfinished_business
```

Once the folders are created, let's copy the data files to the respective folders.

```
$ Hadoop fs -copyFromLocal ./Data/mobydick_summary.txt /tmp/moby_dick
$ Hadoop fs -copyFromLocal ./Data/jurassic_world_review.txt
/tmp/jurassic_world
$ Hadoop fs -copyFromLocal ./Data/unfinished_business_review.txt
/tmp/unfinished_business
```

Let's verify that the file is copied:

```
$ Hadoop fs -ls /tmp/moby_dick
$ Hadoop fs -ls /tmp/jurassic_world
$ Hadoop fs -ls /tmp/unfinished_business
Found 1 items
-rw-r--r--   3 samzer Hadoop       5973 2015-06-18 18:34
/tmp/moby_dick/mobydick_summary.txt
Found 1 items
```

```
-rw-r--r--   3 samzer Hadoop       3185 2015-06-18 18:34
/tmp/jurassic_world/jurassic_world_review.txt
Found 1 items
-rw-r--r--   3 samzer Hadoop       2294 2015-06-18 18:34
/tmp/unfinished_business/unfinished_business_review.txt
```

We can see that files have been copied successfully.

With the following command, we'll execute our mapper and reducer's script in Hadoop. In this command, we define the mapper, reducer, input, and output file locations, and then use Hadoop streaming to execute our scripts.

Let's execute the word count program first:

```
$ Hadoop jar /usr/lib/Hadoop-0.20-mapreduce/contrib/streaming/Hadoop-
*streaming*.jar -file ./BigData/word_mapper.py -mapper word_mapper.py
-file ./BigData/word_reducer.py -reducer word_reducer.py -input
/tmp/moby_dick/* -output /tmp/moby_output
```

Let's verify that the word count MapReduce program is working successfully:

```
$ Hadoop fs -cat /tmp/moby_output/*
```

The output of the preceding command is shown as follows:

```
(Queequeg1
A2
Africa1
Africa,1
After1
Ahab13
Ahab,1
Ahab's6
All1
American1
As1
At1
Bedford,1
Bildad1
Bildad,1
Boomer,2
Captain1
Christmas1
```

```
Day1

Delight,1

Dick6

Dick,2
```

The program is working as intended. Now, we'll deploy the program that calculates the sentiment score for each of the reviews. Note that we can add the positive and negative dictionary files to the Hadoop streaming:

```
$ Hadoop jar /usr/lib/hadoop-0.20-mapreduce/contrib/streaming/hadoop-
*streaming*.jar -file ./BigData/word_mapper.py -mapper word_mapper.py
-file ./BigData/word_reducer.py -reducer word_reducer.py -input
/tmp/moby_dick/* -output /tmp/moby_output
```

In the preceding code, we use the Hadoop command with the Hadoop streaming JAR file and then define the mapper and reducer files, and finally, the input and output directories in Hadoop.

Let's check the sentiments score of the movies review:

```
$ Hadoop fs -cat /tmp/jurassic_output/*
```

The output of the preceding command is shown as follows:

```
"jurassic world," like its predecessors, fills up the screen with
roaring, slathering, earth-shaking dinosaurs, then fills in mere
humans around the edges. it's a formula that works as well in 2015
as it did in 1993.3

a perfectly fine movie and entertaining enough to keep you watching until
the closing credits.4

an angry movie with a tragic moral ... meta-adoration and
criticism ends with a genetically modified dinosaur fighting off
waves of dinosaurs.-3

if you limit your expectations for jurassic world to "more teeth,"
it will deliver on that promise. if you dare to hope for anything
more-relatable characters, narrative coherence-you'll only set
yourself up for disappointment.-1
```

This program is also working as intended. Now, we'll try out the overall sentiment of a movie:

```
$ Hadoop jar /usr/lib/Hadoop-0.20-mapreduce/contrib/streaming/Hadoop-
*streaming*.jar -file ./BigData/overall_senti_mapper.py -mapper
```

Let's verify the result:

```
$ Hadoop fs -cat /tmp/unfinished_business_output/*
```

The output of the preceding command is shown as follows:

```
-8
```

We can see that the overall sentiment score comes out correctly from MapReduce. Here is a screenshot of the JobTracker status page:

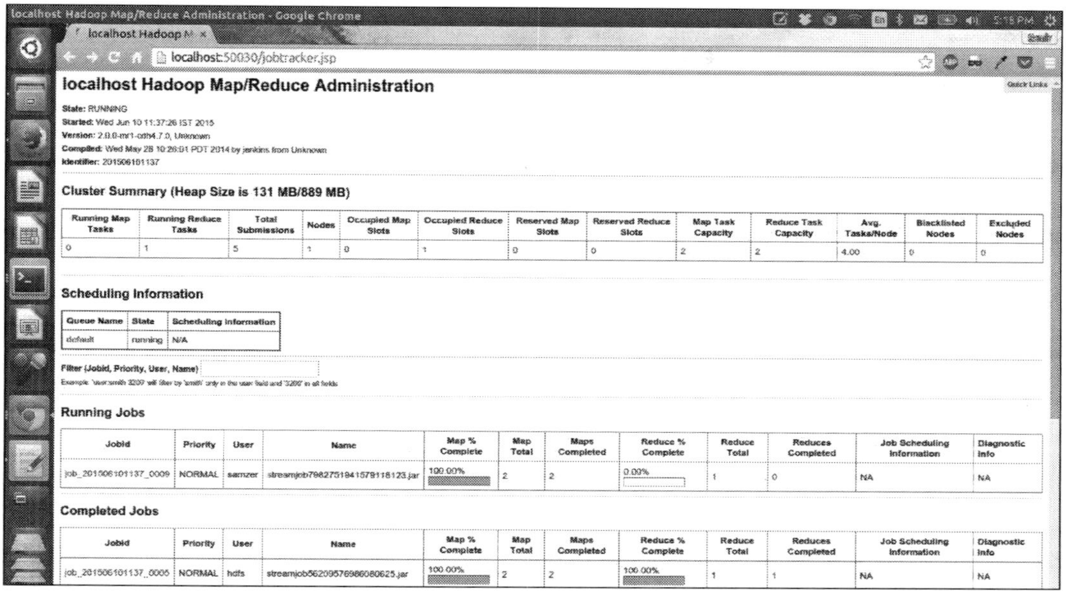

The preceding image shows a portal where the jobs submitted to the JobTracker can be viewed and the status can be seen. This can be seen on port `50070` of the master system.

From the preceding image, we can see that a job is running, and the status above the image shows that the job has been completed successfully.

File handling with Hadoopy

Hadoopy is a library in Python, which provides an API to interact with Hadoop to manage files and perform MapReduce on it. Hadoopy can be downloaded from `http://www.Hadoopy.com/en/latest/tutorial.html#installing-Hadoopy`.

Let's try to put a few files in Hadoop through Hadoopy in a directory created within HDFS, called `data`:

```
$ Hadoop fs -mkdir data
```

Here is the code that puts the data into HDFS:

```
importHadoopy
import os
hdfs_path = ''
def read_local_dir(local_path):
  for fn in os.listdir(local_path):
    path = os.path.join(local_path, fn)
    if os.path.isfile(path):
      yield path


def main():
  local_path = './BigData/dummy_data'
  for file in  read_local_dir(local_path):
    Hadoopy.put(file, 'data')
    print"The file %s has been put into hdfs"% (file,)


if __name__ =='__main__':
  main()
The file ./BigData/dummy_data/test9 has been put into hdfs
The file ./BigData/dummy_data/test7 has been put into hdfs
The file ./BigData/dummy_data/test1 has been put into hdfs
The file ./BigData/dummy_data/test8 has been put into hdfs
The file ./BigData/dummy_data/test6 has been put into hdfs
The file ./BigData/dummy_data/test5 has been put into hdfs
The file ./BigData/dummy_data/test3 has been put into hdfs
The file ./BigData/dummy_data/test4 has been put into hdfs
The file ./BigData/dummy_data/test2 has been put into hdfs
```

In the preceding code, we list all the files in a directory and then put each of the files into Hadoop using the `put()` method of Hadoopy.

Let's check if all the files have been put into HDFS:

```
$ Hadoop fs -ls data
```

The output of the preceding command is shown as follows:

```
Found 9 items
-rw-r--r--   3 samzer Hadoop          0 2015-06-23 00:19 data/test1
-rw-r--r--   3 samzer Hadoop          0 2015-06-23 00:19 data/test2
-rw-r--r--   3 samzer Hadoop          0 2015-06-23 00:19 data/test3
-rw-r--r--   3 samzer Hadoop          0 2015-06-23 00:19 data/test4
-rw-r--r--   3 samzer Hadoop          0 2015-06-23 00:19 data/test5
-rw-r--r--   3 samzer Hadoop          0 2015-06-23 00:19 data/test6
-rw-r--r--   3 samzer Hadoop          0 2015-06-23 00:19 data/test7
-rw-r--r--   3 samzer Hadoop          0 2015-06-23 00:19 data/test8
-rw-r--r--   3 samzer Hadoop          0 2015-06-23 00:19 data/test9
```

So, we have successfully been able to put files into HDFS.

Pig

Pig is a platform that has a very expressive language to perform data transformations and querying. The code that is written in Pig is done in a scripting manner and this gets compiled to MapReduce programs, which execute on Hadoop. The following image is the logo of Pig Latin:

The Pig logo

Pig helps in reducing the complexity of raw-level MapReduce programs, and enables the user to perform fast transformations.

Pig Latin is the textual language that can be learned from `http://pig.apache.org/docs/r0.7.0/piglatin_ref2.html`.

We'll be covering how to perform the top 10 most occurring words with Pig, and then we'll see how you can create a function in Python that can be used in Pig.

Let's start with the word count. Here is the Pig Latin code, which you can save in thepig_wordcount.py file:

```
data = load '/tmp/moby_dick/';

word_token = foreach data generate
flatten(TOKENIZE((chararray)$0)) as word;

group_word_token = group word_token by word;

count_word_token = foreach group_word_token generate
COUNT(word_token) as cnt, group;

sort_word_token = ORDER count_word_token by cnt DESC;

top10_word_count = LIMIT sort_word_token 10;

DUMP top10_word_count;
```

In the preceding code, we can load the summary of Moby Dick, which is then tokenized line by line and is basically split into individual elements. The flatten function converts a collection of individual word tokens in a line to a row-by-row form. We then group by the words and then take a count of the words for each word. Finally, we sort the count of words in a descending order and then we limit the count of the words to the first 10 rows to get the top 10 most occurring words.

Let's execute the preceding pig script:

```
$ pig ./BigData/pig_wordcount.pig
```

The output of the preceding command is shown as follows:

```
(83,the)

(36,and)

(28,a)

(25,of)

(24,to)

(15,his)

(14,Ahab)
```

```
(14,Moby)
(14,is)
(14,in)
```

We are able to get our top 10 words. Let's now create a user-defined function with Python, which will be used in Pig.

We'll define two user-defined functions to score positive and negative sentiments of a sentence.

The following code is the UDF used to score the positive sentiment and it's available in the `positive_sentiment.py` file:

```
positive_words = [ 'a+', 'abound', 'abounds', 'abundance',
'abundant', 'accessable', 'accessible', 'acclaim', 'acclaimed',
'acclamation', 'acco$ ]


@outputSchema("pnum:int")
def sentiment_score(text):
  positive_score = 0
  for w in text.split(''):
    if w in positive_words: positive_score+=1
  return positive_score
```

In the preceding code, we define the positive word list, which is used by the `sentiment_score()` function. The function checks for the positive words in a sentence and finally outputs their total count. There is an `outputSchema()` decorator that is used to tell Pig what type of data is being outputted, which in our case is `int`.

Here is the code to score the negative sentiment and it's available in the `negative_sentiment.py` file. The code is almost similar to the positive sentiment:

```
negative_words = ['2-faced', '2-faces', 'abnormal', 'abolish',
'abominable', 'abominably', 'abominate', 'abomination', 'abort',
'aborted', 'ab$....]


@outputSchema("nnum:int")
def sentiment_score(text):
  negative_score = 0
  for w in text.split(''):
    if w in negative_words: negative_score-=1
  return  negative_score
```

The following code is used by Pig to score the sentiments of the Jurassic World reviews and its available in the `pig_sentiment.pig` file:

```
register 'positive_sentiment.py' using
org.apache.pig.scripting.jython.JythonScriptEngine as positive;


register 'negative_sentiment.py' using
org.apache.pig.scripting.jython.JythonScriptEngine as negative;


data = load '/tmp/jurassic_world/*';


feedback_sentiments = foreach data generate LOWER((chararray)$0)
as feedback, positive.sentiment_score(LOWER((chararray)$0)) as
psenti,
negative.sentiment_score(LOWER((chararray)$0)) as nsenti;


average_sentiments = foreach feedback,feedback_sentiments generate
psenti + nsenti;


dump average_sentiments;
```

In the preceding Pig script, we first register the Python UDF scripts using the register command and give them an appropriate name. We then load our Jurassic World review. We then convert our reviews to lowercase and score the positive and negative sentiments of a review. Finally, we add the score to get the overall sentiments of a review.

Let's execute the Pig script and see the results:

```
$ pig ./BigData/pig_sentiment.pig
```

The output of the preceding command is shown as follows:

```
(there is plenty here to divert, but little to leave you enraptored.
such is the fate of the sequel: bigger. louder. fewer teeth.,0)
(if you limit your expectations for jurassic world to "more teeth,
" it will deliver on that promise. if you dare to hope for anything
more-relatable characters, narrative coherence-you'll only set
yourself up for disappointment.,-1)
(there's a problem when the most complex character in a film is the
dinosaur,-2)
(not so much another bloated sequel as it is the fruition of dreams
deferred in the previous films. too bad the genre dictates that those
dreams are once again destined for disaster.,-2)
```

```
(a perfectly fine movie and entertaining enough to keep you watching
until the closing credits.,4)
(this fourth installment of the jurassic park film series shows some
wear and tear, but there is still some gas left in the tank. time is
spent to set up the next film in the series. they will keep making
more of these until we stop watching.,0)
```

We have successfully scored the sentiments of the Jurassic World review using the Python UDF in Pig.

Python with Apache Spark

Apache Spark is a computing framework that works on top of HDFS and provides an alternative way of computing that is similar to MapReduce. It was developed by AmpLab of UC Berkeley. Spark does its computation mostly in the memory because of which, it is much faster than MapReduce, and is well suited for machine learning as it's able to handle iterative workloads really well.

Spark uses the programming abstraction of **RDDs** (**Resilient Distributed Datasets**) in which data is logically distributed into partitions, and transformations can be performed on top of this data.

Python is one of the languages that is used to interact with Apache Spark, and we'll create a program to perform the sentiment scoring for each review of Jurassic Park as well as the overall sentiment.

You can install Apache Spark by following the instructions at `https://spark.apache.org/docs/1.0.1/spark-standalone.html`.

Scoring the sentiment

Here is the Python code to score the sentiment:

```
from __future__ import print_function
import sys
from operator import add
```

```
from pyspark import SparkContext
positive_words = open('positive-words.txt').read().split('\n')
negative_words = open('negative-words.txt').read().split('\n')
def sentiment_score(text, pos_list, neg_list):
  positive_score = 0
  negative_score = 0
  for w in text.split(''):
    if w in pos_list: positive_score+=1
    if w in neg_list: negative_score+=1
  return positive_score - negative_score
if __name__ == "__main__":
  if len(sys.argv) != 2:
    print("Usage: sentiment <file>", file=sys.stderr)
    exit(-1)
  sc = SparkContext(appName="PythonSentiment")
  lines = sc.textFile(sys.argv[1], 1)
  scores = lines.map(lambda x: (x, sentiment_score(x.lower(),
  positive_words, negative_words)))
  output = scores.collect()
  for (key, score) in output:
    print("%s: %i" % (key, score))
  sc.stop()
```

In the preceding code, we define our standard `sentiment_score()` function, which we'll be reusing. The `if` statement checks whether the Python script and the text file is given. The `sc` variable is a Spark Context object with the `PythonSentiment` app name. The filename in the argument is passed into Spark through the `textFile()` method of the `sc` variable. In the `map()` function of Spark, we define a `lambda` function, where each line of the text file is passed, and then we obtain the line and its respective sentiment score. The output variable gets the result, and finally, we print the result on the screen.

Let's score the sentiment of each of the reviews of Jurassic World. Replace the `<hostname>` with your hostname, this should suffice:

```
$ ~/spark-1.3.0-bin-cdh4/bin/spark-submit --master
spark://<hostname>:7077 ./BigData/spark_sentiment.py
hdfs://localhost:8020/tmp/jurassic_world/*
```

We'll get the following output for the preceding command:

```
There is plenty here to divert but little to leave you enraptured. Such
is the fate of the sequel: Bigger, Louder, Fewer teeth: 0

If you limit your expectations for Jurassic World to more teeth, it will
deliver on this promise. If you dare to hope for anything more—relatable
characters or narrative coherence—you'll only set yourself up for
disappointment:-1
```

We can see that our Spark program was able to score the sentiment for each of the reviews. The number in the end of the output of the sentiment score shows that if the review has been positive or negative, the higher the number of the sentiment score—the better the review and the more negative the number of the sentiment score—the more negative the review has been.

We use the Spark Submit command with the following parameters:

- A master node of the Spark system
- A Python script containing the transformation commands
- An argument to the Python script

The overall sentiment

Here is a Spark program to score the overall sentiment of all the reviews:

```
from __future__ import print_function

import sys

from operator import add

from pyspark import SparkContext

positive_words = open('positive-words.txt').read().split('\n')

negative_words = open('negative-words.txt').read().split('\n')

def sentiment_score(text, pos_list, neg_list):

  positive_score = 0

  negative_score = 0
```

```
  for w in text.split(''):
    if w in pos_list: positive_score+=1
    if w in neg_list: negative_score+=1
  return positive_score - negative_score
if __name__ =="__main__":
  if len(sys.argv) != 2:
    print("Usage: Overall Sentiment <file>", file=sys.stderr)
    exit(-1)
  sc = SparkContext(appName="PythonOverallSentiment")
  lines = sc.textFile(sys.argv[1], 1)
  scores = lines.map(lambda x: ("Total",
  sentiment_score(x.lower(), positive_words, negative_words)))\
  .reduceByKey(add)
  output = scores.collect()
  for (key, score) in output:
    print("%s: %i"% (key, score))
  sc.stop()
```

In the preceding code, we have added a `reduceByKey()` method, which reduces the value by adding the output values, and we have also defined the `key` as `Total`, so that all the scores are reduced based on a single key.

Let's try out the preceding code to get the overall sentiment of Jurassic World. Replace the `<hostname>` with your hostname, this should suffice:

```
$ ~/spark-1.3.0-bin-cdh4/bin/spark-submit --master
spark://<hostname>:7077 ./BigData/spark_overall_sentiment.py
hdfs://localhost:8020/tmp/jurassic_world/*
```

The output of the preceding command is shown as follows:

```
Total: 19
```

We can see that Spark has given an overall sentiment score of `19`.

The applications that get executed on Spark can be viewed in the browser on the `8080` port of the Spark master. Here is a screenshot of it:

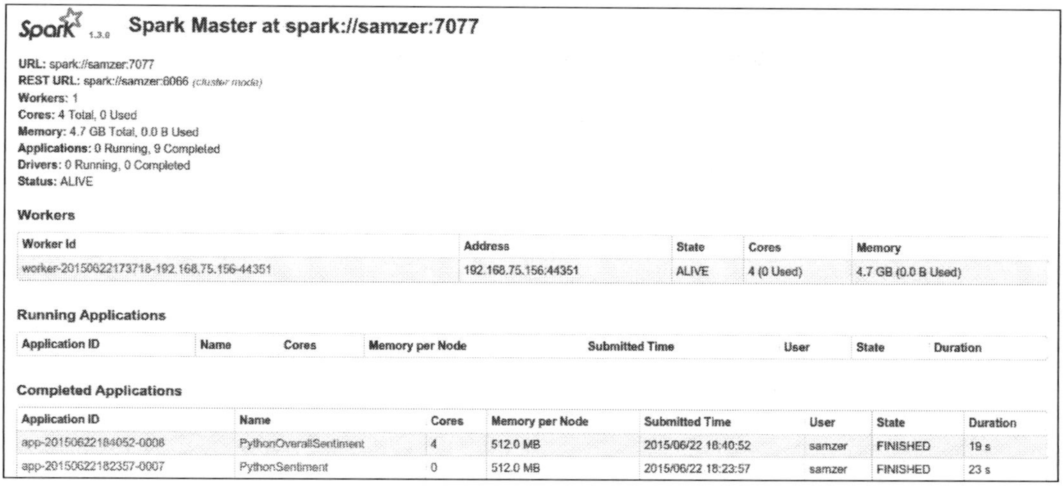

We can see that the number of nodes of Spark, applications that are getting executed currently, and the applications that have been executed.

Summary

In this chapter, you were introduced to big data, learned about how the Hadoop software works, and the architecture associated with it. You then learned how to create a mapper and a reducer for a MapReduce program, how to test it locally, and then put it into Hadoop and deploy it. You were then introduced to the Hadoopy library and using this library, you were able to put files into Hadoop. You also learned about Pig and how to create a user-defined function with it. Finally, you learned about Apache Spark, which is an alternative to MapReduce and how to use it to perform distributed computing.

With this chapter, we have come to an end in our journey, and you should be in a state to perform data science tasks with Python. From here on, you can participate in Kaggle Competitions at `https://www.kaggle.com/` to improve your data science skills with real-world problems. This will fine-tune your skills and help understand how to solve analytical problems.

Also, you can sign up for the Andrew NG course on Machine Learning at `https://www.coursera.org/learn/machine-learning` to understand the nuances behind machine learning algorithms.

Index

D

E

F

G

H

I

J

K

L

M

N

O

P

R

S

T

U

W

X

Z

Thank you for buying

Mastering Python for Data Science

About Packt Publishing

Packt, pronounced 'packed', published its first book, *Mastering phpMyAdmin for Effective MySQL Management*, in April 2004, and subsequently continued to specialize in publishing highly focused books on specific technologies and solutions.

Our books and publications share the experiences of your fellow IT professionals in adapting and customizing today's systems, applications, and frameworks. Our solution-based books give you the knowledge and power to customize the software and technologies you're using to get the job done. Packt books are more specific and less general than the IT books you have seen in the past. Our unique business model allows us to bring you more focused information, giving you more of what you need to know, and less of what you don't.

Packt is a modern yet unique publishing company that focuses on producing quality, cutting-edge books for communities of developers, administrators, and newbies alike. For more information, please visit our website at `www.packtpub.com`.

About Packt Open Source

In 2010, Packt launched two new brands, Packt Open Source and Packt Enterprise, in order to continue its focus on specialization. This book is part of the Packt Open Source brand, home to books published on software built around open source licenses, and offering information to anybody from advanced developers to budding web designers. The Open Source brand also runs Packt's Open Source Royalty Scheme, by which Packt gives a royalty to each open source project about whose software a book is sold.

Writing for Packt

We welcome all inquiries from people who are interested in authoring. Book proposals should be sent to `author@packtpub.com`. If your book idea is still at an early stage and you would like to discuss it first before writing a formal book proposal, then please contact us; one of our commissioning editors will get in touch with you.

We're not just looking for published authors; if you have strong technical skills but no writing experience, our experienced editors can help you develop a writing career, or simply get some additional reward for your expertise.

[PACKT] open source
community experience distilled
PUBLISHING

Python Data Science Essentials

ISBN: 978-1-78528-042-9 Paperback: 258 pages

Become an efficient data science practitioner by thoroughly understanding the key concepts of Python

1. Quickly get familiar with data science using Python.
2. Save tons of time through this reference book with all the essential tools illustrated and explained.
3. Create effective data science projects and avoid common pitfalls with the help of examples and hints dictated by experience.

R for Data Science

ISBN: 978-1-78439-086-0 Paperback: 364 pages

Learn and explore the fundamentals of data science with R

1. Familiarize yourself with R programming packages and learn how to utilize them effectively.
2. Learn how to detect different types of data mining sequences.
3. A step-by-step guide to understanding R scripts and the ramifications of your changes.

Please check **www.PacktPub.com** for information on our titles

[PACKT] open source
community experience distilled
PUBLISHING

Practical Data Science Cookbook

ISBN: 978-1-78398-024-6 Paperback: 396 pages

89 hands-on recipes to help you complete real-world data science projects in R and Python

1. Learn about the data science pipeline and use it to acquire, clean, analyze, and visualize data.
2. Understand critical concepts in data science in the context of multiple projects.
3. Expand your numerical programming skills through step-by-step code examples and learn more about the robust features of R and Python.

Practical Data Analysis

ISBN: 978-1-78328-099-5 Paperback: 360 pages

Transform, model, and visualize your data through hands-on projects, developed in open source tools

1. Explore how to analyze your data in various innovative ways and turn them into insight.
2. Learn to use the D3.js visualization tool for exploratory data analysis.
3. Understand how to work with graphs and social data analysis.
4. Discover how to perform advanced query techniques and run MapReduce on MongoDB.

Please check **www.PacktPub.com** for information on our titles

59811203R00163

Made in the USA
Middletown, DE
22 December 2017